Norma

by
Norma Zimmer

Published by
World Wide Publications
1303 Hennepin Avenue
Minneapolis, Minnesota 55403

Original clothbound edition
published by Tyndale House
Publishers, Inc., Wheaton, IL

NORMA
LIBRARY OF CONGRESS CATALOG CARD NUMBER 76-42117

FOREWORD

How pleased and honored I was to be asked to write the foreword to Norma Zimmer's book. To my way of thinking, Norma comes as close to perfection as anyone I've ever known, both as a performer and a human being.

Throughout the many years she has been with us on television and recordings, she has consistently demonstrated the complete preparation and total dedication which mark a real artist.

Norma, like myself, had a difficult, rather poor beginning in life. And yet no one I know has learned to live as closely to the way God intended us to, as she has.

I have great admiration not only for her serene religious faith which animates her entire personality, but also for her devotion to her family, and her sunny disposition which keeps all us folks in the orchestra feeling bright and happy! Everyone in the band has the same great respect for her that I do, and we all know that a large percent of our loyal audience has been brought to us through her beautiful, well-nigh perfect performances.

We all have tremendous gratitude in our hearts for this wonderful lady. It could be the mold was lost when the Good Lord created her.

Lawrence Welk

ACKNOWLEDGEMENTS

Through the years, many friends and several publishing houses have urged me to write the story of my life, but I have held back, feeling that the time wasn't right. But when Tyndale House's editor-in-chief, Dr. Victor Oliver, approached me through our mutual friend Everett Tigner, I felt a peace about the project that I'd never experienced before. I agreed to try—but where to begin?

First I must express thanks to my brother, Max Larsen, for helping me recall family history and events that happened early in my life. Next, Ruth Peterman helped me get the episodes in chronological order and work out organization and continuity. Ruth has become a dear friend and I am so appreciative of her skillful assistance.

Then I spent several months at our dining room table, writing page after page of past experiences—trying to recapture my thoughts and inner feelings as the scenes unfolded before memory's eye. As I wrote, I was able to see in a new way how clearly God's plan for my life has been revealed step by step through the years. How I wish I could name every person who has helped me along life's pathway, but this would not be possible.

I do want to thank Tyndale House's senior book editor, Virginia Muir, for her work in smoothing out the final manuscript. She too has become a precious friend and I'll be eternally grateful to her for her help.

I pray that this book will bring glory to God and that it will be a spiritual blessing to each one who reads it.

Norma Zimmer
Philippians 4:13

CHAPTER ONE

It was Christmas 1964.

My loved ones were gathered about my table and it should have been a happy occasion. But the mood was tense. While I loved them all, they didn't all love each other.

I looked across the table at Randy, whom I had loved at first sight more than two decades ago. Our eyes met across the table in complete understanding of the situation. Still handsome, his hair dark with streaks of gray, his skin still firm, he was as dear to me as he had ever been.

My eyes moved to our good-looking blond sons, Ron and Mark, fifteen and twelve. Randy and I were proud of them—with their fine young bodies and quick minds. Beyond them sat dad, even better looking in his old age than in his youth. He sat in embarrassed silence most of the time, only occasionally flashing his Clark Gable smile, feigning gaiety, casting loving but furtive glances at my mother.

And on the other side of the table sat mother, stately, regal in her beauty, her lips set in a hard thin line.

My mother hated my father.

It hadn't always been so. True, she had married dad to get off the farm. But what love there was on her part might have ripened through the years if life hadn't been so hard for her—for them— for in marriage no partner ever suffers alone.

But neither was able to cope with the reverses, the vicissitudes of life. Dad turned to liquor. And neither of them knew God.

While still a very young man, he had experienced the greatest disappointment of his life. His career as a concert violinist had been ended by an accident in the shipyards in Seattle.

Later, after he had met and married mother, and the financial stress grew desperate for them, they decided to move back to northern Idaho where my grandfather had said they could return any time and occupy the little log cabin he had built when he had homesteaded the land. He had since then built a much larger house for his own growing family.

With two children, six-year-old Max and little Kay, a toddler, my parents returned to Idaho. Mother was eight months pregnant.

One Sunday afternoon, mother and dad left the children in the care of mother's brothers and sisters and went for a walk. A mile from the farm they encountered a band of gypsies camped under a tree.

What happened in the gypsy camp changed my whole life and affected the future of every member of my family.

A dark-eyed gypsy woman sat in front of her wagon watching my parents' approach. She stood with a swish of her red and purple satin skirt and beckoned to them, her heavy gold bracelets jangling softly. "I'll tell your fortune," she called gaily. "I'll tell your fortune by reading your palm."

"Oh, you will, will you?" Dad laughed. To mother he said, "Let's have some fun!" Smiling broadly he took his coin purse out of his pocket and threw the gypsy a coin, "Catch!"

She sat down again and indicated a chair across from her where dad was to sit.

Laying his hands, palms up, on a small table between them, dad teased, "All right, tell me my fortune!"

The gypsy gasped at the sight of the middle finger of his left hand, curled back toward the palm. "You are a most unhappy person because of what has happened to your finger," she said. "Your life, because of this injury, will always be hard. You have wanted many times to die but your marriage has spared you for a time."

The gypsy looked sadly at mother, then turned back to father. "You—you and your wife—will have three children. Two are born already; the first was a son."

Dad and mother exchanged glances.

"The second is a daughter."

Father winked at mother.

"And the third child will be a daughter."

Mother returned dad's smile.

Agitated now, the gypsy continued. "Very soon, you will work at a hopeless task. Nothing will stop you from starting it. Not even what I tell you. But within a year you will have another bad accident."

Father wasn't smiling anymore. Awkward with her late pregnancy, mother shifted her weight and leaned forward to hear better as the gypsy spoke in a low sad voice.

"Your life will always be influenced by your appetites. At times you will enjoy great moments of elation and exuberance. You like to feel that you are a supreme being. Wine gives you this feeling. You have too wild a nature to withstand discipline or control for any length of time. As a result you will never hold a high position. Any position you hold will never be with any feeling of security."

Dad accepted with amazement what she said about his character. Now he listened with his head cocked to one side.

"You will be a teacher," the gypsy said. "Teaching will give you the greatest joy of all you do in life. And one of your pupils will become famous."

"Well!" father said. He looked triumphantly at mother.

The gypsy looked from the open palms into dad's face, to mother's face and back to dad's.

Then, as though sorrowful to be the bearer of such evil tidings, she made a terrible prediction that was forever to affect my father's life—and mine—hanging like a dark shadow over us all.

CHAPTER TWO

The peace and quiet of the day had gone. They walked back to the farm in silence. As they approached the house they slowed their walk. "Peter," mother said, "don't take it too seriously."

"Well, that's easy to say—she seemed to have me pretty well figured out. She knew a lot about me. Don't you agree?" He was getting disturbed. "Wasn't it true that I like wine—you've said so yourself. And haven't you said that I should keep one job and not move around so much? And haven't you complained that I have a wild nature? Haven't you?" His eyes were shooting sparks of fire. "How do you think she knew all that—"

"Well, a lot of people—"

"She knew about our son and our daughter—"

"Yes," mother agreed reluctantly. "But that could have been chance. Just luck." Mother talked fast as he tried to interrupt her. "And now if this child I'm carrying turns out to be a girl, remember there's a fifty-fifty chance—"

"Kay!" Father stopped and took her by both arms and looked sternly into her face. "Kay, she got it all right so far. You know she hit the nail square on the head—"

"Pete, Pete, I don't know how she did it, but let's try to forget about it. Please! And don't ever tell Max! Besides, how could such a sweet child ever—"

Father laid his hand across her mouth. He gulped hard.

Mother's eyes filled with tears and she pulled herself gently back from him. "She said one of your students would become famous. Do you know what I thought of? Pete, do you suppose you could give violin lessons?"

Father tried to straighten the middle finger of his left hand which stubbornly curled back toward his palm. "I can't play like I used to. You know that, Kay. How can I teach what I can't do myself?"

"Won't you try, Pete? I know how disappointed you are that you and Minnie had to break up your act. I know how much you love to play and perform—but maybe you could practice and improve enough to give lessons. You know so much about it, Pete."

3

Father shook his head slowly. "Those were good days when Minnie and I used to travel. I hope our daughters will sing like my sister." Turning to mother, he talked to her as though he had never told her before. "She had the most beautiful coloratura soprano—"

"Well, I hope if we do have another daughter she will be a—"

"A contralto. Yes, I know you like that better."

They were walking very slowly now, reluctant to join the boisterous family group on the farm.

My parents had moved back here from Seattle when father gave up his job as an engraver. He had started to drink steadily and had become so irritable at work that he lost the only job available to him at the time. Mother had left the hard work of the farm when she got married, anticipating life as a city woman—a life of greater ease. But liquor and dad's bad temper had already brought them back to the farm and once more mother was compelled to work hard from morning until night. At the age of sixteen she had been free of the tedium of tending little children. Now, only six years later she was back, caring for her mother's children besides two of her own, enduring an unwanted third pregnancy. Dad had found work in the silver mines near the farm.

"It's terrible—terrible," father said, unable to shake off the gypsy's spell of gloom.

"Please, Pete!" mother pleaded. "Don't take it so hard. We never should have—look, if the first things she prophesied come true, then there's still time to worry about the last thing." She took a few more steps, then thoughtfully said, "I wonder if you shouldn't give up your job in the mines. You could have an accident—"

"Oh! So you *do* believe in what she said. You do! Don't you?"

"Something like that could so easily happen, Pete. With or without a gypsy's prophecy."

"To go through life with the thought that my own son will grow up to—"

"Oh, Pete, I beg of you." Mother had laid her hand across dad's mouth this time. "Don't take it so hard. Put it out of your mind, Pete. Will you? Besides how could such a fine boy—"

"People change as they grow."

"But we can't think about it."

"All right. All right. As you say."

"We must *never* tell the children!" Mother was pale. Her knees felt weak.

"No! Never! Not as long as we live!"

But when they made that pledge to each other neither of them reckoned with liquor.

4

CHAPTER THREE

My family's history begins in Norway and Finland.

Ole Huseby, a carpenter, emigrated from Trondheim, Norway, toward the end of the 19th century. He traveled to North Dakota where he met and married a widow with a small son. In 1891 my father, Peter Magnus Huseby, was born.

Because Americans found "Huseby" hard to pronounce with a good Norwegian inflection, grandfather changed the name to "Larsen."

Early in their marriage, the Larsens moved to Seattle, Washington, where work was plentiful. Here my uncles, Albert and Morris, and Aunt Minnie were born.

The family felt no need for either education or religion. In fact they never owned a Bible, although my great-grandmother was called a "religious fanatic." Dad had an eighth-grade education and spent most of his time around the pool halls of Seattle. He joined a gang of youths who called themselves "The Dirty Dozen." The group elaborately planned burglaries and the gang carried them out. However, my father always managed to be absent when the crime was being committed. Street fights and his old gang soon lost their glamor for him. He had a desire to take up music and learned to play the violin.

Dad's interest in music rubbed off onto Uncle Albert and Aunt Minnie. Uncle Al bought an old saxophone which he had to learn to fix in order to keep playing. Aunt Minnie began to take singing lessons. At first her vocalizing drove the family wild, but after many months of practicing she began to show real talent. For a time, father and Aunt Minnie traveled with a vaudeville troupe throughout the Northwest. They both soloed, then for a final act dad would play a violin obbligato while Aunt Minnie sang. Their popularity grew and bookings became more and more numerous.

Uncle Al opened a small instrument repair shop in Seattle where he also sold instruments. Many evenings found him playing for local dances. Uncle Morris moved to Tacoma where he married and became successful in business. In spite of their lack of education, the whole family was doing well at work they enjoyed.

Suddenly World War I broke out in Europe.

Entertainers were drafted, so father, still single, went to work in the shipyards in Seattle where he stayed until the tragic accident to his hand put an end to his dreams. Without the comfort of a knowledge of God or any sense of direction in his life, dad turned to liquor.

Mother was born to immigrants from Oulo, the northern province of Finland. My grandfather, Augustus Lindroos, and my grandmother, Louise Nasi, emigrated at different times.

Louise Nasi was only ten when her foster parents brought her to America and settled on a farm in Michigan. Louise did farm chores during her childhood and developed into a beautiful, strong, healthy girl, inclined to be impetuous and irresponsible.

Handsome young Augustus Lindroos arrived in America in his early twenties. He set out at once for the Midwest where he had agreed to work a year for an uncle who owned a dairy farm in Michigan. He worked and saved every penny, with the hope of eventually owning his own farm.

Augustus loved Michigan but found land so expensive he decided that as soon as he could save enough money he would travel farther west where he might still get land by homesteading.

He met my grandmother at a Saturday night barn dance in Michigan. Augustus was not a good dancer but Louise loved dancing. A few dances, a few picnics, and they fell in love. The uncle's farmhouse which had provided a home for Augustus was the first home for him and Louise, and he and his bride settled down, he as a farm laborer, she as milkmaid and kitchen helper. They threw themselves into the farm work and diligently saved what they could for the day they would be free to go to Idaho.

For Louise, the Saturday night dance was the bright spot that relieved the drudgery of the week's hard work. Even when she found she was pregnant, she kept going to the dances as long as possible.

In later years, whenever this fun-loving grandmother of mine found responsibilities too heavy she would dance off for a fling with another partner and leave her family for a time without wife and mother. Eventually she divorced Augustus.

Two years after the birth of my mother, Katherine Lempi Lindroos, my grandparents finally realized their dreams of moving to Idaho to start a farm of their own.

Near Mullan, Idaho, in the northern part of the panhandle, my grandparents acquired the land for their dairy. A railroad track and a road leading to other farms bordered a ten-acre section. It was here they dug a well and built their first house, a small log cabin.

With the help of his Finnish neighbors, Augustus cleared land on which to build and plant crops and raise his cattle. He dreamed of having a large farm. He put up many buildings, including a sauna bathhouse, icehouse, blacksmith shop, and a long open shed. He added to his herd with great pride. He was coming up in the world.

Fun-loving Louise had little time for fun now. Five more children arrived after my mother. Her brothers and sisters were Waino, Emma, Henry, William, and Eva. Soon the little cabin was overcrowded and they planned a larger house.

Remembering the grand log houses of Finland, grandfather built a spacious two-story structure with an attic. By this time, he had a thriving herd of cattle, a good milk route, and was the local blacksmith.

Grandfather had everything an immigrant could want. He was successful—even wealthy by local standards. He had six children. But he had a rebellious wife.

Mother remembered hearing loud and bitter quarrels. Her mother complained about being tied down to working her life away. Grandfather begged her to be patient while he was building his business. There was an easier life ahead for them—a few more cows, a few more customers—

This would anger grandmother. "More, always more! Why can't we ever have enough?"

As daughter Katherine grew into her teens, her mother trained her carefully and depended on her to shoulder more and more of the work load. And so Katherine inherited the life her mother hated and was trying to avoid.

When Katherine was sixteen, she begged to go to a dance with her parents one evening. Peter Larsen was the violinist for that dance.

As his fingers moved over the strings, his eyes followed the pretty girl with the graceful figure. Her auburn hair shone in the light, and her violet eyes often met his blue ones across the room. When he finished a piece he would flash her a wide smile as he pushed his heavy dark hair into place.

That was the beginning of a fast courtship. Peter fell in love with mother that first night. She realized she didn't fully return his love, but she hated her life on the farm, and agreed to marry him and go with him to Seattle.

It was a great disappointment to Peter that his sister Minnie had become a waitress. They used to argue about it. His injury didn't prevent her from singing. Why did she give up her career just because of his tragedy?

Peter's brother Morris lived in Tacoma; the younger brother, Albert, was in the army; and Pete went back to the shipyards, this time as a bookkeeper. His exquisite penmanship soon attracted the attention of his boss and he was called to the front office. "You have beautiful handwriting—so easy to read, such well-formed characters. Have you ever thought of using that skill to better advantage?"

Pete was curious. "I'm open to suggestion."

"Well, I'm the vice-president of my athletic club. You see, every year we give award cups to the winning athletes of each of our sporting events. If you did engraving, you could earn a little extra money."

"I've never done any engraving."

"Well, I have. And I have a set of tools I could lend you. I think we could give you a few damaged cups to practice on, just to see what you can do. I'd really like you to try it."

Dad liked the idea and accepted the tools and the cups. He then went to the Seattle Public Library and studied the art of engraving.

His young wife watched him engrave his first cup and exclaimed, "Oh, Pete. How can you do that so beautifully the very first time? Why, it looks almost perfect!"

The shipyard official was pleased. And dad began supplementing his bookkeeping salary with income from engraving, building a new profession.

In 1917 my brother was born. They named him Max Irving Larsen.

When World War I ended, Uncle Albert and his wife, Peg, whom he had married while in the service, returned to Seattle to resume the instrument repair business. Dad got a letter from Uncle Morris in Tacoma saying, "My friend who owns a jewelry shop needs another engraver. Come on down. You can stay with us until you're situated."

So my parents moved to Tacoma. When they could, they moved into an apartment of their own and began to save for a down payment on a house. They went further into debt to buy furniture, including a Steinway grand piano. Mother had always dreamed of playing one.

Dad began arriving home from work many evenings, carrying a large bottle of wine. Little Max learned to stay out of dad's way. As father drank, he would complain to mother, "I'm getting tired of doing all the hard jobs at work. Those other fellows leave all the tough ones for me."

One night, as mother sat at her beloved piano, playing the "Londonderry Air," dad came in noisily. "Well, I gave my notice."

"Pete!" mother exclaimed, breaking off in the middle of a phrase.

"Two weeks. They're not going to give *me* all the hard jobs. I'm quitting!"

Mother knew better than to argue with dad although she was terribly upset. What would they do? There were payments to make on the house and furniture. And she was pregnant.

"I'll get another job." Dad had already poured himself some wine. "I'm a good engraver! One of the best in the country. I'll get a better job. Nobody's going to shove *me* around! And I've still got money in the bank."

Uncle Morris hurried right over to tell dad what he thought of his impulsive act. "What's the matter with you, Pete? You have to learn to get along with people. What's eating you, anyway?"

It took some prying but finally the truth came out.

"It's the violin. I...I can't play like I used to. You just don't know how much that hurts." His voice had grown husky.

"So that's it. It's your finger."

Dad was looking at the crippled finger, doubling back toward his palm. "I'll never be able to play well again. It seems to me that middle finger gets in the way of all the others."

"But Pete," Uncle Morris reasoned. "You can't change that. You have to adjust. Life goes on—finger or no finger. You're not single—"

"You said it!" dad said, bitterly eyeing mother.

"You've got payments to make. You've got to work."

"I'm not going back there!"

"Pete, Pete!" Uncle Morris pleaded. "I'll try to find something else for you. Pete, if I can get you another job will you take it?"

"Sure. I'm not afraid to work. Don't misunderstand."

"No, I know you're not lazy. But you mustn't expect perfection."

"I doubt if I can get a good reference."

"I'll see to it that you get a good one," Uncle Morris promised.

Uncle Morris kept his promise and soon dad was working again. He liked the employees of this new firm and everything went well.

Mother continued practicing on her Steinway grand. She started borrowing books from the library. Seeing mother engrossed in books, dad began to read too: *War and Peace, The Brothers Karamazov, Les Miserables, Pride and Prejudice, Great Expectations,* Shakespeare's plays and Chekhov's short stories— together they read constantly.

And as he read, dad drank more and more wine.

CHAPTER FOUR

Enormous political turmoil characterized the Northwest as the communists tried to gain control. Father's sympathies were with the labor union and he wasn't shy about expressing himself. His remarks soon led to the end of his employment as an engraver in Tacoma.

Mother's exasperation over his failure to hold a job made dad despondent. "Nobody appreciates anything I do," he complained.

"Pete, we've got so much to lose. Please go out and look for another job right away. We'll lose our house and our furniture." Most of all she feared losing her piano.

It was during this period of uncertainty that my sister, Katherine Maxine, was born. Now mother had her perfect family—a boy and a girl. She wanted no more children.

Dad asked Uncle Morris to lend him money so he could keep his house and furniture. "You know I'll pay it back."

"I know you would but I don't have it! A little maybe, but not enough to pay on a mortgage and a piano. I'm buying a house myself, you know."

Mother and dad decided all they could do was to move back to Idaho to the farm my grandparents owned. Uncle Morris agreed to lend them the money for the train fare. Baby Kay was too young to notice the change, but Max cried bitterly at being uprooted from the familiar home scenes.

When they arrived it was haying time on the Lindroos farm. Augustus received them joyfully but became solemn when he told them his bad news. "My dancing girl has run off with one of her dancing partners," he explained rather philosophically. "She'll come back. She always has—but she left me at a bad time, with haying and all. She's such a good worker."

So mother, who had married to get off the farm, now found herself back on the farm, busier than she had been when she left. Besides the ever-present farm chores and her mother's children to care for, mother had two of her own. But the work had to be done, and she plunged into the cooking, canning, and ever-present house-cleaning. By Thanksgiving she began to suspect what soon became an inescapable fact—like it or not, she was indeed pregnant again. She fiercely resented this intrusion into her "perfect family" and shed many angry tears into her pillow at night.

Grandmother Louise did return after her fling. For her, at least, life became more bearable for a time as she had mother's companionship. But the farm work never let up. Barn dances were her only diversion.

Dad helped grandfather with the farm work to pay for the keep of his family, but since he had debts he decided to go to work in the mines. My parents saw very little of each other as dad's work day was long.

It was at about this time that they encountered the fortune-teller.

In an effort to forget their unfortunate meeting with the gypsy, both mother and dad drank heavily of dandelion wine that night. Eventually mother got into bed, but dad stood for a long time over Max's bed, muttering to himself.

Some time after the fortune-telling experience, dad approached grandfather with a proposal. "You know, I've been thinking. If there's silver and lead in those hills, why can't there be some right here on this farm? I've got my debts paid off and I've got some money. No," he said, seeing grandfather's objection. "No, it won't cost you a red cent. I know the precautions to take for blasting ore-bearing rock, and you've handled dynamite to clear your land. What do you say we run a test on the upper end of your land? The rock there looks a lot like the kind they have around Kellogg."

"Well, Pete—if it don't cost me anything. I need a new milk delivery truck very badly and I'm not interested in spending my savings—"

"No, no, it won't cost you a dime!"

"Okay then. I'll help you but I can't put my money in it."

"Fine!" With characteristic enthusiasm and excitement for another project, dad quit his job in the mines. Mother didn't object, because she had worried that he might have an accident there. However, when he told her of his intentions of digging for silver and lead, she wondered if he might not be embarking on the hopeless task of which the gypsy had warned him.

Within a short time, his savings depleted, dad asked Augustus to help out financially. Grudgingly, grandfather invested a little cash, but it, too, soon was gone. Dad still believed in his venture even though he had to go back to work in the mines at Kellogg. "I can be a weekend miner on the farm," he told mother.

Dad was at work that July 13 when mother sent her brother Waino for the midwife. The delivery was normal and mother promptly name me Norma Beatrice. It was a hot breathless afternoon in the tiny log cabin. Max examined me soberly, then ran out into the fields, returning with a huge bouquet of Indian paintbrush which made a bright splash of color in the bedroom. Mother lay quietly, musing on the gypsy's prediction that her third child would be a girl.

After nine months of blasting in the hills, a new problem developed for dad and a neighbor who had joined in the mining venture. Water from a small spring was flooding the bottom of the shaft. Each weekend they had to bail out the water before they could begin to blast and haul up the rubble.

One rainy Saturday, while the neighbor was in the pit below, dad was cranking the winch, hauling up a very heavy bucket of water. The crank handle slipped out of father's damp hands and as he lunged forward, his left hand disengaged the holding ratchet. On the first free unlocked turn in reverse, with two or three hundred pounds of water in the bucket behind the blow, the crank handle whipped back and caught dad full in the mouth. Smashed backward by the blow, he caught his balance and groped at his wounds.

Blood spurted from his mouth and broken teeth lay on his tongue. Spewing out broken teeth, father fell to the ground, cursing as he blacked out.

The neighbor carried him back to the cabin.

When mother saw him unconscious and bleeding, she knew the gypsy's prediction of a serious accident had come true.

Dad's upper lip needed twelve stitches to hold it in place for healing. Six of his front teeth were gone. "This world is a hellhole of torture," dad cried out to mother. "Why does everything I touch always go wrong? I'm a man accursed! Believe me, I'll never go back down into another mine shaft!"

And they knew another of the gypsy's predictions had come true: He had embarked on a hopeless venture in spite of her warning.

Five months later, a dentist in Spokane extracted the roots of the broken teeth and made bridgework for him. Dad grew a moustache to hide the scar on his upper lip. "Now you're handsomer than ever," mother said, "especially when you smile." Dad was annoyed that the moustache grew in red, so he borrowed mother's mascara and darkened it to match his thick brown hair.

They worked through the second winter on the farm. Mother made the little cabin into a nice home and become reconciled to having three children. Fortunately, I was a quiet, happy baby and made few demands on her. She painstakingly hemstitched curtains for the windows and braided rugs for the floor. She planted flowers and always kept bouquets around the house. She made little cushions of bright chintz and scattered them around for color. The cabin looked homey and with the fragrance of coffee perking and bacon frying, mother was content. But dad was restless. He became resentful of Augustus for laying tasks on him that were too menial for a man of his talents. "After all," he said, "I can make a lot of money engraving."

When I was two years old, dad persuaded mother that it was time to go back to the city.

CHAPTER FIVE

I remember our house in Tacoma. We had a big front porch with a swing. A hedge and a white picket fence enclosed the large yard where Kay and I played happily.

Mother let us wear her old dresses and high-heeled shoes. We loved her hat with huge flowers and colored feathers. She gave us each an old purse full of trinkets and we carried our own compacts and lipsticks from which we still managed to rub our lips a little red.

One day, mother undressed Kay and me down to our panties. She put us in one of her dresser drawers and took a picture of us. I treasure that little photo to this day as there are so few pictures remaining of our family.

Dad's financial condition worsened steadily and soon we had to leave the white house with the big front porch and swing and move into the fourth floor of a tenement. In order for us to play outdoors, mother had Max carry our toys downstairs while she carried Kay and me. Then we would all walk to a public park where we could play. Kay and I loved the sandbox and Max chased squirrels and pigeons.

Father had found work doing engraving in a jewelry manufacturing plant. It was a poorly-ventilated, run-down place and acid fumes soon began to irritate dad's throat. He kept on working in spite of this. Dad wasn't lazy; he always managed to find work, sometimes in far from ideal working conditions. At this time he and mother were paying off their debts and dreaming of a time when we could move to another house with a yard.

That winter, dad caught a bad cold which grew steadily worse. He just couldn't shake it. The fumes at the factory irritated his sinuses and on weekends he stayed inside. Mother went alone on Saturdays to hunt for another house. Dad baby-sat while he drank, smoked, and read library books.

One Saturday when mother returned, dad's flushed face, bright eyes, and chattering teeth told her he had a high fever. She called a doctor. This alone sent a tingle of fear up my spine. We just never called a doctor. Max, Kay, and I stood wide-eyed while the doctor listened to dad's chest.

"Pneumonia. Bronchial pneumonia." The old man lifted his head and looked over his glasses at mother. "You'd better get him to the hospital."

They took dad away in an ambulance. I looked at my father lying on the stretcher, burning up, a wild look on his face. Mother got in the ambulance with him. We three children were left at home with nine-year-old Max in charge.

What if my father should die? I loved him. There were times when dad would hold me close to him and chuckle as I wriggled away from his scratchy kiss. I knew by his tender touch that he loved me, even though he seemed angry with the world most of the time.

During dad's long stay in the hospital he was too weak to light his own cigarettes. Now mother rolled them, struck the match, and took the first pull on each one to get it burning. This was how mother started smoking, a habit that remained with her the rest of her life.

Several weeks passed before dad was finally allowed to come home, but he was too weak to work. The doctor advised him to stop smoking and drinking and take a long rest. "Otherwise you'll have a relapse. If you go to work too soon you'll wish you hadn't."

Mother was a genius at preparing tasty food with next to nothing to work with. With her care and plenty of rest and by abstaining from smoking and drinking, dad was able to get back to work. But soon he caught another cold and again it lingered. Again the acid fumes aggravated his bronchial condition.

Once more dad had bronchial pneumonia and spent a long period in the hospital. "You ought to get outdoor work, Mr. Larsen," the doctor told him. "That plant's going to finish you off if you're not careful. I mean it. Another bout with pneumonia and you just might not make it."

Father recovered slowly and the family survived on borrowed money. When he was well, it was spring and dad took the doctor's advice and applied for a job with the county road department. Later he told mother, "I told the superintendent I was good with a pick and shovel from working in the mines. I told him of all the experience I'd had with dynamite, too, and that seemed to make an impression." He got the job.

Those were better days. Dad was sober and there was a little money coming in. The debts were being paid. Mother was happy and we children laughed and played with lighter hearts.

Then dad started smoking and drinking again. Working out of doors, he seized every chance to join the other road workers for a cigarette. This would send him into a fit of coughing after each puff.

Mother reminded dad that we should look for a different place to live. "Living on the fourth floor of a walk-up tenement isn't so nice for me and the children," she said.

One night father came home with a light step. "Kay," he called. Mother stood up at the excitement in his voice. "One of the fellows at work says he has a house for us."

We all looked at each other in happy anticipation.

"He says we can have it real cheap. He lived in it himself with his family until they put up a new house. I said we'd come and look at it."

We all went. Young as I was I recognized the look of horror that sprang into mother's eyes. It was a tiny tarpaper shack on a weed-infested lot. The back of the shack was precariously supported by tall stilts and the hill fell away sharply beneath it. A wood shed and an outdoor privy also stood on the lot.

"Pete, what are you thinking of?" mother cried. "I'd rather stay in the tenement. There at least I have water and a bathroom." She shuddered and pulled herself away from dad. "A privy! And a strong wind would blow that miserable shack over!"

Little did she know! We found out that in a strong wind the place would start to sway and the family would hurry out to seek refuge with some kind neighbors who welcomed us in to wait out the storm. The house never did fall over; God must have had his hand on it.

We kids loved to stand near the base of the stilts and with our shoulders start the house swaying by pushing rhythmically. Mother would scream out the windows, "Don't rock the house!"

I have since wondered how my father felt. He had been ill and had run into debt. Surely he must have longed to provide a better living for mother.

His argument was that the rent here was cheaper and the school district outside the core of the city was better. "Now that the children are of school age, we should give them the benefit of a school with a higher rating."

We moved our meager belongings into that dismal two-room shack. A small wood-and-coal-burning stove had to keep us warm and cook our food. Kerosene lamps were our only light. We had a round galvanized washtub for our Saturday night baths. The tiny bedroom held a double-deck bunk for us children to sleep on. Mother and dad slept on a fold-out couch in the main room which was a combination living room, dining room, and kitchen.

There was absolutely no privacy. We heard every sound my parents made. When they didn't want us to understand them, they spoke in Norwegian or Finnish. They quarreled in English. We never talked about their fights the next day. We pretended we had not heard the argument of the night before.

With mother's amazing genius for turning a hovel into a home, this house soon took on a cheerful coziness. We picked dogwood and found room to place huge bouquets.

Mother had a box of other people's cast-offs and from it she took a large piece of black cloth with blue forget-me-nots and green leaves done in a dainty embroidery. She gathered the sides to form a soft ruffle and with this she made a cover for the iron daybed, transforming it from a stark monstrosity into a thing of beauty. She put ruffled curtains at the windows and arranged pictures on the walls. We children accepted it as the only refuge we knew.

Kay and I found the landlord's daughter to be a wonderful friend. We spent hours playing "dress up" and "house." In warm weather we ran barefoot. Shoes were a luxury we couldn't afford unless we were in school or it was cold.

School started. Little Max worked a few hours a week for the Yokoyamas, who owned a vegetable market. Each night when he came home he would bring with him the outside leaves of romaine and lettuce and the dirtiest and most wilted stalks of celery that Mr. Yokoyama gave him. Mother knew these were full of the vitamins her children needed and she accepted them gladly.

We had no running water and had to carry it a pailful at a time from the neighbor's house. Since we couldn't use all the water we wanted, mother kept a pailful handy and used it over and over to wash the vegetable leaves. In 1974 when I was having a physical examination the doctor told me that I had in my blood the highest arsenic content he had ever seen in a person still living. I could only attribute it to the outer leaves of these vegetables, since at that time arsenic was used as a pest killer.

We seldom had visitors but dad's brother Al and his wife Peg never stopped coming. In retrospect, it's amazing, for their visits always ended the same—in a hot argument with dad.

I can remember seeing them get out of their car and in my excitement I would get my tongue twisted and call out to mother, "Mommie, Eg and Pal are here!" I was proud to have their shiny car parked in front of our house.

Uncle Al was a very affectionate man. He would sweep me up in his arms and hug me. I loved him so much and his kisses weren't scratchy as my dad's were. When they arrived everyone would be in a good mood. Mother always begged dad not to argue with them, so for a few minutes he would be a perfect host.

We children would hurry away with our cousins Dorothy and Bill and play as fast as we could for we knew that almost immediately dad and Al would start to talk politics and the war would be on. We would hear voices rising: "You just ought to read Upton Sinclair," dad would say. "That book *The Jungle* really lays it on the line." Al would snort, "He's a communist!" and dad would argue, "He's a socialist. Don't you know the difference?"

Soon dad and Al would be shouting at each other. Our mothers would anxiously try to soothe them and comfort each other. "You don't know what you're talking about!" would be Al's parting shot as he said to Peg, "Let's go home." Then he would hustle Peg and the children into the car and hurry away, vowing as he went that they would never come back. But of course they did. A month or two later, there they would be and the whole scene would be reenacted.

Their family was so different from ours. Uncle Al would take his children boating, fishing, and ice skating—they rented skates for our family once and we all had a marvelous time stumbling around the rink as the organ played "The Skaters' Waltz."

Uncle Al had a ten-foot fishing boat and would take his family for exciting excursions out on Puget Sound. It seemed to me they were always laughing together. Once or twice they took mother and us children on a fishing trip. Dad wouldn't get into the boat—even watching the bobbing of the craft at the dock was enough to make him queasy. Those were precious times when we could go somewhere with Uncle Al and Aunt Peg.

Al was as dad might have been if he had handled his accident and subsequent disappointments differently. Oh, dad enjoyed a good laugh too and when Al told a funny story, dad's laugh was so infectious that we would all have to laugh with him. For a few moments, the entire climate would change.

There was precious little laughter in our home. I have always loved to be surrounded by people who laugh freely. Perhaps because I enjoy it so much in others, I have developed a real humdinger of a laugh myself—not a tinkle as would befit a petite blonde singer. No, I have a high, hearty "yuk yuk yuk" that sets others to laughing.

CHAPTER SIX

I'm not wearing these shoes anymore!" Max announced bitterly as he came in from school one afternoon.

Mother put her arm around his shoulders. "They're too big for you, aren't they, dear?"

The cheap shoes bought for school in the fall had long since come apart. The paper soles, never intended for the Seattle climate, lasted only until it rained. One afternoon, Max had lost the soles entirely and was ridiculed by his classmates for wearing the tops without soles.

That night, father had dug up an old pair of his oxfords. They were full of holes but dad laid cardboard on the soles to help keep Max's feet dry. Then, because they were far too large for a small boy, dad stuck newspapers in the toes to keep Max's feet from moving all the way forward. "Put 'em on," he had ordered. Max did, and had been shuffling about in them ever since.

"Look at this!" Almost in tears, Max demonstrated his awkward walk. "The kids are all making fun of me."

Mother stood watching him, her lips in a hard line. "There's no money, Max. We can't get you new shoes.''

Now I realize how painful it must have been for both of my parents not to be able to provide the most basic needs for their children.

Frustrated by the loss of his own career with the violin, dad decided to make a violinist out of Max. Dad borrowed a three-quarter-size violin from Uncle Al's music store. ''I've got to make something of this boy,'' he said to mother.

His determination had the opposite effect on Max. He hated the violin from the start and resisted dad's efforts with all the force of will a young boy could muster.

One whole winter, our digestions were ruined by dad's tirades at the table. When his hunger was satisfied, dad would lay down his fork and put his knife across the top of his plate. He was finished, and I could feel my stomach muscles tighten as I anticipated the scene he was about to launch.

''How long did you practice today?'' His tone was stern, his look challenging.

Max stiffened and his eyes dropped.

''How long?'' Dad's voice would rise and his eyes would flash angry sparks. When he was angry, one eyebrow would shoot up higher than the other, giving him a really fierce look!

Mother interceded, ''He didn't have much time, Pete—''

Dad turned a cold eye on mother, then back to Max. ''I got you that little instrument to use, not to gather dust.'' Turning to mother, he said, ''You see to it that he practices. How can you sit at home here and neglect your duties as a mother?''

''He practices when—''

''I've got to go to work every day. I want this boy to make something of himself.''

Mother said, ''He's playing beautifully, Pete. He'll—''

Max interrupted. ''I'd rather help pick berries and go fishing.'' He took a deep breath, then flung at my father, ''I *hate* that violin.''

The long cold pause made my stomach jump right into my throat. Now the tirade began in earnest.

Standing stiff-legged, he glared right into Max's face and shouted, ''Go ahead, you stupid oaf! Throw your life away! I try to help you make something of yourself and all you want to do is play and fish.''

Max was already contributing to the family income by helping put food on the table. Mother relied on the fruit we picked and the fish Max caught. But dad overlooked that right now. He ranted on, ''Go ahead, play with your imbecile friends and waste your life, you jackass. Here I'm slaving six days a week. Working on the

18

roads, ruining my hands with callouses. I'd be glad—'' Dad's voice broke a little. "I'd be glad to play the violin, but I have to get these hands hard and calloused. And I'm doing it so you can make something of yourself. But you talk about fishing and playing with your friends.'' He pushed his chair back roughly and left the room. We all relaxed a bit.

I was very young at the time, but I wanted to tell dad that I would like to play the violin. I wanted to say, "I'll practice, daddy. I'll practice real hard and learn to play it real good.'' But I didn't.

Dad finally gave up trying to teach an unwilling pupil. In despair he returned the instrument to Uncle Albert.

For many weeks after returning the violin, dad was grouchy and upset. Every meal was lecture time. Both mother and Max would catch a scolding.

One night after dinner, dad sat down as usual to drink his wine. This time, though he didn't pick up a book. Instead, he just sat and glowered at Max, muttering. Finally he said loud enough for all of us to hear, "You'd like to kill me, wouldn't you, Max?'' With his eyes lowered, he hissed between his teeth, "*How* are you going to kill me?''

"Pete!'' mother screamed. "How could you? You promised me—we said we never would—Oh, Pete, how could you?'' Sobbing, mother threw her arms around Max. Bewildered and frightened, we all began to cry.

Our hysteria seemed to rouse dad from his stupor. He realized he had disclosed the secret he and mother had vowed never to tell the children.

All the gypsy's prophecies had now come true except: "One of your students will become famous,'' and "Your son will grow up to kill you.''

CHAPTER SEVEN

Not all our days were as black as that one. We had a few happy evenings when dad could scrape up a few extra cents and take us to a funny movie. He roared at Will Rogers and Charlie Chaplin and laughed throughout the Looney Tunes. When he wasn't drunk or dissatisfied with us he could be wonderful. We were a touching and kissing family. Even after we were quite grown we never left the house without kissing mother goodbye and when we went to bed we always kissed both of our parents good night.

Mother deserved a good husband and a better life. Through the years she took more abuse than I even knew until many years later. Kay and I used to ask her, "Why is daddy always angry with us? Are we naughty?"

Tears would well up in her eyes and she would take us in her arms and whisper, "Don't worry, my babies. You're not naughty. Daddy loves you."

"Then why does he shout at us so much?" we would ask.

"When you're older you'll understand better. All he wants is for you to make something of yourselves."

"What does that mean?"

"Well, you should know what that means. Max could have earned a lot of money playing in an orchestra if he had learned to play the violin."

Perhpas *I* could make something of myself. I longed to start taking violin lessons. I ran to mother, reaching my arms up for her to take me on her lap, and said, "*I* want to play the violin, mommy. Someday I want to play for big audiences like daddy used to do."

"That's nice, Dee Dee." Mother laughed. "But now the violin is still bigger than you are."

I drew myself up. "I'm big."

"Of course you are. But you have to grow up a little more." I studied mother's face. Was that a tear in her eye?

I remember mother as the gentlest of women. To me she was always beautiful. Her wardrobe was pathetic. She had two dresses— her house dress and her "Sunday" dress, though we never went to church. Her house dress was a faded cotton that had once been an orange print, and her good dress was of green silk with long wide sleeves, a cowl collar, and a little flare at the bottom of the skirt. She had a black wool coat, worn and graying with age at the cuffs and collar. The glowing auburn hair that had caught dad's eye at the dance when they first met was already turning gray. But the violet eyes were as beautiful as ever. Since she believed that "smiling gives you wrinkles," she didn't smile often. But she spoke soothingly and gently and her voice was soft and low.

Every morning, mother carefully applied her makeup. I sat on her bed and watched every move. First she put on lipstick, then a touch of rouge and powder. Her eyebrows were thick so she kept them neatly plucked. Last, she did her eyes and unconsciously my face copied hers as she raised her eyebrows and opened her mouth to form an "O" as she brushed the brown mascara onto her long lashes.

Mother's arms provided strength and comfort. She played small innocent jokes on us children to keep us in good spirits through all the hard times.

Dad provided the challenge for our lives. He expected far more of his children than we were ever able to achieve. He was never satisfied. "What are you going to do with your life?" rang like a steady refrain through my early years. But I responded to his challenge and to this day I'm grateful to dad for driving me to develop self-discipline.

And dad gave me my initial training in music.

CHAPTER EIGHT

Dad's third bout with pneumonia occurred the following spring. He almost died of suffocation but was saved when the doctor cut out a rib section and inserted a lung drainage tube. The doctor told him it was time he left the damp climate of Seattle and lived in drier air. "Without it," the doctor warned, "you're sure to have a relapse."

Mother made it her business to carry out this order. She got a map of Washington and pointed out to dad a town named Yelm, just west of the Cascades.

"But Max is in school," father protested.

Mother went to Max's teacher and explained the problem. It was spring; would it be all right if she took Max out of school for the rest of the term?

Teacher and principal both consented; Max would be promoted to fourth grade.

Mother appealed to Augustus for funds and he came through without delay. It was little more than our train fare, but it got us to Yelm. The owner of our tarpaper shack assured us we could move back into it when we returned after father regained his health.

Kay and I carried our dolls. It took very few bags to hold our clothes and personal items.

We had no definite destination in Yelm. For us children it was an adventure. Now when I think about my mother and father leaving the only home and security they had, and dad in poor health, I marvel at their daring to move the five of us out as they did.

Dad and mother went to the town hall where the "help wanted" notices were posted. "Farmer needs family for berry picking." Eagerly we applied for the job, but the farmer shook his head at the sight of us. "I meant a couple with bigger kids," he said. "I need a more grown-up family." He looked down at Kay and me and asked, "What kind of work could such cute little girls do?"

Kay promptly answered, "I can pick berries!"

Not to be outdone, I echoed, "Me too!"

"OK. We'll give it a try," he said, his eyes searching the area as though still hoping a better prospect might come down the road. "Hop in my truck."

Max and Kay and Mother and I climbed up into the truck bed. Dad rode up front with the farmer. We children squealed and laughed. Mother seemed happy. The wind blew my hair into my eyes and mouth as we bumped down the country road.

As the farmer lifted me down from the truck and set me beside Max and Kay he said, "Now, I expect you children will be my best berry pickers." He led us to the row of cabins where the workers lived and we crowded into the small drab room that was to be our home. If mother felt any disappointment, she didn't show it. There was a kerosene lamp, a kerosene stove, a table and chairs, and a washstand with a place for a pail of water and dipper. We would carry water from the farmer's well. Two double-deck wooden bunks with straw mattresses were our beds.

Mother opened up a small bag and took out the carefully folded flowered curtains she had brought from the tarpaper shack. She strung them up at the two windows of our new home and immediately the room looked more cheerful. She laid red-and-white checkered oil cloth over the table and sent us girls out to pick wild flowers. As we went, we saw father take mother in his arms and kiss her.

These were extraordinarily happy days. Dad wasn't smoking or drinking. He worked hard helping the farmer prepare the bushes for their harvest. Mother and the farmer's wife did farm chores. Kay and I played with their little girl and Max fished in a large irrigation ditch near by. Our work would start when the berries began to ripen.

While we were working at the berry farm our grandfather, now divorced from Louise, came to visit us. He was a handsome man with a white moustache and startling white hair. No wonder mother worshiped him. Easygoing and gentle, he soon won our hearts completely.

Finally the farmer decided it was time to pick his crop and now life became more exciting for me. All the berry pickers hurried out to the bushes very early in the morning. We girls ate almost as many as we picked of those delicious sweet blackcap raspberries. It was a bumper crop.

We soon found out that it was hard work. My back got tired and

I longed to quit. But no. We were migrant workers and we had signed with Mr. Jones as a family.

When the farmer came to see how we were doing, he said, "Well, now, if you aren't the best little workers I've got! Your row is one of the cleanest picked of all I've seen."

We stood there smiling broadly at him, revealing purple teeth and lips.

He said, "Even though you aren't the fastest pickers, I'm happy with you because your berries aren't crushed." Then he noticed our lips. He laughed and said, "You'd better not eat too many of those berries."

Mother, alarmed that we would lose our job, turned on us and warned, "You mind Mr. Jones, do you hear?"

But Mr. Jones laughed again and said, "Better keep an eye on those kids. If they get a bellyache, they'll need a good dose of castor oil."

"Oh?" mother questioned.

"There's an old Indian saying about them berries, 'Eat'm too much, plug'm up fast!' It's the seeds, ma'am."

We did indeed all get stomach aches. Dad had to go to town and get us some castor oil.

At last the berries were all picked and it was time to be paid. It seemed there was nothing to do but return to Seattle.

The tally of our earnings showed that we had only enough left for trainfare back home after the farmer deducted what he had advanced for kerosene and groceries. Father and mother were depressed and their mood affected us children. We had all worked so hard, thinking that every berry was money in our purse.

Then there was a knock at our door and one of the workers said, "I'm driving to Lake Chelan to pick apples. If you want to help buy gas and oil for the trip, I'm sure you can find work there too."

That ride bore much resemblance to the trip to California of Ma Joad and her family, depicted in *Grapes of Wrath*. After a series of flat tires and much engine trouble, we arrive in apple country in plenty of time to find work. The man who hired us said we children should pick all the apples that were within reach as long as we kept our feet on the ground. "I don't want any kids climbing ladders," he warned.

We worked hard all week. Kay and I had found a new girl to play with and on Sunday Max went fishing with the local Indian boys. Dad and mother read Westerns, and we girls played house under a big apple tree.

When dad had collected the money we all earned, he said it was time to return to Seattle. "You kids should be in school," he said.

Max was ready for fourth grade and Kay was eager to start first grade. School was already in session, as it was near the end of October.

CHAPTER NINE

We came home to the tarpaper shack, now surrounded with weeds. If mother felt depressed it didn't show. She put the curtains back at the windows and the embroidered cover back on the daybed. As always, she put a vase of flowers on the table.

Now that Kay was of school age, dad said he would start her on the violin. Once more he borrowed a three-quarter-size instrument and once more tried to force the violin on an unwilling pupil. He had no patience. He was too full of anger. Kay's fumbling attempts infuriated him and every lesson ended with father shouting and Kay in tears.

One evening after school, Kay told mother, "I wish I didn't have to play the violin."

"Your father wants you to, dear. Wouldn't it be nice if you could play as well as daddy wants you to?"

"But why does daddy get so mad at me?"

"Just keep trying, darling. When you learn to play a little better daddy will be happy with you."

Mother was able to keep Kay practicing and she was becoming better at it but the tension was always there. The more anxious father became, the more nervous it made Kay. One night she was playing "Humoresque"—very badly. Dad stamped his foot and his hair fell down over his forehead. "That's terrible! You've got to practice more! *Concentrate* when you play."

Mother said, "She's practicing every night after school, Pete. It's just that you make her nervous. She played it fine for me."

By this time Kay was crying. Dad stopped shouting and his face softened. "You've got to try, child," he said now in a gentler voice. "You shouldn't cry. Try to learn what I'm telling you. You've got everything you need to be a violinist—long tapered fingers, strength in your hands and arms, finger dexterity, and a good ear for music."

Kay was listening now and he repeated, "You're pretty even now but you're going to be tall and slender and beautiful. And if you can play the violin well, you'll always be able to make a *good living*."

24

Kay started playing again and seemed almost to enjoy it. If only father could have used praise more often and held up goals rather than resorting to the harsh criticism which had turned Max against the violin.

That evening when we kissed our parents good night, dad held Kay a little longer than usual and seemed more gentle with her. Then we went to bed. Dad rolled a Bull Durham cigarette and puffed at it, trying not to inhale because of his delicate lung condition. He and mother sat by the kerosene lamp and read Steinbeck.

One chilly day that winter I was playing with a neighbor child. My friend's mother handed me an envelope.

"Here, Norma," she said. "Take this envelope." She bent down and explained. "Go to all the neighbors. When they answer the door, show them this writing on the envelope. That's a note to them. Then wait a few minutes and they will give it back to you. Then you go to the next house and do it all over again. Is that clear?"

That sounded like fun so I was off, the loose soles of my worn shoes flapping with each step. I went to the first door and knocked. The neighbor read the note on the envelope and glanced at my shoes.

When she returned the envelope to me, I proceeded to go around to all the neighbors, doing the same thing.

When I got home I showed the envelope to mother. Dad looked up from his book. "What's that?" he asked curiously. He set down the glass of wine he held and came over to mother. She drew a handful of money from the envelope. She gave dad the note and he read, "Dear Neighbor. You will notice that our little friend needs shoes. If you can help, please place a contribution in this envelope."

Dad's face grew very red. "Begging!" he exclaimed in utter shock and disbelief. "You've been begging!" I wasn't sure what begging was, but it sounded dreadful, and I was overwhelmed with guilt. Shoving the envelope into my hands, he pushed me toward the door. "You go right back. You go back to every house. Tell 'em we take charity from *nobody!* Tell 'em to keep their blankety-blank money."

Timidly I went back to every house. As each neighbor came to the door I spoke my piece, my face hot with embarrassment. "Please take out the money you put in the envelope, because my daddy doesn't want it."

One night we three children climbed into our beds on our wooden bunks built into the wall. "Tell us the story about the haunted castle," we demanded of Max. We never grew tired of Max's marvelous stories. He was five years older than Kay, and she and I considered Max grown up all our lives. I imitated him in an extreme form of idol worship. If Max did somersaults, I did somersaults. If Max walked on his hands, I walked on mine. If Max walked on his hands up the stairs, I walked on my hands up the stairs. In following him around, I became the world's foremost tomboy.

"Once upon a time," Max began in his beautiful expressive voice, "in a land far across the sea, lived a happy little family, the Pfeffernuses—"

"Pfeffernuses," I laughed.

"Pfeffernuses!" Kay giggled. We rolled the name over our tongues, as we always did. Max chose the best names for his characters and we laughed every time we heard the name "Pfeffernus."

"Now be quiet," Max warned. "They lived in a tiny village near the edge of a deep dark forest.

"Mr. and Mrs. Pfeffernus had three charming children: Pumpernickel, age ten; Tya, six; and Weetina, four.

"Mrs. Pfeffernus was always worried when her children went outdoors to play because many youngsters from the village had strayed into the woods and had never been found. One day, in spite of their mother's warning, the Pfeffernus children chased after a big butterfly. Across valleys and meadows, over rocks and fallen trees they scampered, happily unaware that the morning had passed into afternoon and that the afternoon had turned into early evening. All day long they had listened, enraptured, to the sounds of nature, but now suddenly they were alarmed by the raucous call of a crow. As they listened their eyes wandered upward.

"Looming above them were the ruins of an ancient castle and vultures were circling menacingly around and around in the sky.

"Pumpernickel said, 'What a scary place! It looks haunted.'

"It was getting darker as clouds scudded overhead—the wind hissed and moaned through the trees.

" 'I'm afraid!' said Weetina.

" 'Me too,' said Rya.

"At that moment a great crash of thunder nearly frightened the three of them to death. As if their troubles were piling up around them, it started pouring rain.

"They huddled together, trying to protect themselves from the chilly wind and rain.

"Pumpernickel said, 'Oh, why did we have to disobey Momma and go into the woods?'

" 'Cuz I wanted to catch that butterfly,' said Weetina.

"Just then, illuminated by a sparkling flash of lightning, a wicked—"

Max laughed. "That's all for tonight. We'll continue tomorrow night. Good night!"

"Aw c'mon, Max, tell about the wicked witch. Please, c'mon."

But he just laughed. He always kept us in suspense until the next night even though we knew the story as well as he did.

Later, when I should have been asleep, I heard dad take out his violin and practice for a while. But he soon gave it up and put it back in its old worn-out case.

"It sounds beautiful, Pete," mother said. "Don't stop yet."

I agreed. In my fantasy, I was the one drawing the bow across the strings. I was standing in front of a huge audience, playing a violin concerto brilliantly. The audience burst into vigorous applause and I bowed repeatedly.

Something was compelling me to learn music.

During his struggle to regain his health, dad had controlled his drinking completely. But now, back at work on the roads, the wine bottle again became his evening companion.

One night dad was in an ugly mood. He sat drinking and glowering at the rest of us. We tip-toed around him, hoping no one would come to the door and witness our shame. Mother had an intuition about when dad would be hardest to live with and this night she hustled Kay and me off to bed earlier than usual.

"Is Max coming to bed?" I asked, looking longingly at my brother doing his homework.

"Not just yet, darling," mother whispered. "Max, you hurry up now and finish," mother said with a nervous glance at dad.

There was trouble in the air. I felt it deep down in my stomach. From the time I could understand words, I had gone through this —these awful times when father would drink until he got ugly. Then he would start in on one or all of us—mother and Max more often than Kay and me.

Mother must have felt it too. As soon as Max finished his homework mother sent him to bed.

Kay and I were overjoyed. "Finish the story about the haunted castle," we begged.

"No, I'm tired tonight."

"Aw, please, please!"

"Well, OK."

It always took a little begging, but we knew he'd do it even though he wouldn't finish the story. He had already spent three nights telling it this time.

"Let's see," Max pretended to be trying to remember. "Where were we?"

"Where the Pfeffernus children were hanging by their hair in front of that smoky old fire—" I said.

"No! No, sir! That was the night before!" Kay said. "You were at the woman giving the children a broom to fly on."

"To escape the dancing ocarinist," I said, savoring the word. Max chose the most exciting words in his stories. I clasped my hands over my chest and kicked my feet in the air.

"Dee Dee! Stop shaking the beds!" Kay shouted.

"Keep still or I won't tell it!" Max threatened.

I put my legs down and lay perfectly still.

"Oh, yes!" Max said in a very grown-up way. "The dancing ocarinist threw everything he could lay his hands on upwards, trying to knock them down.

"Weetina, with a quick eye for flying objects, was able to dodge the missile.

" 'What do we do now?' asked Rya.

" 'Fly low through the forest! And hurry before morning dawns! Once the first cock crows you are doomed, unless you reach a village and fly into the first church belfry you see! You will be safe there!'

"Out through the big open window, amidst a hail of cups, spoons, knives, and sundry items, Weetina guided the broom into the night.

" 'Quick,' warned Pumpernickel. 'Remember the woman said that we should fly low! Through the trees!' "

I became aware of my parents' voices rising. Then a loud thump as a body hit a wall.

"Pete, please, please," mother begged.

We heard loud slaps. I clenched my teeth and buried my face in my pillow.

The next morning, mother came into our room and went to each of our beds. "Max," she called and kissed him. Then, "Kay," and then, "Dee Dee," her nickname for me. We sleepily got out of our beds and found our clothes. Mother already had her hair combed and her makeup on. But the makeup couldn't hide the bruise she had between her eyes. Usually we pretended we hadn't heard the fighting, and we wouldn't let on that we noticed her bruises. But this morning, seeing her eyes almost swollen shut, we all exclaimed, "Oh, mother!" I ran to her and flung my arms around her waist. Kay stood speechless, wide-eyed with concern.

Max clenched his fists and said through his teeth, "I could kill him! He can't do that to you!"

Mother was quick to answer. "Don't say that, son. It won't help to be angry. Your father will die young enough—the way he abuses his body. Attacking him will only make things worse."

"I'm not going to let him do that to you."

"Be patient, Max. When you children are grown you will leave."

"But what about you?"

"I will, too."

That afternoon on his way home from work, the landlord stopped by to collect the rent. "What happened to you?" he asked mother, eyeing her with obvious curiosity.

"Oh, I...tripped on the step...and hit my head on the handrail."

"You did, huh?"

It was plain even to us children that the landlord didn't believe her.

That night, he warned my father that he was getting upset about all the loud arguments going on at our house at night.

That was our first warning that we might be evicted.

CHAPTER TEN

The first years of school were painful for me. I felt I didn't belong, and I was careful not to call attention to myself. To this day I have difficulty feeling like "one of the gang." It's a problem I am still trying to overcome, along with being too sensitive.

When summer came, school was out, and I reveled in being able to go barefoot all day.

One June day dad brought home a twenty-gallon crock. "Picked this up at the secondhand store," he explained to mother. "I want you to brew me some beer. I'm getting sick and tired of this prohibition nonsense."

Mother inspected the earthenware crock, putting her fingers in the chips and superficial cracks. "It's still watertight."

"You clean that up and make me some brew," he ordered.

Father hoisted the crock up to the attic above the woodshed. Mother carried pails of water up the ladder and filled the container to the proper level. She measured and stirred the ingredients until she got the right proportions. Each day she climbed up the ladder to skim the froth from the top as the fermentation began.

One night dad came in and made a point of kissing mother. She tried to turn her face away, but he pulled her closer. "Don't avoid me," he scolded. "You've been into the beer again, haven't you?"

"Just sampling it to see if it's ready," she said. "You shouldn't complain if I sample it since you told me to make it."

Much annoyed, father hurried out to the woodshed and climbed the ladder to the attic with me right behind him. He struck a match and lifted the gauze that covered the crock.

He swore and threw the gauze back. I had to hurry back down

the ladder to keep him from stepping on my fingers.

I followed father back to the house. He confronted mother angrily. "It's down an inch!" he shouted. "You must have drunk three quarts today!"

"No, Pete," she pleaded. "It evaporates. You know that. I'm sure it does."

Father unlocked his toolbox where he kept his wine jug and poured a waterglass full of wine. As he drank it, he lectured and scolded mother, growing more abusive with each sip. We children kept out of his way. Kay and I were frightened, but Max was scowling and his fists were clenched.

As our summer vacation drew to an end, mother had the beer all bottled and had started brewing a new batch.

Being curious little girls, Kay and I decided we'd like to sample it. We stole off to the shed and dipped our cups into the brew.

We looked at each other and grimaced. "It's bitter," Kay said.

"It tastes like straw," I observed. I saw Kay going back for more so I giggled and did the same. My head began to feel as it did when I whirled around in circles. I couldn't stop laughing. Kay started to snicker, at the same time trying to quiet me so we wouldn't be discovered. But the more we tried to stop, the louder we became, till we heard footsteps coming up the ladder.

Dad's expression when he saw us was one of disbelief, then anger.

We tried to be serious, looking at the floor and pressing our lips together primly. Then a snicker broke through my sealed lips and we both burst out again in boisterous laughter.

Dad gave us both a good spanking and sent us to bed with a warning to leave his home brew alone!

In the fall, father bought us our annual pair of cardboard shoes and I entered second grade. I'll never forget my second grade teacher, Emma Lou Douglas. She singled me out for many special acts of kindness. Perhaps she knew what our home was like. She would let me stay after school and help with her work. Sometimes she would give me an apple or a sandwich—even candy.

I sensed that she really cared for me. It has made me realize what choice opportunities a teacher has to encourage a lonely child.

The teachers had initiated a program where families could bring usable clothing for needy students. Sometimes Kay and I were given warm coats and shoes.

One day during lunch hour an older girl pointed to my shoes, and said, "Those shoes used to be mine."

Before I could think of an answer, she rejoined her friends and I saw them looking at my feet and giggling.

Not for the first time, I felt the sting of being poor.

One afternoon Kay and I raced home from school. She beat me and threw open the door. "Mother," we called. There was no answer. The breakfast dishes were still in the sink. This wasn't like mother. She always kept a spotless house. Dad never wanted her to let us girls do housework. "They've got to develop their talent," he would say, "or they'll never make anything of themselves."

Thinking mother must have gone to buy food, we washed the dishes and swept the floor, making a game of it. Mother had still not returned when we finished.

We were both feeling very silly that day. Everything made us laugh. "Tell you what," Kay said. "I'll give you a violin lesson."

Now the reluctant pupil became the tyrannical teacher. "Play!" she ordered in imitation of dad.

I drew the bow across the strings.

"Not that way, you stupid fool!" We both doubled up in laughter. She yelled at me in mock rage every time I touched the strings. "You idiot! You'll never make anything of yourself!" Her imitations of dad were letter perfect, sending us both into such gales of laughter that we just gave up the violin and rolled on the floor.

Suddenly I began to feel uncomfortable. Making a joke of the violin? That seemed wrong, for some reason. Without telling Kay my feelings, I quietly took the violin and put it back. "Let's go look for mother," I said.

On the doorstep we met Max carrying two quarts of milk from the market where he worked. "Where's mother?" he asked.

We said we didn't know. "We've been home a whole hour and mom's still not here."

"Can't blame her if she ran away," Max said. "She better be here when dad gets home or she'll catch it."

When dad came home, we innocently told him, "We haven't seen mother since before school this morning."

His expression prompted me to follow him to the woodshed and up the ladder. We heard heavy breathing. There by the crock lay mother in a dead sleep, slumped back against the attic wall, her head fallen to one side. Dad lifted the gauze and looked into the crock. Cursing, he grabbed mother's shoulders and shook her violently. She opened a bleary eye. He pulled her to her feet, and somehow got her down the ladder and into the house.

That night we had a late supper. After we were in bed, mother and dad had a long, loud argument.

The next day we were asked to move.

Our next house had electricity, running water, and a real bathroom. It had electric wiring, but we couldn't afford to have it hooked up, so the old kerosene lamps continued to do service. The rent was not much higher than we had been paying before. The house was better than the last one, but it was still much too small.

Kay seldom had violin lessons now but when she did I watched and listened carefully to everything that was said as I waited for the day I could try.

One day I approached mother. "Mother," I whispered, "would you let me play the violin when dad isn't home?"

"Do you want to play it, honey?"

"Oh, yes, mother."

"I will let you when just the two of us are at home."

That day came and mother took the treasured violin out of its old worn case. I had listened so carefully and observed so much that I had learned many scales and arpeggios.

A short time later I stood practicing the violin, trying to imitate the beautiful tone my father made. There was a quality to his music that brought tears to my eyes, even then, when I was a young girl. I carefully went up and down the scales, drawing the bow slowly so that it touched only one string, shaking my left wrist to make a fast vibrato the way I had seen dad do it. I heard a sound and turned around—there was dad with tears streaming down his cheeks. He rushed to me, and knelt down to hug me, saying, "At last I've got a violinist in the family."

"You won't have to worry about me practicing, daddy," I assured him. And I meant it.

"Well, you're pretty small, Dee Dee, but I'll be happy to start you on lessons every day," dad whispered, obviously thrilled that one of his children loved his precious instrument.

Later that night I heard dad tell mother that it was surely too bad that the only one in the house interested in the violin was the runt of the family. "If only she had Kay's long fingers and arms. If she was only tall and slender—"

I put my fingers in my ears. I wanted to look like Kay more than anything in the world.

In spite of his criticism, I was determined to learn. Dad was right. My hands were too small, my arms too short, but I wanted lessons. Gradually I learned to sightread any music set in front of me. What an asset that has been to me in my singing career!

CHAPTER ELEVEN

I always loved Aunt Eva's visits. She was mother's youngest sister—a sparkling, vibrant girl. When she first arrived in Seattle to look for work, dad gave her a bad time. "You ought to try to make something of yourself," he'd say. "What can you do to further yourself in the world? What talent are you going to develop?"

When Eva took a domestic job with a well-to-do family, dad's indignation spilled over. "Can't you do something better than be a maid for rich people?"

Every time Eva visited us, dad would start lecturing her. "What are you going to make of yourself? Now's your chance. You aren't going to give yourself away for the rest of your life, are you?"

Eva was unflappable. She handled dad with a light touch. Throughout my life, Eva always provided fun and laughter. There wasn't much laughter in our home, but when Eva would come, the mood always lifted. Many years later, Eva and her husband, Ivar, lived near us for almost two years. She still affected me the same way. I loved her very much and do to this day.

Mother's older sister, Emma, and her husband Gus, made infrequent visits to our home. They drove a beautiful, shiny green Olds—and would let me sit behind the wheel, pretending to drive. I dreamed of owning a car of my own some day.

Max had developed a beautiful soprano voice. Dad wasn't much impressed. "That'll change in a few years," he said. But it gave him the idea that Kay and I should develop our voices and perhaps we could be coloratura sopranos like his sister Minnie.

Somehow he managed to save enough money to buy a used phonograph and some old records, scratchy and cracked. There was music by Kreisler, Heifitz, Caruso, Schumann-Heink, Ponselle, and Galli-Curci, plus some Russian ballet music by Tschaikowsky.

Mother loved the music, as we all did. From the time we came home after school, right through the dinner hour, we had music. We got to know all the numbers. When the needle came to a crack in the record we all bore with it patiently until it had passed that part. The music even soothed dad, making him far more pleasant during dinner. Much to the delight of both of our parents, Kay and I soon started imitating Galli-Curci.

Mother reminded dad that he had listened to Minnie doing her vocal exercises. "Why don't you teach the girls how to do it?" she asked. "You could teach them to sing."

"I will," he said, "but first I will teach Max."

We all dreaded that. Max rebelled, as we knew he would. Dad raged and drank heavily.

The next night I asked father, "Will you teach me how to sing?"

He looked down at me briefly and said, "You just concentrate on the violin for now."

Max gave dad no cooperation so he started in on Kay. She showed absolutely no interest.

"I suppose you'd rather sit and draw," dad sneered. "You'll never make anything of yourself drawing!"

The two children he felt had potential in violin and voice rejected his teaching. Disgruntled, he continued to give me violin lessons and I practiced daily for about two hours. I felt this was the only encouragement my father had in life, so I worked extra hard. Meanwhile, when he was away from the house, mother would let me practice what I had heard father teaching Max and Kay about voice.

Again, I asked dad to teach me how to sing, and this time he took me seriously.

Slowly I was overcoming my father's reluctance. By sheer determination I was learning to play the violin and I was learning how to sing. Father, who held no hope of my ever becoming a great violinist, one day made my day bright. There was admiration in his voice when he said, "You're doing very well, Dee Dee. You are ambitious and willing to work hard."

The winter of 1932 was the hardest winter of my life. We suffered from hunger and malnutrition. Even the plain macaroni with salt gave out. I believe I came close to starvation. At times I was too weak to stand and I lay on the cot most of the time, missing a good deal of school. My chest felt terrible and my mouth had a foul taste day and night. I thought I was going to die.

At Thanksgiving that year we had hardly any food at all. The day before the holiday, several ladies appeared at the door. Dad answered their knock. Cheerfully, one of them spoke for the group. "Happy Thanksgiving, Mr. Larsen! We brought you a turkey!"

A turkey! That brought me to my feet. I staggered to the door, peeking out at them.

Dad swore. Taking the heavy basket, overflowing with food, from the woman who held it out to him, dad threw it violently out onto the ground. "I don't take charity!" he bellowed. "Remember that! Peter Magnus Larsen doesn't take charity!" He slammed the door!

I watched through the window as the women picked up the turkey, a bag of cranberries, potatoes, yams, and assorted cans. With an indignant glance at the closed door, they went on their way.

Mother was crying. I was hungry—we all were.

For Thanksgiving we had bread.

Young as we were, we all experienced great embarrassment when our peers discussed the radio shows of the day. We just couldn't join in the conversation when they wondered how Li'l Orphan Annie was going to get out of her latest predicament or what the next Jack Armstrong episode might hold.

In 1933, though, Max used some of his earnings from the Japanese market to buy a crystal set, which he put together. Now at last we had a radio. We three children still slept in the same room and when we went to bed early at night to be warm, we took turns with the earphones, savoring the triumphs and setbacks of our radio characters. Now we could discuss the programs in school. We were "in." Later, when times were better, we got a radio the whole family could listen to, and mother loved to listen to "Ma Perkins" and "Pepper Young's Family."

But there was a new cause of embarrassment at home. We couldn't be sure that we would find mother sober when we got home from school. From occasional nipping she had become alcoholic.

From the time I was ten, mother drank heavily. Some days after school we would find her under the bed. Whether she crawled there to hide her shame or to spare us, we never knew. When she had slept it off she would come out and make our dinner or join us in the evening's activities.

CHAPTER TWELVE

As we approached our teens, Kay and I became more competitive and there were many scraps. Sometimes mother would get so disgusted with our fighting she would come and take our hands and make us hit each other. "Go ahead," she'd say, "get it out of your system!"

But Max! Oh, how I adored him! I always considered him grown up; he grew to six feet while still in his teens. Max was an ardent sports enthusiast and because I admired him so much I followed him wherever he would let me. I lifted weights because Max did; stood on my head when he did. And I still stand on my head regularly because I want to be able to do it when I'm eighty!

I developed a firm bond with the creatures of nature. I loved birds and pitied and petted the snakes. More than once I shocked mother and Kay by appearing at home with a garter snake around my neck. I think I identified with them because they were hated. "Oh, you poor thing," I would say. "I love you."

Not only was I persecuted in school for wearing clothes out of the poor box, but also because my father so often embarrassed us when he was drunk.

There was still another reason why I felt unloved. One day when I came home from school, I overheard mother talking with our landlord's wife. Hearing my name, I listened under the window.

"We really wanted only two children," mother calmly told our neighbor. "We really didn't want to have Norma. In fact I tried to lose the baby by riding my horse every day. After she was born there was a well-to-do woman who wanted to take her but we decided not to adopt her out."

I stole quietly into the house. I went to the bedroom and threw myself on my bed and wept. My heart was deeply hurt as I heard that my parents hadn't really wanted me.

It was not to be the last time I would hear that story. My folks didn't seem to feel the least bit ashamed to tell this, and they weren't careful about my hearing it.

One Saturday mother returned from house hunting. She was flushed with excitement. "Oh, Pete," she exclaimed, "I met the nicest family! They have a house for rent right next door to the one they live in. They want me to bring the family right over—"

We all went back with her and met Bob and Del Robertson. Mother and Del hit it off from the start. They had a son Jerry, just a little younger than Max, and a beautiful shepherd dog, Pat, who considered our house home. Much to our delight, he adopted us.

Fortunately dad hadn't been drinking that afternoon. He had just returned from teaching his violin students. He knew he couldn't go to the homes of his students with liquor on his breath. When he did, he sometimes lost a student and the loss of $2.50 a week would be catastrophic. If dad had been half drunk that afternoon, it's doubtful he could have been so charming and we might not have pleased the Robertsons so much.

After meeting us the Robertsons said we could rent the house for $17 a month, which was only $4.50 more than we were presently paying.

We moved in. Kay and I had an upstairs bedroom all to ourselves. A large window overlooked a vacant lot. Max had a smaller room across the hall. Downstairs, we had a large living room with a fireplace, a kitchen and dinette, and a master bedroom. It was heated with a wood stove and our bedrooms had registers in the floor that brought the warm air up from downstairs. We thought it was a mansion. It was the last house we children were to occupy with our parents.

The house was wired for electricity and finally we were able to afford to use the lights. But since we couldn't buy an electric iron we still used old stove irons. Mother did the laundry in a round tin tub, patiently scrubbing out the dirt on a glass washboard.

Max brought in the extra money for the rent by collecting bottles and selling them to the grocer. Then, at the very worst of the depression, dad was laid off by the county road department. They too had run out of funds.

Now dad tried hard to get more violin students. Occasionally he would report, "I got a new student today. That's another $2.50." Reluctantly, he had applied for welfare but was too proud to carry home the food they gave us. Max and mother borrowed Jerry's wagon and brought home the surplus commodities that helped keep us alive that winter. Many times the fish and meat were bad and weevils had gotten into the cereals, but mother was grateful to have anything at all.

Dad got permission from Del to make a garden in the empty lot behind our house. That summer we had green onions, potatoes, carrots, peas, and string beans. The raspberry bushes produced a generous crop in season.

We were delighted to find that the strawberry patch that went with our house yielded large, delicious berries. "The folks who lived here before must have carefully tended that patch," dad said to mother. "If we do the same, we'll have strawberries as long as we live here."

One day, dad set out to give lessons. He turned back and said to Max, "Spade up the ground around the strawberries today. Don't forget."

Not quite knowing what dad meant, and not asking mother, Max carefully spaded under all the strawberry plants. When dad came home he was furious and all the rest of us cried.

The Robertsons never pressed dad for the rent. We appreciated their kindness and generosity during those desperate times.

I spent a lot of time with a vivacious blonde neighbor girl, Virginia Viewig. Her mother seemed to know that I always craved something good to eat. She would offer me a slice of her delicious German kuchen or give me a piece of homemade apple strudel.

The Viewigs had all kinds of recreational equipment—bicycles, skates, horseshoes, and badminton rackets. We spent happy weekends playing at their home.

It embarrassed me to bring my friends to our house because dad not only drank but he also lectured my friends. "Virginia," he'd say, "what are you going to make of yourself? You should be planning now. Don't be wasting your time. Be somebody. Don't just get married and have a bunch of kids."

Virginia heeded him well. She had a flair for business and designing of ladies' apparel. After World War II, working out of her own little house, she took orders for designing and sewing for entire weddings. Later she got orders from department stores. As her business grew she hired help. Eventually she needed more space and rented a large factory in downtown Seattle. Soon her clientele included many of the nation's outstanding apparel and department stores.

She married and had two children. After five years of assisting her husband in his business she accepted a position as consultant for a pattern company and eventually developed what had been the program of her dreams—making individual patterns that really fit, and holding classes where she taught women how to design their own clothes. She has written and published several books on personal pattern development.

Virginia is only one of many women who have proved that women can "make something of themselves," and still have a family.

My friendship with Virginia was to have far-reaching consequences. If it hadn't been for her, I might very well be an old maid—a very shy one. For it was through the Viewigs I met my husband, and through him that I gradually overcame my shyness.

Another close friend in our class was Dorothy Reddy. We three played together for years, never suffering the petty jealousies many girls playing in "threes" encounter. She, too, frequently caught the unabridged lecture from dad.

Whenever the county had money for roads, they would call dad back. Each time he would give up his weekday students and go back to work for the county. On Saturdays, he would give as many violin lessons as he could. I still remember watching him clean up to go. His callused hands were thick with grime from the road work. But dad was so fastidious, he couldn't bear to handle the violin with dirty hands. I can still see him at the wash basin, brushing his cracked, bleeding calluses, gasping with the pain.

He would don his old suit, which mother always kept neatly pressed. He always wanted his hair *just so,* but couldn't afford to go to the barber shop, so mother would cut it. He sat holding a mirror, and watched every snip with an eagle eye—always anxious that she not cut too much. Last, he applied a little mascara to his red moustache. Then he was off with his violin in its old worn leather case.

It seemed he could have built a good business of teaching the violin if he hadn't always returned to the roads when he was called. For the few extra dollars so badly needed by his family he allowed his career to be interrupted by the hard work of road maintenance.

During our teens, Kay and I found it increasingly hard to get along peaceably in our shared bedroom. Like mother, I was very neat. No matter how drunk mother got, she always kept the house in apple pie order. Kay was downright slovenly. She would leave her shoes in the middle of the room or wherever she took them off. She tossed her clothes on my bed as if it were her own. We had to share a comb, and Kay would invariably leave her hair in it.

She sewed clothes for herself whenever she could lay her hands on a piece of material, new or used. I couldn't sew; consequently Kay was always much better dressed than I. Five feet, seven inches tall, she was a natural beauty with mother's violet eyes and heavy auburn hair.

In contrast to Kay, I was homely and felt even homelier. Dad called me a runt; I had a bad complexion and drab coloring. My hair, which had been blonde when I was a child, was turning darker and my eyelashes were light. My stomach protruded and other kids teased me about my thick ankles.

One day Kay was teasing me about the way I wore my hair. "Straight! With just a bobby pin in it," she taunted. "You look like a freak!"

Furious, I went after her, but she was so tall she could just put her hands on my shoulders and hold me away from her. I swung my short arms, but I couldn't reach her. I ran away, sobbing with frustration.

Later, still nursing my hurt feelings, I came downstairs to find dad in an ugly mood. He had run out of wine, and it was raining. When I came into the room he started in on me. Cursing sullenly, he found fault with everything about me.

Enraged, I looked about me for something to throw at him. My eye fell on a pair of long-bladed scissors lying on the table. I grabbed them and hurled them at my dad, swearing violently as I let them fly.

He ducked just in time, and the scissors flew past him. Immediately, I was appalled at what I had done. I burst into tears and ran to him. He started to cry, too, and we fell into each other's arms. "Oh, dad," I sobbed. "I'm so sorry!" We just stood there weeping helplessly.

That day I realized that my frustration, bitterness, and anger had built up into an almost continual state of bad temper and that I had to do something about it. I was terrified when I realized that I might have killed my own father. I knew that I desperately needed self-control—and peace—and love. What I did not yet know was that *only* God could supply what I needed.

CHAPTER THIRTEEN

In 1938, dad bought a '24 Essex. He had owned a Model T Ford with isinglass curtains when we lived in Tacoma. At that time I was only a few years old, but I have memories of an exciting ride with dad at the wheel. He always drove too fast. He was an angry driver, shouting epithets at other drivers. A screech of the brakes, a fast turn, lurching over a curb, accompanied by, "Fool!" "Stupid!" "Dirty bum!" or whatever might come to his mind. He couldn't stand to have anyone pass him. If they tried, he stepped on the gas, his face set like a rock.

Now that we again had a car, I begged dad to let me learn to drive. After much coaxing, he agreed to show me what to do. "But I'm not going with you," he said.

We went out to the car and he explained the procedures. "This is how you start it. You push the clutch in and then you shift like this. Push the gas pedal *slowly*. After it's going along you push the clutch in again and shift up here. Then after you're going right along you push the clutch in again and shift to *this* position. When you want to stop, here's the brake. Every time you stop, you start over with the clutch again. Be careful. Don't you ruin the car."

That was my driver training.

I started the car. It lurched forward. I slammed both feet down and jerked to a stop. My heart racing, I started again, more slowly this time. The car seemed to have the hiccups. After several attempts I managed to get through the starting procedure without using the brake and I was moving along smoothly. Then I met a car. What to do? Nobody had told me. I gave him a wide berth, turning sharply toward the ditch. I jerked the wheel in time and got back onto the road.

I went home trembling from head to foot. A few more such attempts and I did learn to drive entirely by myself. I didn't get to drive very often, though. Gasoline was too costly to waste.

Dad tried to teach mother how to drive, but for her the ditch was like honey to a bee—she steered straight for it every time. Dad got disgusted with her and gave up.

Now I realize that God had a plan for my future, and that he sent into my life the people whose encouragement would help me develop my talents. One of the most important of these people was Carl A. Pitzer.

I first heard of Mr. Pitzer when Max started high school. Max talked constantly about his music teacher. "He wants me to join the choir at his church, too, mother," he said, as though going to church were a regular occurrence in his life.

So Max, and later Kay and I, joined the choir of the University Christian Church of Seattle. Mr. Pitzer not only invited us—he said that in order to get an "A" in glee club at school, we had to join his choir at church. How thankful I am today that I sang in both of

Mr. Pitzer's singing groups. The University Christian Church of Seattle is where I first heard and believed the gospel of Jesus Christ. And what a change that made in my life!

Dr. Hastings was our minister, and I clung to every word he preached. He told how God loves us no matter who we are or what we've done: "He loves *you*; he has a wonderful plan for your life." I didn't see how God could love me, but oh, how I wanted that eternal life he promised!

I was a poor, shy, insignificant little sinner who felt she couldn't stand before God—but I did turn to him. I asked God to have mercy on me, and I acknowledged my need for the Lord Jesus to become my personal Savior.

It was so simple to become a child of God—a Christian. I gave him my whole heart and gradually I became a new person—the person he wanted me to be. I began to know in very practical ways the reality of God's love.

Along with his church choir work, Max was getting excellent vocal training at school. In his senior year, he sang the male lead in the operetta "Sally," by Jerome Kern. Mother was thrilled that Max got the part. Dad boasted that good voices ran in his family. "Why shouldn't our children have good voices?" he asked. "Look at Aunt Minnie."

It proved to be an excellent performance. When Max sang his main solo, "Look for the Silver Lining," I glanced at mother. She had tears rolling down her cheeks. And no wonder. Max had the most beautiful baritone voice I had ever heard.

I looked over at dad. He was frowning. No, he wasn't satisfied. Later, at home, he scolded Max. "You should have sung louder, with more vigor. Put more gusto into it!" When he had exhausted his criticism of Max's singing he reminded Max that he was through high school. "You'd better get a job and start to pay for your board and room."

Finding work was no easy matter in those days, but Max finally did get a job as a page at the Seattle Public Library at $30.00 a month, working from 3:00 to 9:00 P.M. By working Saturdays, he was able to get Thursdays off and to continue to sing in Mr. Pitzer's choir.

Dad charged Max $25 a month for room and board.

When I auditioned for the junior orchestra, Mr. Pitzer praised my musicianship. "You're more advanced than any of the other students who auditioned," he said, "and I'm going to put you in the senior orchestra."

Silently I gave dad credit and breathed a silent prayer of thanks to God.

"However," Mr. Pitzer continued, "your hands are very small, and I fear you will be limited in your technique. For this year, though, I'm going to put you in the first violin section."

I was thrilled. I never imagined I had come that far on the violin. But I had sightread a piece Mr. Pitzer set before me, and he was impressed. I determined to practice even harder.

I also tried out for the glee club. On my applicaton I stated that I was a coloratura soprano. Now as Mr. Pitzer listened to me sing scales and arpeggios, he seemed a little disturbed about my voice. He had me do the notes in the high coloratura range again and again. Finally, he said, "You have ability, but you're definitely not a coloratura. You're a lyric soprano."

I was surprised. Father had convinced me I was a coloratura.

"I think," Mr. Pitzer said, "that you're too young to be singing E's and F's above high C." Then he turned to me and with a smile I shall never forget he said, "I'd like to offer you a scholarship to study voice with me privately."

I was so happy I nearly cried. Later I was to learn how rarely he offered a student that privilege. I studied voice with Mr. Pitzer all through high school and had the additional training and blessing of singing in two groups under his leadership. There is no way I can ever repay Mr. and Mrs. Pitzer for the many kindnesses they extended to me through those years. I can only give my thanks to God and use my training for him. (Many years later I surprised Mr. Pitzer by singing at a banquet honoring him at his retirement as choir director at University Christian Church.)

When I got home from school that day and told what Mr. Pitzer had said, dad turned a deep red. People just didn't contradict my father and he had said I was a coloratura. To prove he was right, he commanded me to sing scales. Urging me on, he had me vocalize higher than ever before. When I had sung F# above High C he tried to get me to sing G. I tried, but the tone never came out. By that time my throat was sore and my larynx felt as if it had been seared.

The next day I tried to sing for Mr. Pitzer. Alarmed, he asked what had happened to my voice. When I told him, he warned me, "To try to extend the vocal range by forcing is risky. Eventually you will cause nodes or blisters to form on the edges of the vocal cords." He showed me a chart of the throat. "See the bands here? Ideally, the perfect sound production should never produce blisters or nodes on either of the vocal bands. A tone produced correctly will always be a more pure sound for people to listen to. This was the approach of the Italian Bel Canto teachers who produced the greatest singers the world has ever known. So, Norma, it's up to you."

I promised to try to learn the way he wanted me to, knowing I would have problems with my father.

When my throat was healed, I returned to Mr. Pitzer. He started me humming scales pianissimo and doing five-note "mm ahs," humming up and ahing down. Staccato vocalizing came next. My efforts brought broad smiles to my teacher's face and this new approach was a great relief to me.

Now when father insisted that I sing louder and higher I refused. He was infuriated. Somehow, I knew that my voice was mine more than my father's and that it was my most precious possession. Even then, I realized it was a gift of God.

Mr. Pitzer had found that I could read violin music. Now he placed an opera score in front of me and asked me to sing the notes on vowel sounds, interpreting the music by paying strict attention to the signs. Today I still follow the musical signs in every song I sing, saving the voice here, spending it there, saving energy for the climax of the song.

Father didn't give up easily. He couldn't seem to comprehend that I was dedicated to learning the Italian Bel Canto style. When I would refuse to do the strenuous vocal gymnastics, he would throw up his hands and exclaim, "You used to sound like a singer! Now you sound like a child!"

It really disappointed him that I had switched my loyalty to Mr. Pitzer. One night, he became so angry he threatened to go to school and punch Mr. Pitzer in the nose for ruining my voice. I cringed at the thought. Dad fought with me about my voice night after night. "You'll never become a singer, humming and crooning all the time. How can you be so stupid as to let a mere high school teacher ruin your voice? You could learn to sing well if you would do what I've been teaching you."

When the wine would wear off, he would forget his threats against Mr. Pitzer. And in time dad's keen ear began to notice a change for the better in my voice. Gradually he stopped trying to get me to vocalize so strenuously.

I realized that having me as an apt violin pupil was one of the high spots in dad's life. I practiced more than ever to please him, usually three to four hours a day. When my freshman year ended, he purchased two books of violin music for me to study during summer vacation, *How to Study Kreutzer,* and *The Rudolph Kreutzer Violin Method*. These were advanced for me but provided just the challenge I needed.

At the beginning of my sophomore year, Mr. Pitzer said, "You've made amazing progress with your violin this summer. You've been studying!"

Proudly I told him about the books father had bought. Mr. Pitzer expressed surprise. "Kreutzer! Those are considered college level. Was your father able to teach you that?"

"Yes." I smiled proudly.

"Who was your father's teacher?"

"When he was young he studied with a pupil of Leopold Auer."

"That's wonderful! Your father was fortunate to find such a teacher. Heifitz is the epitome of Auer's teaching method," he said, "and there has perhaps never been a finer violinist than Heifitz."

I began to realize then, and have come to realize more since, what a deep loss my father suffered when that accident in the shipyards ended his concert career. I was beginning to appreciate how much dad knew about the violin, and to be grateful for everything he taught me. Because of dad's abilities as a great teacher, I was now able to learn under Mr. Pitzer—to enjoy the disciplines of a fine conductor, the tremendous strength of Beethoven, the beautiful sweeping melody of Tschaikowsky, the lilting charm of Strauss, and the genius of composers like Moussorgsky, Grieg, Smetana, and Rimsky-Korsakov. It was a glorious reward for learning to play the violin.

Early that year, Mr. Pitzer started teaching me how to sing the beautiful songs of Victor Herbert, Sigmund Romberg, Vincent Youmans, Rogers and Hart, and Jerome Kern. I found it easy to memorize and sang without looking at the music. Mr. Pitzer commented one day, "Your good memory will be very helpful to you in the future."

Time has proved how true that was. Today, I must memorize every song I sing on the Welk show and all of my other appearances.

My junior year in high school was wonderful. Not only did Mr. Pitzer begin giving me voice lessons in his home rather than at school, but he also decided I must learn to play the piano. He would teach me himself.

He gave me a practice room at school where I worked on scales and arpeggios every day during my study period. One afternoon a week, Mr. Pitzer taught me in his home. I'll never forget my first visit. Myriads of flowers and blossoming trees and shrubs surrounded the white brick house, situated on the shore of Lake Washington. From the entry hall I stared in amazement at the huge living room, the oriental rugs on shiny oak floors, the oil paintings in ornate gold frames. A fire was burning brightly in the immense fireplace. A grand piano stood near a large arched window which framed the lake and the Cascade Mountains towering in the distance. It was there I stood to take my lessons. I had never seen such beauty; it was like a dream.

My piano playing was greatly impeded because I couldn't stretch my hands wide enough to reach an octave. "Runt of the family" still echoed in my ears. Mr. Pitzer finally conceded the hopelessness of spending more time with piano lessons.

Under Mr. Pitzer's voice training I gradually learned to stop straining, and to sing naturally. That season, Mr. Pitzer decided it was time for me to sing my first solo in church.

One Sunday the solo of the day was to be "The Lord's Prayer" by Albert Hay Malotte. Everyone assumed it would be sung by the regular tenor soloist. Mr. Pitzer didn't want the congregation or the choir to know that I was going to do it, so it wasn't announced. He felt I would be less nervous if no one was expecting me to sing the solo.

To everyone's surprise I stood up and sang. I was a little nervous at first, but gradually my heart stilled as I sang the beautiful words of that prayer. By the time I sang, "And lead us not into temptation but deliver us from evil," I was almost calm. I was deeply stirred by the power of the words of the song and my voice soared to the climax with perfect freedom. "For thine is the kingdom and the power and the glory forever! Amen."

As I finished, I looked at Mr. Pitzer. He smiled and bowed ever so slightly, so I knew he was pleased.

I have sung "The Lord's Prayer" many times since but I shall never forget the thrill of that first solo. And how well I realize that if I had not come to know personally the Lord who taught those words to his followers, I could never have sung that song with the true feeling it deserves. When I sing the great religious classics of musical literature, I'm singing words that are real in my own life and experience—and what a difference that makes to a singer!

CHAPTER FOURTEEN

The musical training Mr. Pitzer gave me continued in violin and voice. In my junior year I sang the role of Yum Yum in the "Mikado." Kay designed all the costumes for the operetta and everyone acknowledged that they were truly professional.

In my senior year Mr. Pitzer told me he would like me to become one of his featured church soloists. When my parents learned that I was going to sing a solo at church, both insisted that they wanted to come to hear me. Before this time, dad had always steadfastly refused to attend church, so I realized how much it meant to him to hear me sing.

The day arrived and I left early to rehearse with our organist,

Nadine Conner. I was excited and elated at the prospect of singing again. The choir processed down the middle aisle and as we walked I stole glances at the congregation, trying to find my parents. We made our way up the stairs and back to the choir loft. I still couldn't spot mom and dad.

Then in horror I saw them—weaving down the aisle in a state of disheveled intoxication. They were late. Few empty seats were left. My parents stumbled over the feet of other people to reach a place in the middle of a row. The whole congregation stared.

I don't know how I ever got through that morning. The invocation, the congregational hymn, the prayer, the offering—and then I stood up to sing. "How beautiful upon the mountains are the feet of him that bringeth good tidings—" The song seemed interminable. I tried to think only of the words and kept my eyes from turning to the row where my parents sat.

I took my seat, my heart pounding, my cheeks burning. Dr. Hastings started to preach. At first I hardly heard him. Then his words reached me, "God is our refuge and strength, a tested help in time of trouble."

My own trouble seemed to bear down on me with tremendous weight that morning. I felt I had more than my share of grief, and I knew I needed help. I realized how desperate life in our family was without God and that day I recommitted my life to him. As Dr. Hastings preached that morning, Jesus came into my life not only as Savior but for daily strength and direction.

The spring of my senior year I sang the lead in the operetta "New Moon" by Sigmund Romberg.

Mr. Pitzer said he planned to keep me busy singing at church too. "Pastor Hastings wants us to present a whole evening of music. It will be a big event. We're going to advertise in the papers and use the money we raise for the community projects the church has taken on. So you be thinking what you'll want to sing in that."

"Do you want it to be a sacred song?"

"Not necessarily."

I had added "Girls of Cadiz" to my repertoire under Mr. Pitzer's training and he agreed that I could sing that for the musical evening.

When the printed program came out, I saw I had a position near the end of the concert, a place cherished by performers. I thanked him and he said, "I want you to sing your very best because there will be many prominent people in the audience—people who could be important to your future."

This news both thrilled and terrified me. I prayed that mother and dad wouldn't created another scene.

The featured soloist was Lee Sweetland, a young baritone who had graduated from high school with Max and had gone to Los Angeles to study voice. He had just completed a tour with Sonja Henie's ice skating troupe.

It was a marvelous concert. The church was filled; my parents arrived and found a seat inconspicuously. They were both sober. I breathed a silent "thank you."

At last my turn came to perform. With a prayer, and remembering that "important people who could affect my future" were in the audience, I sang my very best.

When I told Lee Sweetland how much I had enjoyed his singing he surprised me by saying, "And I enjoyed yours. If you ever come to Hollywood, be sure to get in touch with me. I might be able to help you with your career." I hadn't given much thought to what I might do after high school. Could it be that I would ever find a career in Hollywood?

After the concert, Mr. Pitzer made a suggestion. "If you want to take an extra year at Lincoln High School as a special student, I'm sure there are courses that could be of help to you. I'd like to give you more voice lessons and coach you in diction while we add to your repertoire."

I readily accepted and made plans to graduate, with the intention of returning the following fall.

Now people began asking me to sing for weddings and for this I received $5. I sang, "I Love You Truly," "Oh, Promise Me," "Oh, Perfect Love"—standard wedding songs at that time.

I was to have a dual honor at graduation. Not only would I sing but I would also play a violin solo. When the programs were being printed I learned that all the graduates must wear formal clothing. This caused me great anxiety which I shared with Kay. She was making great progress in her art and designing while I was developing my musical skills. Though she was older than I, we were in the same class and would be graduating together.

I could almost see the wheels turning in Kay's pretty head. "If we could get some material, I could make you a dress," she said. "But how to get..." Together we worried about it. There just wasn't any extra money. Everything we all could earn went into the household budget.

"I know!" she exclaimed. She beamed as she pulled a box out from under the bed. A neighbor had intended to throw out her curtains and Kay had said, "Don't throw them out. Give them to me." They were an off-white dotted Swiss, slightly discolored with age. Out of this, Kay designed two charming dresses. There was no money for zippers, so the night of graduation we sewed each other into our formals. I'll never forget how Kay made it possible for me to be on stage, properly dressed, on that important night. Mr. and

Mrs. Pitzer had bought me silver sandals and a white jacket—the perfect accessories to my outfit.

When the evening arrived, we came down from our room, feeling like twin Cinderellas. When we entered the living room, dad handed each of us a small gift box. He cleared his throat and smiled proudly. "Something for your graduation, girls. It's not much."

I opened mine. It was a watch—to me it seemed the most beautiful one I'd ever seen. Kay's was identical—yellow gold with a dainty black band.

"Dad, how did you ever—?"

"Been saving for it." He'd not been able to give us many gifts. I can only guess how much it meant to him to give us those watches.

The day after graduation I went swimming at Haller Lake with some friends and walked into the water wearing my precious watch. Almost at once I realized what I had done. "Just keep it wet and it won't rust," my friends said.

I went home crying, with a watch that had stopped running—and it did rust. We all wept. Dad had worked hard and sacrificed much to give me that watch and I felt guilty for my carelessness. It seemed that even our happy moments were marred with misery. For years I wore the damaged watch as a bracelet, hoping no one would notice that it wasn't working.

By this time, Kay and I were earning money in every way we could. I did housework from morning till night, earning twenty-five cents a day. I worked in Mrs. Cloyd's grocery store across the street. Some days I would wait on customers. Other days I would take care of her two tiny daughters. Often she would send home milk or a small piece of meat. We were able to live better now that we were all bringing home some money.

Another of my early jobs was to clerk in the Bon Marche Department store, in the sportswear department. I was so shy I often stood at the counter hoping no one would ask for anything.

One customer picked out a sweatshirt. I grabbed it and crammed it into a bag. When I returned from the cash register with her receipt, the lady had taken the shirt out of the bag, folded it neatly, and was carefully putting it back. Her disgusted look seemed to say, "You're hopeless—this is the way it's done." I was miserable with embarrassment.

Now I was earning $13.50 a week. I carried a bag lunch, kept just enough money for carfare, and gave the rest to my parents every payday.

My next job was with the Army Engineers as a timekeeper. My salary jumped to $25 a week.

CHAPTER FIFTEEN

During Christmas vacation, Virginia Viewig asked me to go to the mountains with her to ski. We were invited to stay in a friend's cabin. When the day arrived, Virginia couldn't go, so her sister Betty went with me instead. I didn't have skis or ski clothes so Mrs. Viewig let me borrow hers. Mrs. Viewig was much larger than I and her clothes hung on me loosely. Both her skis and poles were inches too long. Nevertheless, I was thrilled to be going—there weren't many just-for-fun days in my life.

As we rode on the bus to Snoqualmie Pass, we saw beautiful homes such as I never knew existed. The foothills of the mountains were thick with evergreens and underbrush. Cattle grazed here and there in the sweeping meadowlands.

It was almost dark when we arrived. As we got off the bus, Betty saw someone she knew and stopped to speak to him. I took one look and my heart skipped a beat.

He was about my age. He had dark hair and a rugged, handsome face. As he talked with Betty I thought I had never seen such a beautiful smile. I stood for a moment, watching him. His complexion was ruddy but I couldn't see the color of his eyes because he almost closed them when he laughed. Betty turned to me and introduced us—"Norma, this is Randy Zimmer."

As he greeted me, he gave me that terrific smile. I smiled shyly, but I couldn't make a sound. He joined his group getting on the bus. "Well, we're going to get something to eat," he called back as he disappeared inside.

Betty and I watched the bus leave. "Gee, I hope we get to see him again," I sighed. "He's so good-looking, and seems so nice."

We hurried through the deep snow to our cabin. We flipped the light switch but nothing happened. "The electricity must be shut off," Betty exclaimed. "We'd better get a fire going quick."

There was plenty of wood by the huge fireplace and we struggled to get it to burn—but it stubbornly refused to blaze properly. We realized something was wrong there too. Smoke billowed into the room. "Open the damper, open the damper," Betty called as she ran to open the door.

I fumbled with the handle. I could hear the damper opening and closing but the smoke was just as bad, no matter what I did.

Betty flung the door open and the smoke poured out. Coughing, we went outside to bring in some snow to put out the fire. Just then some young fellows who were going by gave us the answer. "The chimney's probably blocked with snow." They helped us put out the fire and invited us to come up to the Sahalie Ski Club for the night.

We had no choice, as it was too cold to stay in the cabin without heat. Gratefully, we followed them to the club and they pointed out the girls' dormitory. We were tired and went right to bed.

In the morning, when we entered the cafeteria, my heart started to pound when I saw Randy Zimmer there, having breakfast.

Betty, who wasn't shy, took her tray and headed for Randy's table. I shuffled along behind her, feeling awkward in my borrowed boots and baggy outfit. Randy was friendly to me, but I couldn't think of a thing to say.

"Would you like to go out and try skiing?" he asked.

"I've—I've never skied before," I stammered.

"I'll help you," he promised.

We made our way to the slopes together. To me he looked like a Greek god and I became more clumsy and tongue-tied than ever.

Patiently he tried to teach me to ski. "First of all," he said, "just think of it as walking. One foot ahead of the other, slide your skis along like this. As you're sliding your right foot, you put your left pole ahead of you a little and as you slide your left foot you put your right pole—that's right!" he encouraged.

We practiced until I was tired—which didn't take long. Randy said, "You rest a little now and I'll go up for a couple of runs." He grabbed a rope tow and was pulled up a long hill. He skied back down to me, making long sweeping turns. He made it look so easy!

When he returned he said, "There's a good restaurant about five miles from here—you know—the place my friends and I were going last night when you got off the bus. Would you like to go there for dinner tonight?" I nodded happily.

That night we boarded the bus together. The food at the restaurant was delicious, but I was too shy to talk. Randy was completely at ease and gradually I began to relax as he told me about his skiing experiences.

"A couple of years ago," he said, "I broke my back. The doctor said I'd never ski again, so I'm mighty glad I'm back on skis. I was in a downhill race at Mt. Ranier and skied into the fog. I was doing 65 or 70 miles an hour when I hit a snowbank. My back was bent so far in the crash that my seat actually hit the back of my head!" He carried the conversation alone.

Virginia had told me in high school about this handsome friend of hers who was injured skiing. She had even suggested I go with her to see him in the hospital, but I was too bashful. She told how Randy had been semi-conscious when he heard the doctor say, "Five vertebrae are crushed. I'm afraid this boy will never walk again," and how Randy had thought, "I'll lick it! I *will* walk again." Through sheer determination, he had concentrated on one toe—then the foot—then the leg—until he was moving and walking again. "He has real grit!" Virginia had said.

After dinner, instead of taking the bus, we walked the five miles back to the ski club. The snow crunched under our feet. Randy held my arm firmly in his and talked as though he had always known me. "This injury disqualified me for the army. You see, I had signed up with the Ski Troops and was to leave the following Monday." We trudged along in silence for a few moments.

"I still have a lot of trouble with my back. I'm pretty embarrassed about not being in the service because I look so healthy. I signed up to go to Recife, Brazil, with an army engineers' group, but that fell through, too."

I found my tongue. "You did? So did I! I work for the army engineers. I signed up to go, but it fell through for me, too."

"You're kidding! And then I applied to Sun Valley to be a ski instructor just as they closed it down to the public and turned it into a naval hospital."

I pulled at his arm. "I applied for a job at Sun Valley too—to work as a maid..."

"At that time? When they closed down?"

"Yes! Yes!" I was smiling.

We had stopped walking and were facing each other. Randy took me in his arms and kissed me. I believed he felt as I did—that we were meant to find each other—that it just had to be. In a husky voice he said, "Norma...I love you. I know we haven't known each other long, but I really do love you."

There was no doubt in my heart that he was sincere. Because I was sure I loved him too.

I had to ask him an important question then. "Randy, do you believe in God?" I awaited his answer anxiously.

"Yes, I do. I trust him completely," was his welcome reply.

He drew me close for another kiss. I had never felt so happy—so at home—in my life. And God's love put the seal on it all.

For once, the thought of my father's reaction never entered my head.

The next day, Randy taught me how to climb up the hill. "With your skis parallel to the hill, like this, you keep raising the higher one and bringing the lower one up to it."

Then he taught me how to go down beginners' slopes. "You snow plow by putting the tips of your skis together pigeon-toed, bend your knees like this with your skis apart a little—just like you're sitting. Then you just let the skis go flat downhill. If you want to stop you just bring the edges in like this," and he stopped.

When he saw I was getting tired he left me and took a few runs by himself. It was a delight to watch his marvelous skiing form.

Sunday was clear and cold. Randy asked Betty and me if we

would like to go with him and his father to Soap Lake. "It's only an hour from here," he said.

We said we'd love it and so I met Hugo Zimmer.

He greeted me warmly and I liked him from the start. He looked quite old. His was best described as an "old country" face. Dancing blue eyes peeked out from under heavy eyelids, laughing as though life were a perpetual joke. Laugh lines came from the corners of his eyes, forming paths deep into each cheek. He was a jolly person. Betty and I felt comfortable with him—he was like one of us kids.

Mr. Zimmer had a summer home in Soap Lake that he wanted to check. When we got away from the ski resort and out on the road, Randy tied a rope to the back bumper of his father's car and was pulled along at forty to fifty miles an hour on his skis. It was clear to me that this Randy Zimmer loved adventure.

Betty and I had to catch the bus back to Seattle that afternoon but Randy was staying for a week at the Pass, so we went back to the ski club where the Zimmers dropped us off. Instead of taking my borrowed skis on the bus I left them with Randy. I gave him my address and asked if he would please bring them to me when he got back. We had just time for a quick hand-clasp as we said good-bye, and our hearts were in our eyes.

Bashful little Norma had come a long way.

CHAPTER SIXTEEN

From the time I left the ski area until a week later when Randy brought the skis, I worried constantly about how dad would take the news about the friend I had met skiing.

I had had only one date in high school and remembering it still made me grow hot with embarrassment.

A boy with beautiful manners, a member of the school orchestra, had become very friendly with me and I had agreed to go out with him. When I announced to dad that I had agreed to this date with "a nice young man," he nearly had a stroke. "There is no such thing as a nice young man!" he snorted.

Just as we were arguing about that, Del Robertson came over and said a "Mr. Bill Sloane" was on the phone and wished to speak to Kay.

Turning furiously on her, father raised his voice, "I don't want either of my daughters getting phone calls from mashers on your line.''

Mother gasped but Del, smiling sweetly at dad, said, "But Mr. Larsen! You must realize that you have two very attractive young ladies here. Do you mean you would deprive them of boyfriends? You must know that young people are attracted to each other!"

"Not when it's going to ruin their chances to succeed in life!"

"Excuse me! If you're serious about that, I'll just take a message." But Kay had slipped out of the house to take the call herself. Meanwhile, mother picked up the subject of my having a date. With Del there backing her up, dad was outnumbered and he seemed to realize it.

That didn't deter him from embarrassing me. When Walt arrived in a beautiful Chevrolet coupe, dad started in, "Now see here, young man. You bring my daughter home before 10:30 or I'll get the police after you."

"But Mr. Larsen, we won't even be out of the movie by then!"

Soft answers often unsettled father. He cleared his throat. "What time will the movie be over?"

"Maybe by eleven, sir."

"All right. Eleven-thirty! No later!"

"But, Mr. Larsen! When the movies let out, everyone goes out to eat and that takes a while. It might be after midnight before I can bring Norma home!"

Father said, "How long after?"

"That depends, sir. Places are awfully crowded on Friday nights!"

Dad said, "See that you leave as soon as you can. Understand?"

Pleasantly, but slightly dazed, Walt said, "Mr. Larsen, have a heart, will you, please?"

I marveled at dad. Expecting him to go straight up in a fit of temper, I saw him temporarily confused. No longer able to negotiate, he turned to me and firmly said, "Norma, I expect you to get home as soon as possible."

I was dreadfully anxious about getting home on time. One has to be young to be able to understand how I could be so anxious and yet completely forget what time it was. After eating out, a group of us went to Walt's home to dance. Time just flew. I had never danced but I found that I loved it. We were having a great time.

Suddenly, one of the girls said, "Oh-oh; I'd better go. It's twelve-thirty!"

I hurried to find my coat. I tried not to show how afraid I was.

The moment the coupe pulled up, dad appeared at the car window, his face contorted. "It's about time you got home," he shouted, swaying drunkenly.

We tried to explain but he wouldn't listen. "Don't you realize that you have to make something of your life? Fool around with these playboys and all you'll do is end up raising babies." Turning to Walt, dad snarled, "I don't want you to have anything more to do with my daughter. You're just the type she doesn't need. She's trying to make a success out of her life. What are you doing with yours? I'll bet you do nothing but try to seduce every girl you take out in this fancy wagon of yours."

Walt started to answer, but dad pulled me out of the car and toward the house. I heard my friend say, "I'm sorry, Norma, but he's really impossible. Mr. Larsen, I can't understand how a man like you ever had such a charming and intelligent daughter." The car door slammed, and he drove away.

Of course, he never asked me out again, and I was always too embarrassed to speak to him when I saw him at school.

I had been watching for Randy all weekend. Though I was anxious to see him again, I was afraid dad might scare him off too. On Sunday afternoon, Randy drove up. He came to the door and I introduced him to my parents.

Dad had been drinking and his expression was menacing. "Well, young man, tell me—what do *you* do?"

Randy told him what he had told me at the restaurant the week before. "My sister and I have a juice business."

Dad fixed a bleary eye on him. "A *juice* business? What might that be?"

"Well, we make fresh fruit and vegetable juices and sell them."

"Where?" dad demanded scornfully.

Randy amazed me. I expected him to turn away insulted, but he kept on respectfully answering my father's questions.

"At the Seattle public market. We also deliver to health food stores. I help my dad build, too. My father's a baker, but he builds houses in his spare time."

Dad set down his glass and brushed his lips with his hands. "You oughta make something of yourself!" he declared. I knew he was going into his speech, and he did. "My girls are going to *be* somebody. They're not going to get married and raise a bunch of kids, and don't you forget it!"

I couldn't look at Randy. I wanted him to leave. I knew I'd probably never see him again.

He listened with a little smile on his face. Then, as dad reached again for his glass, Randy said, "Well, I've got to be going now. Be seeing you!" He winked at me and was gone.

Kay wanted a phone so badly that she had one installed. She was very popular and the telephone rang often for her. She was now working in one of Seattle's finest jewelry stores.

Kay's charming personality attracted boys to her and she dated frequently. To avoid confrontations with dad, Kay would have her friends drop her off a half block from home. Dad seldom noticed Kay's absences since she came home alone and on time.

One Saturday the phone rang and it was for me. This was unusual and made dad curious. "Hello," I said and could already hear dad demanding, "Who is it? Who is it?"

"Hello. This is Randy."

I had recognized his voice. My heart leaped with excitement.

"How would you like to go with me to a movie tonight?"

"I'd—I'd love to," I said, glancing apprehensively at father.

Randy said he'd be over in an hour to pick me up.

We had a good time. Dad was asleep on the couch when I got back. He grumbled, "First thing you know you'll get married and have a family. Then how can you amount to anything?"

Randy and I dated a few more times during that winter. He took me to see his sailboat in Lake Washington and one night he took me to dinner at an Italian restaurant overlooking Lake Union. I marveled each time he called or came over. I thought surely he wouldn't be back for more of dad's lectures and insults. But each time we were together we grew to care more and more for each other.

It had been rainy much of that spring but one day the sun shone bright and hot. Kay's phone rang and it was for me. It was Randy. Alerted by the ringing of the telephone, dad immediately asked, "Who is it? What does he want?"

"It's Randy. He wants me to go to the beach with him."

"To the beach?" dad shouted. "Absolutely not! You're not going to the beach with any boy. Nosiree!"

Randy had heard him. I said, "I'm sorry but I can't go."

I was almost twenty years old but I had to live with dad, and that was impossible if I went against his will.

I was getting desperate. Was my life to go on like this forever—with dad interfering constantly? I loved Randy and I felt sure he would never call me again.

While I was brooding about this and thinking how much I wanted to be with Randy, dad said, "Well, if you want to go to the beach that badly, why don't we go? I'll take you."

I almost laughed. It was a poor substitute for going with Randy, but I thought it might get my mind off my trouble, and it *was* stifling hot in the house. So I said, "All right. Let's go, dad."

We got in the old Essex. Dad drove, and as always when I rode with him I was scared to death. A new Ford tried to pass us, and each time he'd get about even with us dad would step on the gas and stay ahead. "That jerk!" he growled. "That'll teach him."

"Well, here we are," dad said as the car lurched to a stop. We got out. Dad leaned up against an old tree, pulled his hat over his eyes for shade, and started to read.

I plodded through the warm sand and tested the water with my toe. The salt water was still icy cold, but I waded in slowly and swam out a little way. A group of young people nearby was having a good time. I envied them. I seldom was in a group because I was still painfully shy, yet I loved the laughter and enjoyed listening to the kidding and conversation.

Suddenly I recognized a voice, and as I looked toward them, Randy saw me. With a puzzled look, he came right over and said, "Hi! I thought you couldn't come."

With a hundred beaches in the Seattle area, the Lord had led me to Golden Gardens where Randy and his friends were!

I felt an honest answer was all I could give him. "My father didn't want me to go out with you."

"I see." The hurt showed in his eyes and I felt he really did understand. I felt that for the first time he saw it was hopeless, that we could never go on with dad forever standing between us.

Dad meanwhile had observed us and was calling to me. Randy started back to his friends. "Goodbye," he said—not, "Be seeing you."

All the way home, dad ranted about that "raucous bunch of hoodlums that juicer was with." To hear dad, one would have thought he was the epitome of good culture and gentility. "Folks like that would just be a ball and chain to you," he said. "You'd never get ahead. Cut 'em off. You don't want to get married, Norma. You don't want to have to cook and tend babies. You've got a voice. God gave you that voice. Your mother and I couldn't do that for you. With talent like yours, you owe it to God and to society to be a singer."

I wanted to be a singer. But that day all I wanted was Randy. Deep down I knew he wouldn't call me again.

And this time I was right.

I was deeply hurt. I knew dad didn't want me to go with boys anyway. But a new dimension had come into my life. During my high school years I had turned more and more to the Lord with my problems. Now I went to him with my heartache. "What shall I do?" I cried in despair. The Bible was beginning to be a great comfort and I recalled John 14:27, "Peace I leave with you. My peace I give unto you. Not as the world giveth give I unto you. Let not your heart be troubled, neither let it be afraid." Gradually I began to believe that God would take care of this too. If he wanted me to meet Randy again he would give me another opportunity.

Weeks went by. I was still working for the Army Corps of Engineers in Seattle. Two years had gone by since I first met Randy at Snoqualmie Pass. No one asked me for dates. I was still far too shy to talk easily with boys.

Five days a week Kay rode the 5:15 bus home from work. She noticed a good-looking, well-dressed young man sitting in the same seat every evening. His fine tweed jackets, shiny shoes, jaunty tyrolean hat, and poised manner intrigued her. He stepped off the bus at the same stop and would touch the brim of his hat, bow his head in a friendly "So long," and walk around the corner to one of the nicer houses in our neighborhood.

Naturally, Kay, being the friendly outgoing type, sat beside him. It was always easy for Kay to make new friends and before long she found out that Hank owned a sailboat, loved jazz music, and had a collection of hats. He was extremely good looking and possessed a dazzling smile. He had Kay daydreaming about finding her ideal man. She pictured herself and Hank sitting in front of their fireplace, she stroking his hair—or sailing Puget Sound with the wind whipping the sails in a rosy sunset. She spent hours at night conjuring up all kinds of romantic scenes.

Finally she came in one evening, her eyes glowing.

"Hank wants to take me sailing next Saturday! Why don't you invite Randy to come along?" she coaxed.

"I can't call him, Kay," I moaned. "A girl just doesn't phone a boy."

"Don't be so old-fashioned," she scolded. "Besides, it's different asking him to go sailing. He'd love it—he has a boat of his own, doesn't he?"

"Yes, but it's just a 'flatty.' "

"Well, then, imagine how excited he would be to go out on Hank's forty-footer."

That did it. I pocketed my pride and went to the phone. Nervously I dialed the number. I recognized the voice as he answered.

"Chateau Bedlam!" he shouted.

"Randy." I cleared my throat. "Randy, this is Norma Larsen."

"Oh, hi there! I'm glad to hear from you." The obvious sincerity in his voice reassured me.

"Would you like to go sailing on a forty-foot sailboat next Saturday?"

"Sounds good!" he said with enthusiasm. "What time?"

"How about coming to my house at 7 A.M.? I'll bring the picnic lunch."

"Swell! I'll look forward to it, Norma. See you then."

I hung up. My hands were shaking and I could hear my heart pounding.

I didn't tell dad. I was feeling more and more like an adult. I told myself I couldn't have dad ruling me forever.

What should I wear? Virginia! Surely she'd let me borrow some slacks. Bless her. She let me use some white ducks and a windbreaker. With a bright scarf for my head I felt ready to face the world.

Hank's boat was dreamy! Randy and I lay on the deck and spoke of how someday we'd love to sail around the world in something similar to this. God had given us a rare warm sunny day. The wind gusted at times, then suddenly it would be calm.

When noon came, Kay and I went down into the galley to prepare the food we had brought. Kay handed me some tomatoes. "Here, slice these," she said.

I remember the incident so clearly. Believe it or not, I had never sliced a tomato before. I put it down on the drainboard and bore down on it, squashing it and causing all the juice to run out.

"Oh, can't you do anything right?" Kay scolded. "Go up on deck and get out of my hair."

I was crushed. She confirmed what I already felt. I was only a runt—always short of what I should be.

After lunch we all went back on deck. Kay sat admiring Hank at the wheel, handsome in his white and navy sailing outfit—the captain's hat placed at the right angle on his fine head—when suddenly, *whoosh*! A gust of wind lifted Hank's hat and blew it into the water.

Kay's jaw fell. Her already large eyes bulged.

Hank was as bald as a honeydew melon.

Kay looked stunned. Randy and I couldn't hold back the giggles. Poor Hank.

Gone were Kay's fantasies of cozy nights in front of the fireplace, stroking Hank's hair.

"Oh, Norma," she wailed, when were alone. "That's why he always wears those smart hats! I can't believe it's the same man."

She made her way to the galley. We watched her sit down glumly, disbelief registered in her eyes. Suddenly she stood up. "Randy, help me get the dinghy out. I'm going to sunbathe."

Randy attached the line to the small dinghy. Kay climbed in and for the rest of the day she trailed the sailboat by 75 to 100 feet.

There she lay, her arms under her head, oblivious to Hank, totally without pretense. The obvious conclusion for Hank was that Kay was completely disillusioned.

We watched the sun set over the Sound, then Randy brought me home in his car. He kissed me good-night at the door. My heart felt as if it would burst.

Fortunately, dad didn't come raging out of the house. He had been drinking before I left.

Randy said, "Norma, when will I see you again?"

"That's up to you, Randy," I said, and this time I knew he would call.

It was through my job with the Army Corps of Engineers in Seattle that I met Anne O'Brien, whose friendship I enjoyed from the start. Like Virginia Viewig, Anne was to help me meet someone who would be important in my future.

Anne was a petite girl with huge brown eyes set in a tiny kewpie-doll face framed by black, wavy hair. Her husband, Pat, was a cab driver, and since they lived near us in Lake City they picked me up and I rode with them to work. Full of fun, Anne was a real tonic for me. Pat would sometimes get annoyed with us for "giggling like little kids."

One day, Anne invited me to go on an overnight trip to Victoria, B.C., with her. "I'd like to give you that for a birthday present," she said.

I accepted with excitement. I had never had such an opportunity before.

We had dinner and a pleasant evening on board the ship, then went to bed in our tiny stateroom. The engines kept me awake, but I loved it so much that I didn't mind not being able to sleep. Every so often I would creep up to see the water and the lights along the shore of Puget Sound. Evergreens grew right down to the water, interrupted here and there by little beaches.

We arrived in Victoria before it was light. In the morning, we went to the vine-covered Empress Hotel. It seemed I was in a different world. We walked around all the shops. I had saved just a little money I could call my own and with this I bought a little brushed-blue cup and saucer. The inside of the cup and the center of the saucer were decorated with dainty pink flowers. Anne bought me another cup and saucer with a yellow floral pattern. I still have both sets.

As I walked around admiring the baskets of flowers hanging at each lamppost, I kept thinking of mother. Oh, how I wished I could buy her everything I saw. Years later I had no greater joy than buying her the beautiful things she had missed all her life.

Reluctantly, we boarded the ship to go back in the afternoon. After a couple of hours, someone started singing on deck and slowly the other passengers joined in. After a few songs a gentleman sitting next to me said, "This young lady has a pretty voice; let's ask her to sing a number."

So I sang "Smoke Gets in Your Eyes." When I finished, other passengers said, "Sing another one."

I sang for two hours. I went through my entire religious and secular repertoire. I distinctly remember singing "In the Garden,"

"What a Friend We Have in Jesus," "The Lord's Prayer," "Amazing Grace," "Will You Remember?" "Indian Love Call," "My Hero," and all the songs I knew from Jerome Kern and Victor Herbert.

After entertaining the passengers all afternoon, I learned that the man who had asked me to sing was a Hollywood agent. He introduced himself as Joe Chandler. "I would be happy to arrange auditions for you if you ever make your way to Hollywood." His wife urged me, "Now you be sure to try to come to Hollywood. He's offering you this opportunity; you be sure to take it." They gave me their address and phone number, and their kindness kindled real hope in my heart that I might find a career in singing.

This was the second person to offer me help if I ever came to Hollywood.

I arrived home flushed with excitement. I poured out my story of the encounter with Mr. Chandler. Dad said, "That's great, Norma. That's just great!" And I was glad I had pleased him. All too seldom did I feel he approved of me or my plans.

About the same time, I was offered a full four-year scholarship in voice to Seattle University, a Jesuit school. I sensed that for some reason dad didn't want me to take that opportunity for a college education. Mother did. It had disappointed her deeply that Max had to turn over so much of his money to dad and was able to get so little education before he went into the navy. Mother later told me father's objection to the Catholic college was their opposition to birth control. He had a deadly anxiety that "having babies" would prevent his daughters from "making something of themselves."

Now I was faced with these two opportunities. By this time I had formed good habits of prayer—and how I prayed about this decision! I asked God please to let me know what to do. When would I ever again have such a chance for a college education? What if I gave up this chance to be introduced around Hollywood by Mr. Chandler? When would such a chance ever come again? Surely God had found that chair for me next to Mr. Chandler on the boat.

I thought it all through very carefully, and finally I felt sure I should go to Hollywood. Dad borrowed sixty dollars for my fare and a few dollars to spare. It was clear to me that dad was excited about my prospects for a Hollywood career. At last he felt assured that I was going to make something of myself.

CHAPTER SEVENTEEN

Randy did call me again. He asked if I would come to a party at his house.

Excited, I prepared to go. My selection of dresses was small. I ignored the black and red dress I'd worn for years with the fuchsia coat. Ugh. Memories of that coat made me wince. Dad had bought it for me when I was entering high school because then I had loved the color. After wearing it for four years, I couldn't stand the sight of it anymore. I had to wear it with that black and red wool dress, a hand-me-down, and the reds clashed.

When I had started earning a little money I went to the other extreme. The first thing I bought was a coat. I wanted a neutral shade that I wouldn't get tired of and that would blend with other colors. The one I had chosen looked like an army coat, very drab and severely tailored. Later, I had bought a gray dress. I dressed up for Randy's party in my tasteless attire.

It had been two years since I had met Mr. Zimmer at Snoqualmie Pass. Now the thought of meeting Randy's mother made me nervous.

I was in no way prepared for the surprise of seeing their impressive two-story house which Randy had helped his father build. Located on Queen Anne Hill overlooking Puget Sound, their front yard was adjoining Kenear Park. With wide glass windows on two sides, their huge living room—it must have been twenty by forty feet—seemed an extension of the Sound. From it we could watch the ferries and ships coming into Seattle.

I went down to the rumpus room where the party was in progress. As I walked into the large room, I noticed the player piano and I thought, "How could Randy ever look twice at me, coming from all this luxury?" I appreciated him and loved him all the more for caring for me regardless of my poverty.

Once during the evening I saw Mrs. Zimmer sitting at the dining room table. I had tried to plan what I would say, "You have a lovely home, Mrs. Zimmer." No, I thought, she'll think that's a silly thing to say. I tried to think of something else. I often found myself wishing later that I could take back things I'd said—nothing ever seemed right.

Fortunately Mrs. Zimmer was very talkative and didn't seem to notice my embarrassment. A large woman, she had a ready, hearty laugh—much like her husband's.

I admired her cut glass—she must have had twenty or more pieces. I walked around looking at their pictures—real oil paintings. I commented on one of a sunset over Mt. Rainier. There were Oriental rugs everywhere and many ferns and tall palms in enormous, expensive-looking pots. I observed the beautiful rose-satin drapes, the two luxurious couches, and still another piano.

Upstairs, Randy's sister Arline took me to her room. She had a huge dressing table with a large circular mirror. *You could walk into* her closet! Arline had rows of stylish dresses and smart pointed-toe shoes. Her room had its own little balcony overlooking the Sound. Each floor had its own bathroom. The one on this floor was decorated in light blue.

Later, Randy showed me his room. He too had a walk-in closet. Tossed on a shelf in the closet was money—lots of paper money and coins. I knew Randy and Arline had a juice business in the public market but had no idea how successful it was. Here was a comfortable amount of money just lying around. Apparently no one had urgent need of it. I couldn't believe my eyes.

Arline was a charming girl with a wonderful personality. I grew to love her. Her curly shoulder-length hair framed a peaches-and-cream complexion and beautiful smile. I was grateful for the messages of welcome I received from her expressive eyes.

Never had I seen such a buffet as was provided for us that evening. I can almost see it now: sandwiches of all kinds—salami, cheese, fish, ham—a relish platter filled with carrot and celery sticks, olives, and pickles. We drank apple cider—it was the first time I'd ever tasted it. For dessert we had a huge, delicious chocolate cake. I was to learn that Mrs. Zimmer loved to cook and bake. She always prepared large quantities of food so that members of her family felt free to bring guests home at any time. They would just enlarge the table to include any number of extra guests. After we finished eating, we sat around the fireplace and talked. I didn't participate but I loved hearing the others talk and laugh and I followed every word, wishing I could think of something to contribute. At home it was always bickering and arguing but this was warm and pleasant and the conversation moved easily from one interesting topic to another.

The phone rang upstairs. Soon Mrs. Zimmer appeared in the door, flushed and tense. Her eyes met mine coldly. "Norma, it's your father."

I knew at once what had happened. He was drunk and had been rude to Randy's mother. I went to the phone. Dad poured out such foul language that even I was shocked to hear him. "I want you home *right now,*" he concluded, and hung up with a bang.

Randy drove me home quickly. I sat silent, too crushed to cry.

CHAPTER EIGHTEEN

While I was preparing for my trip to California the mother of Harold Siebenick, one of the choir members at church, invited me to go downtown with her and select a new dress. "A going away present," Mrs. Siebenick explained graciously. I accepted gratefully and we decided on a beige twill suit from Graysons. The price tag said $10. I had never bought such an expensive outfit. I was ecstatic. It even went well with my olive drab coat, which I hoped I wouldn't need very often in California. I loved sunshine and would count the rare sunny days in Seattle. I distinctly recall that in one entire year the sun shone only thirty-six days.

Arline had planned to go to California with me, but ever since dad had telephoned their house in a drunken rage, Mrs. Zimmer had been quite cool to me. I felt she didn't like to have Randy go out with me. Now I was afraid I might have to make my way to California alone.

But Arline went and it was a lucky thing for me she did. We stayed at the home of close friends of the Zimmers—Fred and Jewell Fuller, in Venice, California. They were very kind to us. Arline and I helped with the housework, but for six weeks we had no money to give them. They insisted upon giving us their own cheerful room. Jewell was a chubby four-foot-ten and wore her gray hair in soft finger waves. Her eyes twinkled behind rimless glasses and her smile often turned into a little giggle. Fred was a pleasant man—never in a hurry; even his speech was calm and deliberate.

When I would say, "Oh, I wish I could help pay for the food," Mrs. Fuller would say, "Doing the dishes is enough for me." We begged them to take their bed back and let us sleep on the couch, but they insisted that it was we girls who needed to get a good night's rest, "so you'll be fresh for your auditions."

God bless older people who understand the deep hunger in young folks to be respected and understood. I had never in my life been so highly regarded as a person and it came at a most appropriate time, as I was trying to build enough self-esteem to make my way in the entertainment world.

Venice was a lovely area, with many fruit trees and flowers we had never seen in the north. I loved the hibiscus and bougainvillea cascading down sides of homes and garages and marveled at the geraniums growing like bushes and forming hedges. It was a great thrill for me to pick an orange from Fred's prize tree in the back yard.

On the Saturday after we got there, I called the agent from NBC studios. I hoped my voice wasn't shaking. "I'm the girl who sang on the boat coming home from Victoria, B.C.," I said.

"Oh, yes, I'm so glad you're in town." He asked some general questions about my trip to California, then said, "My wife and I are having some people over tomorrow afternoon for a swimming party. Could you join us?"

I told him I had Arline with me.

"That's great. Bring her along. I'll pick you girls up tomorrow at 1:00."

Arline was as thrilled as I. She thought we should dress our finest. To me that meant my black hand-me-down silk dress and heels, and a wide-brimmed black hat. Arline wore a black, light-weight suit and a fancy felt hat with felt-covered pieces sticking up from it that looked as if they were made out of pipe cleaners. Thus attired, we were picked up for a swimming party!

If the Chandlers noticed anything strange about this, they were far too gracious to show it. They served us a delicious lunch and we met their friends. Late in the day, they took us back to Venice.

Mr. Chandler arranged an audition for me at NBC early the next week. I wore my beige suit and black patent leather sandals. I couldn't believe I was going to a real recording studio.

For my audition, I sang "Un Bel Di" by Puccini. The man I sang for was enthusiastic about my voice and hired me on the spot to do staff programs for $24.00 a show.

I was overwhelmed by my good fortune. Previous to this, the most I had ever earned was $25.00 a week—sitting at a desk all day, five days a week. Now I was to get almost that for doing one show—well, a rehearsal and a show! I got on the smelly old street-car, never noticing the oil fumes that later made me feel ill when I rode the car every day.

Still a very shy person, I would go to work and sit in a corner to wait my turn. Extremely nervous, I would sit and pray that God would keep me calm. "O Lord, use me today—help me to be a blessing to those who hear me." I would pray for each person participating in the show with me and then imagine my audience and pray, "God bless you. God bless you." This is something I still do in every concert or TV appearance.

Praying for my audience has caused many people to say in person and in my mail that they sensed something different about me—that I sing with genuine emotion and seem to be communicating very personally with my listeners. It makes me happy to hear this, for I really do care about the people who hear me; and I'm thankful that they feel that love in my singing.

However, after I had worked a few weeks for NBC they let me go. I wasn't quite as qualified for the job as they had thought. The man told me ever so kindly that he liked my voice and would like to hear me again after I had enlarged my repertoire and had had more training. I left the studio utterly heartbroken. Again it swept over me that I was the runt—just a bit short of what I should have been. I cried all the way to Venice on the streetcar and later wept alone in my borrowed bedroom at the Fullers.

So the audition Mr. Chandler had arranged for me didn't prove to be my immediate passport to success. Nevertheless, it brought me to Hollywood and introduced me to important musicians of that day. I made many friends and today still occasionally work with musicians I worked with at NBC in 1943, one of whom is Charlie Parloto, trumpet player on the Welk show.

Here I was, out of work and still with the Fullers. I had heard of Quirino Pelliocciotti, a prominent voice teacher. Arline didn't have a job yet, but she had some savings which she offered me if I wanted to take voice lessons. I had an audition with Mr. Pelliocciotti. He was pleased with my voice and agreed to teach me.

After several weeks I explained to the maestro that I couldn't keep up the lessons as I didn't have the finances. I didn't expect Arline to keep on lending me money when neither of us was working. "Oh," he said, gesturing widely with both arms, "don't let money stop you. I'll give you lessons free!"

Again, God was 'way ahead of me, working out my problems. Mr. Pitzer's fine training was being followed by Quirino Pelliocciotti! For several years, he gave me voice lessons twice a week. His beautiful wife, Katherine, accompanied me at the piano.

His handsome studio was furnished with Oriental rugs and hand-carved chairs. He was a maestro from the old Italian school and also taught the Bel Canto method used by Mr. Pitzer. This method teaches the singer to place the tone toward the nose, the eyes, the forehead, toward the top of the head—in other words, in the upper resonating cavities for the high notes. But the method doesn't tell you *how* to get there. Now I realize that the soft palate needs to be open.

(After singing on a microphone for years and using the electrical amplification for power to reinforce my voice, I recently found that gradually but surely the function of my support muscles was weakening. I mentioned this problem to my accompanist, Mark Thallander, as I sang at Garden Grove Community Church one Sunday this summer. He in turn told Don Fontana, choir director at the church. The following day Don called and recommended that I read a book, *Singing Technique,* by Joseph J. Klein. I was so excited with what I read that I contacted Mr. Klein, and I am now taking singing lessons with him weekly. It's never too late to "improve yourself"!)

The Pelliocciottis owned a cross-eyed Siamese cat who sat on the piano next to the music as the maestro gave the lesson. As I would sing, this character of a cat would sing along. He had a terrible voice! He could hold a note for the longest time in an ugly, rasping monotone. When I'd stop he would stop and sit there licking his lips; then he'd look intently at Mr. Pelliocciotti, as if waiting for further instructions.

Mr. Pelliocciotti suggested that I go to see the opera *Faust* being rehearsed at Plummer Park on Sunday afternoon. Arline and I went to the auditorium as the rehearsal was in progress. I was surprised and delighted to see that Lee Sweetland was playing Mephistopheles.

The last time I had seen Lee was at the "Musical Evening" in the University Christian Church when I was a high school senior. He finished rehearsing his role and spotted me in the first row. He rushed down the stairs and greeted me warmly. "Well, Norma Larsen, what are you doing here? I remember seeing you that night at the church program in Seattle. I thought you were going to call me if ever you came to Hollywood."

Shyly I told him I hadn't wanted to bother him, not knowing for sure whether he had meant it when he had told me to contact him.

He said, "Well, I did mean it. Here, I want you to come and meet my wife. She can help you in the business."

Sally Sweetland was tall and beautiful. Her dark hair was drawn back into a huge chignon with flowers, and she was wearing the most elegant suit I had ever seen. Her warm friendliness put me at ease immediately.

They invited me to their home for dinner the following evening. After a delicious meal they asked me to sing for them.

Sally was singing with a quartet called the Girl Friends and she knew of a trio, The Tailor Maids, who had just lost a soprano. An audition was arranged and nervously I sang for the group. We ran through several numbers. They seemed pleased and I was hired.

Our thirty-three-week engagement was in a nightclub. It was an unnatural place for me to be and I was always uncomfortable there. The contract read that each girl was to receive $250 weekly but the agent said, "I'll give you $55 a week take-home pay and put the rest in a bank account. Then, at the end of our thirty-three weeks, we'll divide up the remaining money."

The problem was that the small print of the contract provided the agent with an unlimited expense account. He entertained his friends and business associates extravagantly and at the end of the thirty-three weeks he told us there was no money to divide.

I had never enjoyed working in that nightclub and was glad when it was over. But it was a job and kept me in Hollywood. I believe it was meant to be. I had made good friends of the other girls in the trio, Virginia Friend and Marian Short. That experience made me distrustful of agents, and never again have I signed a contract with one.

During those first months in Hollywood, Sally Sweetland did a most generous thing. She arranged for me to substitute for her in various groups so that I would have that exposure in the profession. One doesn't soon forget such kindness.

Randy and I were missing each other badly, so in December he came to Hollywood too and went to work in his Uncle Adolph's plastics factory. Hugo's brother Adolph was a tall, handsome, distinguished-looking man. He had a regal appearance with his perfect posture, his soft gray hair, and white moustache. He was a skillful tool-and-die maker and had designed a beautiful injection-mold clear lucite compact. It was shaped like an octagonal flat diamond with prisms that glowed with rainbow hues. On top was placed a circle of mirror. This beautiful item was sold in top stores such as Saks Fifth Avenue, Magnins, and Bullocks. Randy became foreman in the shop and quickly learned how difficult it was to keep fourteen women happy.

Randy's uncle not only provided a job for him, but gave up his Hollywood apartment for Arline and me. We took turns cooking and cleaning and got along pretty well for several months while she worked at Paramount Pictures in the publicity department. She would come home with thrilling inside stories about the stars and studio life. It was a vicarious thrill for me and I often wondered what it would be like to be famous and rich. I pictured the stars living a life of complete ease: maids drawing their baths, laying out their clothes, serving them breakfast in bed. Of course there would be a chauffeur to drive them in a shiny Cadillac, a cook to shop and prepare exotic feasts. Surely a nursemaid cared for their children. No doubt some magic method was used to feed these stars their lines of dialogue, so that there was no *work* to memorizing the parts they performed. I continued naively to believe these things for years, even while living and working right in Hollywood.

Studio work soon lost its glamor for Arline and she returned to Seattle to continue her education at the University of Washington.

Randy never actually proposed to me. He just spoke of our future together as a fact. He would describe the home he was going to build for us or speak of how beautifully he thought I would age, as our children would grow up and have babies of their own. "What a knockout of a grandma you're going to be, honey," he mused.

In June, Randy said, "Let's go to Las Vegas on your day off and get married."

My heart sank a little at the thought of being married in "Tinsel Town," but since our families were 1,400 miles away and we didn't have enough money for a church wedding I didn't want to hurt his feelings by offering objections.

We pooled our money—we had $100 between us, mostly Randy's. Seventy-five dollars went for my rings—a tiny, but perfect diamond set with four rubies, my birthstone. I wore that ring until just recently when Randy replaced it with a large, beautiful diamond.

As we drove out of town we decided to stop by the home of Larry and Barbara Thackwell, some dear friends Randy had met while skiing in the local mountains. We were anxious to let them know of our marriage plans.

Barbara was shocked! "You are *not* going to Las Vegas to be married!" she protested. "I won't hear of it. You're staying right here and you're going to be married in a darling wedding chapel that I know of right here in Pasadena." We were both relieved at the thought of having a more traditional wedding, so she helped us make all the arrangements. We decided to include Jerry Hiatt and June Roe, two other skiing friends, in the wedding party, so the six of us went to the chapel.

I wore the simple beige suit Mrs. Siebenick had given me. There was to be another wedding that afternoon and the flowers and candles had already been set up. So we had the benefit of flowers and borrowed candles—although of course we couldn't light them. We didn't have any organ music—I missed that. The preacher's services were included with the chapel.

We stood together and asked God to bless our marriage. We were deeply in love and completely committed to each other. The simplicity of our wedding made it all the more meaningful to me. I knew Randy was risking his mother's disapproval to marry me, but I felt secure in his love.

CHAPTER NINETEEN

After the ceremony we left for our brief honeymoon. We drove along the Rim of the World Highway, overlooking all of San Bernardino and Riverside. At one scenic overlook Randy stopped the car. Together we walked to the edge of the highway. A masonry wall bordered the deep dropoff. Randy took me in his arms and held me close.

"It's just different now, holding you near. It's as though we're one. You're the most precious thing in my life. Oh, Norma," he choked, "I love you so!"

How grateful I was that I had saved myself for him alone.

That day at Lake Arrowhead we couldn't resist renting a sailboat. We jumped into the small vessel and hoisted the sail. A cold, brisk wind moved us swiftly over the choppy water. Spray dampened the light blouse and shorts I wore, and soon my teeth were chattering as we tacked across the gorgeous alpine lake. The distant tyrolean village of Lake Arrowhead looked so authentic from our vantage point that we could have sworn we were transported to the Alps. We couldn't have been happier.

Soon after we returned to our quaint room at Arrowhead Inn, the glands in my throat started to ache. Before nightfall I was feverish with a miserable cold. So Randy spent his honeymoon tenderly doctoring a sick wife.

When we got back to our apartment in Hollywood Randy picked up the newspaper at our door. Headlines read, "Allied Armies Invade Normandy." We had begun our married life on the very eve of historic D-Day.

Randy telephoned Earl Carrol and told him I was sick and couldn't work. I suppose because we were just married, Mr. Carrol became suspicious, so he sent a doctor over to examine me. The thermometer showed clearly that I had a fever of 102°. My nose ran and my eyes watered. The doctor told us he thought I should remain in bed, but after he reported to Earl Carrol, Mr. Carrol called and scolded me for not coming to work. "The doctor says you could've made it...you're not all that sick. You kids just want to be left alone!"

Furious, Randy took the receiver from me and slammed it down so hard that the phone box pulled loose from the old plaster and dangled by its wires!

I went back to work the next night, still weak and slightly feverish. How thankful I was that that job would soon end.

We paid $42 a month for our little bachelor apartment with its Murphy bed, and for us it was heaven. The kitchen was ancient and ugly—a real challenge to Randy, who completely remodeled it, to our landlord's delight.

Remembering how mother could make any house into a cozy home, I set out to do the same. I bought criss-cross organdy curtains and colorful pillows. I arranged pictures and plates on the walls and covered an old chair, which, with a maroon, gray and gold-striped couch and chair, came with the rent. We were idyllically happy in our one-room home.

We lived in the Vivian Apartments in Hollywood, only a block from Paramount Pictures. I came home from work one afternoon and there, unannounced, stood Randy's father. I had always liked him and was glad he had come—nevertheless, I felt uneasy.

I brought him into the apartment and fixed him a cup of coffee. He was very jolly. When Randy came bounding down the hall, yodeling as usual, to let me know he was home, I met him at the door with a kiss. Hand in hand, we came into the apartment where Hugo jumped up to greet his son with a hug. While they visited, I prepared our meal of hamburger patties and salad.

I showed Mr. Zimmer the twelve-place set of Dorothy Thorpe china and the sterling silver service for twelve, which were my pride and joy. "We got these dishes and this sterling from Uncle Adolph. His girl friend, Ann Nolan, helped him pick them out," I told Mr. Zimmer. Carefully, I set the table with our new china, and a bowl of flowers. We ate by candlelight. After dinner, Randy and I sat together on the couch holding hands; Mr. Zimmer sat on the chair I had re-covered. Randy described his job at the factory. Conversation seemed cheerful and natural.

The next morning, Mr. Zimmer prepared to leave. Randy and I had to go to work. I can still see Randy's father standing at the door with his jaunty little hat on, shifting his weight from one leg to the other, making small talk. He kept his hand on the door knob and seemed uncertain about leaving. Finally he blurted out, "Well, Berdie told me to come down here and see about having your marriage annulled."

We stared at him in shock. Then he hastily added, "But I couldn't do that to you kids. I can see how much in love you are. May God bless you and give you a long and happy life together. And here's a hundred dollar bill for your wedding present!" He turned quickly and was gone.

I had known the Zimmers didn't want Randy to marry me. My home situation had become apparent to them when dad had cursed drunkenly at Mrs. Zimmer over the telephone the night of the party. She had become aware of our poverty and social inferiority in the weeks after that, before I left for California. When word reached them that I was singing in a nightclub, they must have decided I was really going to the dogs.

In the years to follow, Mr. Zimmer and I grew to love each other. Both Randy and I called him "Pop." But I never did feel completely accepted by Randy's mother.

Randy and I spent every possible minute together but I still didn't seem able to tell him enough how much I loved him. It was only natural that from time to time Randy had some twinges of jealousy about my working with other men in what he thought of as the glamorous entertainment world. I wanted so much to let him know that I had eyes only for him! I developed a little habit of writing him love notes. There was a card shop at the bus stop and I would drop in and pick out a cute card and write something like,

"Dearest, I'm sitting here at the bus stop wishing you were close beside me. I love you with all my heart, and I just want you to know how grateful I am that you're my husband."

I'd slip it in a mailbox and watch for Randy's reaction as he picked up the mail the next day. His pleasure was transparent, and the little reassurances of my deep love for him made his face soften in a special way.

We both loved to walk and knew it helped keep our legs in shape for skiing, so each night that we were both free we would hike the four miles to the base of Mt. Hollywood and then climb the 1,200 feet to the top. Each time, we'd try to beat our time record.

Dad hadn't permitted mother to teach me to cook, but Randy was patient with me while I learned. My meals were the simplest of foods. I *did* know how to boil an egg and since that was Randy's and my favorite breakfast—and still is—we had them almost every morning.

I broiled a lot of lamb chops and fish and we both loved salads and other natural foods. Randy cheerfully ate everything I fixed. He asked me not to make rich desserts, as we were both watching our weight, and suggested that I use only honey as a sweetener.

Our first Thanksgiving together I had to work on the Bing Crosby show. When I got home that night, I found Randy had prepared a complete, traditional Thanksgiving dinner: turkey, dressing, candied yams, vegetables, salad, and pumpkin pie with the flakiest of crusts. He served this on a beautiful table with flowers and candles. I couldn't help but cry. For five months he had bravely eaten the results of my poor efforts, while all the time he was an accomplished cook. It was plain to see there wasn't anything Randy couldn't do. How sweet he was to be so patient with my cooking when he could have done so much better himself!

About the only problem we had in those days was Randy's bad back. It had never been the same since it was broken. Many mornings Randy would groan as he moved to get out of bed. He would slide off the bed, knees to the floor, his chest and arms still lying over the mattress. For a few moments he would try to limber up the stiff muscles before attempting to get up. Some days he would have to crawl for several minutes until he could brace himself on a chair and inch himself to a standing position. Once upright, he'd throw back his shoulders and struggle forward, his knees slightly bent. He suffered like this for years, getting only partial occasional relief from chiropractic adjustments.

There were many months that Randy couldn't ski, but when he could, the rhythm of the sport, the free-flowing body movements, were a tonic to his aching back muscles. He is so at home on his skis and loves the sport so dearly that if he's able to maneuver at all, he improves after a few hours on the slopes.

The whole world was involved in the war. Max had been assigned to a naval office in Pearl Harbor, so he, at least, was comparatively safe.

From time to time we were saddened as we learned of friends dying in Africa, Sicily, Italy, France—and such faraway places as Guadalcanal, Iwo Jima, Tarawa, Kwajelein—islands we had never heard of before.

Randy was embarrassed to be seen by servicemen, of whom there were many in Los Angeles. "I look so healthy," he'd say. "I feel like going up to each one of them and explaining, 'You see, I broke my back the week before I was to leave with the Ski Troops. I was signed up and ready to go.' "

An opportunity for another solo spot on radio presented itself. The part of "Sally Stone" in "The Singing Sweethearts" broadcast was offered to me. I thought it strange to be called Sally Stone, but the turnover in women vocalists was so great the sponsors kept the same name for their character.

My unhappy interlude at Earl Carrol's finally came to an end and I wondered what my next job would be. A phone call from Sally Sweetland solved the dilemma.

"Norma, can you be at CBS Thursday afternoon to audition for my quartet—the Girl Friends?"

"Of course," I said. "But what happened?"

"Lee and I are going to move to New York. It's sudden, I know, but there are opportunities on the East Coast that we can't resist—so be in Studio A at 2:30—OK?"

"I'll be there," I assured her, "and thank you, Sally. How can I ever repay you for all your help? You've paved the way for me and I'll be eternally grateful."

"Don't thank me, Norma. I'm just happy Lee and I could give you a hand. Now don't be nervous. With your ability to read music you shouldn't have any problem at all. You've got the voice, but without your ability to sightread, you'd never be able to hold the job. Good luck, gal!"

I dressed carefully the day of the audition. My hair behaved and lay in golden ringlets on my shoulders. I studied myself in the mirror—just enough makeup—not too much. I knew these girls were refined, and I had heard Sally rave about their personalities. They were tops in the business and were established in all segments of the industry: radio, recordings, movie studios, and commercials. Before I left the apartment, I prayed earnestly that I would suit them.

CBS studios were located on Sunset Boulevard. Many times Randy and I had strolled past, awed by the names on the marquees—Jack Benny, Lucille Ball, Tony Martin, Dinah Shore—and now I was pushing open the huge glass entry doors.

I walked across the lobby, my heels making a hollow click-clack. The girl at the reception desk looked up pleasantly. "May I help you?"

"I have an audition in Studio A," I said.

"Take a seat over there," she said, pointing to a long bench, already lined with girls—beautiful, confident-looking girls. They were not friendly as I timidly sat down at the end of the row.

One by one they were invited in. I had to ask God to calm me again and again. The suspense was almost unbearable. After an eternity my name was called.

As I entered the studio I saw Sally seated at the piano. She called to me. "Norma, come and meet the girls. This is Betty Allan, Betty Noyes, and Dorothy Morton."

"How do you do." I hoped I appeared at ease and confident.

"Hi, Norma, we've heard about you from Sally," Betty Allan said. "Let's get right to it—you read the second part."

My heart fell. I was accustomed to singing lead—and it was so different and confusing to pick out that second part. The four notes looked like a scramble to me.

Fortunately the song, "Dream," was slow and I had a chance to pick out the notes. The blend of the voices sounded right to me, and I could tell by the satisfied look on Sally's face that she was happy. "That sounds beautiful, Norma," she said. "Girls, I think that's the sound. What do you say?"

They all agreed, and told me to report to work the next day at the Annex Studio on Sycamore Street in Hollywood for a Dinah Shore record session.

We arrived a half hour before the session was to begin. The parts were handed out to us and to the four men who were going to carry the male parts. I looked at the long pages. No simple oo's. This was to be a *jazz* session and the intricate syncopated rhythms, plus searching out the second part, made my mind go blank. It was a nightmare. Somehow I got through the rehearsal, but when the band was all set up and we were placed before the microphones to begin recording, my loud heartbeat could have given the drummer competition.

"She's not getting it!" I heard Betty Allan whisper to Dorothy after we had a run-through.

"Give her a chance," was her reply.

I forced my eyes to seek out the notes. Dad's early training in counting out the time came to my aid—but nothing I had done before had ever had such a complex rhythm pattern or such a difficult arrangement. I felt that I was an utter failure.

I was frozen. I couldn't even apologize. I just became a robot.

Thoughts of being fired crowded my mind. I was miserable.

Betty Allan hummed the notes in my ear. Betty Noyes beat out the time on the stand. Dorothy kept giving me a pat on the shoulder to reassure me and three hours later I stumbled out of the studio into the fading day.

In my distress, I hadn't even met Dinah, who did such a fabulous job of those records—in spite of the faltering second soprano.

"I'll practice," I finally managed to murmur to Betty Allan as we walked to her car.

"I'll help you," she said, and that began a friendship that is rich to this day.

Dorothy Morton left the group to go to Wichita, Kansas, with her lawyer husband, Bob, and was replaced by Dorothy McCarty, a beautiful redhead who did secretarial work for composer Victor Young, who wrote "Golden Earrings" and many other popular songs and musical scores for films.

These four girls have always been up front in my cheering squad, wishing me well and rooting for me. They're dear friends.

Now I had to join the union and that took money which I still didn't have. Sally and Lee gave me the money. "No, it's not a loan," they said. "Don't worry about it." I didn't have a proper wardrobe. They outfitted me with clothes, beautiful dresses and suits. I learned how to do my makeup and hair.

Sally had given me opportunities from time to time to substitute for her so that people in the business could hear my voice. I had learned to sightread well. The violin training my father had given me continued to help me in the world of song. I could clearly see how God had brought earlier experiences and friendships into my life as preparations for the career that was now beginning to open up to me in Hollywood.

With the Girl Friends I became a very busy vocalist. We did choral background singing. Life became a round of jobs. CBS and NBC were our constant haunts. Those marquees that Randy and I had looked at in awe never lost their glamor as I became a part of the scene. Guards at the artists' entrance stopped asking for identification and I felt very much at home with all the famous people we encountered.

We sang for the Eddie Cantor Show, the Jack Benny Show, Phil Harris and Alice Faye (who seemed a truly loving couple—and the years have proved that this was true), Dinah Shore and Lucille Ball, Nelson Eddy, Edgar Bergen. And each week we did a show with Bing Crosby and one with Frank Sinatra. To work with all these shows, we had to rush back and forth between CBS and NBC constantly. On Sundays we did two shows, and during my break I would dash over to Hollywood Presbyterian Church, a block from

CBS, arriving just in time to hear the anthem and the sermon.

Waiting has always made me impatient, especially on a street corner. Many nights after finishing radio shows I stood tapping my toe as Randy skidded to a stop, apologizing before he opened the door. Not a clock watcher, Randy was seldom on time. I had explained to him, "Honey, if there's anything I *hate*, it's waiting! Sailors take me for a pick-up. Please be on time!"

Having told him how I felt, I would feel myself growing angrier and angrier when I had to wait. By the time Randy would drive up I'd often be pouting.

One night after working on the Al Jolson show I was standing on the corner in front of NBC. It had been a long day. Sailors drifted by, whistling and asking, "Hi, honey! Waiting for someone?"

How long will it be till he gets here? Furious, I scanned the street for the beige coupe. As I craned my neck to see farther, a new dark-tan car pulled to the curb right in front of me. "Want a lift, little girl?" It was Randy!

I jumped in beside him. "Randy, where did you get this car?"

"I bought it!"

Our Chev had 110,000 miles on it and we had talked of getting a new car. But this! "How could you? How can we ever afford this? It must be brand-new!" I felt the plush upholstery. The dashboard dazzled with shiny buttons and glass.

We had a policy of not going into debt or paying interest, but now Randy assured me, "I gave them $2,600 and the fellow says if we can come up with the last $1,000 soon, we won't have to pay any interest!"

"We should be able to do that. Oh, Randy, it's so lovely." I sank into the comfortable seat. "It's really ours. Isn't it beautiful?"

"I think it's really terrific," Randy said. "It'll take most of our next few paychecks to pay it off, but it will be worth it not to have to pay the interest."

But we'd been taken. When Randy returned with the cash for the car, a different salesman handled the transaction. Patronizingly he said, "We don't do business that way. We never do. *Of course* you'll have to pay the interest."

So Randy decided he might as well pay off the car in small installments and he kept the cash.

That '48 Packard is the only thing we ever bought on time. When we needed something, we watched the paper for sales. When we bought furniture for our house we didn't get anything that wasn't on sale, and we paid cash.

CHAPTER TWENTY

Randy has helped countless numbers of friends, both young people and older ones, to handle themselves with ease on skis. He is a patient and talented ski instructor. It's unusual for a husband to teach a wife to ski without losing patience, but Randy has that easy-going disposition. His careful program of training allowed me to ski for years without taking a spill.

Mammoth Mountains beckoned us on several long weekends each spring. Most of the 300-plus miles to the area were flat desert roads. Snowy, icy conditions seldom affected the roads until we were practically there, making the adventure much more agreeable. With rucksack full of hardtack, cheese, and apples; warm sleeping bags, skis, poles, boots, gloves, and goggles packed in the car, we were on our way. No need for fancy motel rooms; a patch of heather made a good mattress and, as long as the sky was clear, the stars were a perfect ceiling. Randy and I were rugged people—we didn't require the comforts most couples wanted.

I wore my hair in long pigtails—which Randy still prefers over all my other hair styles—and at night I cleansed my face with a pad of cotton and lotion. In the morning we brushed our teeth with water from our canteen.

In those days a rope tow was the only mechanical aid to gaining altitude on the mountain. It didn't extend high enough to give us the long run we desired, so upon reaching the top of the lift, we'd slip sealskin climbers on our skis and continue climbing for several hundred feet. The views from the heights we attained are indelible in my memory. It was like looking out the very windows of heaven. As far as the eye could see were majestic white giants—snow-crowned mountains fading down into the distance. It's a scene no artist could capture, so vast is the panorama.

We'd perch on a chair of jutting granite to breathe in the magnificence, then we'd rub paraffin on our skis and start our swift descent. The exhilarating experience is impossible to describe, but we intend to keep repeating it as long as our legs will carry us.

When prayers for local snow were answered there was no need to travel so far. Within a hundred miles of Los Angeles there are several excellent areas. Randy and I often spent a day at Snow Valley, in the San Bernardino mountains, where both beginners and advanced skiers could have an enjoyable day.

One stormy Saturday morning we headed for the resort. As we approached the parking area, the sun burst through the clouds. This was going to be a great day!

I was still a novice, so Randy found a place for me on one of the beginners' slopes. Then he went off to one of the lifts for more exciting skiing.

I was very cautious and practiced slowly. I got to the bottom of the run and stood for a moment to enjoy the beauty around me. Pines and cedars were heavy with snow; paths ran between the trees where the skiers flew down the slopes. Voluminous clouds wafted about in a sky of periwinkle blue. I inhaled the crystal-clear air, taking with it the marvelous aroma of pine cones. Joyous laughter and excitement rang in the air. It was good to be alive!

I glanced toward the place where Randy had gone to ski, wondering if I might catch a glimpse of him. I saw a group of people, three or four, approaching with someone on a toboggan. They were right in my line of vision as I searched for Randy. Not seeing him, I decided to go back to the top for another run. Glancing once more at the party with the toboggan, I could see now that someone had been badly hurt. "The poor creature!" I murmured to myself sympathetically. He had a white coat wrapped around his head and blood was seeping through the fabric. As they passed me I realized with a shock that it was Randy! It looked to me as if he was unconscious. I slipped off my skis and ran over to them.

"What happened?" I cried, stumbling to my knees as I reached for Randy.

"He got hit by a hammer. Are you with him?"

"He's my husband! A *hammer?* How did it happen?"

"Well, a lift broke down and one of the workers climbed up on the tower to repair it and he called for a peen hammer. They threw one up to him but he missed it, and it fell and hit your husband." I walked beside the toboggan, bending over to touch Randy's arm. I was crying, and praying, "O God, help us! Please protect him, Lord!"

We took him by station wagon to the San Bernardino hospital, where a doctor examined him thoroughly and stitched him up. He didn't think Randy had a concussion so he released him in a few hours. For weeks Randy suffered from severe headaches. He finally went to our doctor for x-rays and found that his skull had been fractured.

Years later, on a ski trip at Mammoth Mountain, we were sitting at a table, having lunch, when we were joined by some good skiing friends of long standing, Tony and Norma Milici. We began to share skiing yarns. Randy told of breaking his back at Mt. Rainier and we told about a narrow escape I had had, when I had fallen on an icy slope and careened all the way down a run, narrowly missing trees and rocks. Finally I hit another skier, but fortunately no one was hurt.

Tony said, "I've often wondered whatever happened to a fellow who was hit by a hammer at Snow Valley."

Randy perked up. "You didn't happen to wrap a white parka around his head, did you?"

"Why yes...yes, I did!"

"I was that guy," Randy explained incredulously. "I often worried about ruining your parka!"

Tony laughed. "You don't mean it!" And so after all these years of skiing together, we learned that Tony was the man who had taken care of Randy that day in the San Bernardino mountains.

Randy grinned. "I heard the man ask for that hammer and a second later it hit me. Boy, did I ever drop! I was just partly conscious but I could dimly hear somebody yelling, 'Get a tourniquet. He's bleeding,' and I thought, 'Oh, no, not that... it's my *head!*' But I couldn't do anything about it. My gosh, they could have choked me!"

"That woulda finished you off right there," Tony chortled.

CHAPTER TWENTY-ONE

Randy was working for the Hawthorne Construction Company and together we were earning enough money to think about building our own home. Randy was a fine carpenter and I was an eager helper. We would do it together.

One weekend we came down from the mountains early because the ski slopes were icy. We had driven through Flintridge on our way up. It was such an attractive area we decided to look around on the way back. It wasn't built up yet; there was a lot of vacant land but we couldn't find any For Sale signs.

We drove through the long winding streets to the top of the hills. The view was spectacular! "Can you imagine living up here?" Randy asked.

"Could I! It would be so inspiring! We'd have to have huge windows and I'd want the patio overlooking the view."

We stood there dreaming of the possibilities. "Well," Randy said, "if the Lord wants us to have it, he'll show us how."

A trip to the real estate office the next day was productive. They gave us a list of fifteen lots with prices ranging from $3,000 to $15,000. Enthusiastically we started our search. It was hard to believe, but the lot with the most promise was the cheapest.

"That can't be the right price," Randy said. "I'm going to check this out."

The realtor told us, "Yes, $3,000 is correct." We gave him the down payment. Later he admitted he had thought it was the steep lot across the street. "If I'd known it was *that* lot I'd have bought it myself," he said ruefully.

Randy drew up the plans for our home. Weekends, he started building a brick fence along the frontage of the lot. For weeks, he worked lovingly, carefully creating a filigree design. It was the most artistic fence I'd ever seen and I praised and encouraged him.

"This weekend stuff has got to go," Randy told me as we drove home on a Sunday evening. He had progressed very slowly and knew that at this rate it would take too long. "I'll quit Hawthorne Construction and work full time on our place. In the long run I'll save money anyway. If we had to hire carpenters it'd cost a fortune."

So he gave up his job and turned his full attention to building our own place. Now things started to happen.

After clearing the brush from the homesite, Randy discovered the ground was decomposed granite. It took weeks of blasting and long jarring hours with a jackhammer to prepare for the foundation. After he poured the cement slab, framing went quickly. I helped by holding the 2 x 4s in place. Costly materials started piling up on the site, and Randy hated leaving at night for fear of theft.

Knowing we would soon have a home and a big yard, we couldn't resist buying a darling boxer puppy. We named him Duffy. Randy built a large box that looked like a tool chest. Each day we sneaked our puppy in and out of the apartment.

Every day, we lost an hour and a half of working time commuting from Hollywood to Flintridge. So we decided to move up to our building site and rough it, living in the small room that was to be a projection booth. The framing was now complete, the roof was partly finished.

As our apartment manager bade us good-bye she added, with a twinkle in her eye, "And don't think you've fooled me with that tool chest. I know you've been keeping a dog!"

Camping in our new unfinished home was a lark! We put army bunks in the small projection room which measured 6 x 10 feet. Two apple boxes with a plank on top made a counter and shelf space. A hot plate connected to the temporary electric light pole was our stove, on which we cooked and heated water for our sponge baths. We hung our clothes on hooks screwed into the framing. We wrapped canvas around the room temporarily for privacy and protection from the wind. I carried water from the spigot outside and (not for the first time in *my* life) an outhouse was our bathroom. Our sleeping bags kept us comfy and warm during the chilly nights.

Now the work began in earnest.

Between singing jobs, I helped in every way I could; holding boards in place while Randy hammered, bringing him tools, finding objects, holding flashlights for night work, cleaning up debris, picking up nails, running errands. When roofing began I could really help. I placed each heavy cedar shake carefully in place and Randy followed along nailing it down. There wasn't a leak in the 2,600-foot home when it was completed.

Uncle Adolph showed up almost every weekend and seemed to enjoy helping. About the only work Randy contracted to have done was plastering and stucco.

While we were working on the house I would silently pray, "Lord, just fill our home with your love and your peace. Be a partner in it. Help us to keep you first in our lives. Guide us in the right paths."

I had known so much misery in my childhood—so much quarreling and bitterness. I wanted a peaceful home more than anything in the world. Randy is easy to keep peace with. He prefers talking things out, too—so we have rarely quarreled. God has abundantly answered those prayers for a serene and happy home.

New singing opportunities kept coming my way, and I enjoyed many exciting contacts with prominent musicians and other entertainers. It was during this time, while I was helping Randy build our new house, that one of my most unique jobs turned up.

In 1947 Meredith Willson, who wrote *The Music Man,* hired me as one of his Talking People. The Beverly Hills *Register* on September 10, 1947, described us this way:

> ...a quintet of unique spielers dubbed the Heads by their creator, Meredith Willson. They talk their heads off, but surprisingly, in a most entertaining manner.
>
> The Talking People are five talented singers—two gals, three fellows—carefully chosen by Willson to take part in his experiment of contriving something unusual, catchy, entertaining, and commercial in the way of radio salesmanship. And it's gone over. College of the City of New York recently deemed it the best radio commercial of the season; radio editors in a poll placed the show among the top five for the good taste and the commercial effectiveness of its sales talks.
>
> Their trick is simple to explain, intricate to accomplish. The whole five of 'em talk, sing, hum, laugh, and emote as one.
>
> Willson's idea of having several persons speaking in unison is not, of course, new. But he gave it a humorously entertaining twist.
>
> The Talking People do not merely recite commercial plugs,

but are a featured unit of the program. Hearing their charming chatter, it's difficult to realize that the words are being spoken by ten lips. They seem to have merged five personalities into one.

But the trick takes long hours of practice, according to John Rarig, the head Head, "We practice at least four or five hours the day before each broadcast and another hour or so before air time."

Willson works a great deal with the group and directs their conversation on the air in very much the same way that he leads his orchestra. He writes the lines, then sets them to actual musical notes which are used as cues and guide marks for the "Talking People."

Working in the "Talking People" was one of the most exciting parts of my early career, and I grew to admire and respect Meredith Willson both as an employer and as a friend. He and his wife were house-hunting. Flintridge offered some really choice homes. He knew that Randy and I were building ours in that area, so one afternoon after rehearsal Meredith said, "C'mon, Norma, let's drive up to see this dream palace you're creating."

We drove through Glendale, then wended our way over Chevy Chase to the top of the foothills, made a left turn on Inverness, followed a pretzel of meandering wooded roads, ending again at the crest of a hill. Just off to the right nestled our beautiful ranch house. Pride welled up inside me as we approached it. It looked so handsome with the heavy shake roof, brick siding, and Randy's artistic fence bordering the entire frontage. I could hear Randy's yodeling as we sauntered down the winding driveway. That meant things were going well. Whether he's skiing or working, life is in tune when my husband warms up the atmosphere with his tyrolean serenade.

"Honey, we've got a visitor!" I called loudly.

Randy bounded up the stairs from the sunken living room.

"Well, welcome, Meredith," he called. "How nice of you to take the time to drive 'way up here."

"Came to see if you're interested in selling yet. I'm in the market for a home, y'know."

"Not for sale at any price," Randy quipped. "But there are some great homes across the valley over there," he said pointing to the south.

Proudly we gave him the grand tour of our dream house. It was still far from complete, so it took imagination to picture the finished product.

"This will be the living room."

"Nice and big. About 25 feet long?"

"It's 18 by 26," I replied. "There will be a long hearth—don't you love this big fireplace? It measures six feet. We plan to bring huge logs down from the mountains."

Randy moved over to the special feature of our house. "We're building a projection room at this end. We'll have recording equipment too and it'll all be concealed behind soundproof glass. We're going to conceal it with a huge picture on piano hinges that will swing out—so it will be artistic. And over where Norma's standing, at the other end of the room, there will be a hidden screen that comes down electrically."

"I'm impressed. What an idea!" Meredith said. "And the room is so light—all this glass."

"We love lots of light and sunshine. That's why we have the whole wall in picture windows. These French doors lead out to the patio."

"Come and see the size of the master bedroom, Meredith," Randy said proudly, leading the way. "It's 15 by 18."

"It's spacious and will be really great when you have it finished," Meredith said, seeming impressed with the layout.

As Randy and Meredith discussed the advantages of building versus buying, I made a pot of coffee on the hot plate.

Visiting over mugs of hot coffee with such an enthusiastic admirer of our work gave us a real sense of satisfaction.

It was not the last time Meredith surprised Randy. Several times he dropped by to watch the progress. Then he'd sit and visit for a while. "I've seen nearly every home that's offered in Flintridge," he said.

Later the Willsons purchased a gorgeous home in Pacific Palisades, where we were often invited to spend delightful evenings.

Our breakfast room became our next living quarters. It seemed spacious as we moved our army bunks, the temporary furniture, and all our worldly possessions into it. Duffy, the boxer, had his little bed in the corner, and charmed us with his antics.

Randy worked constantly trying to finish the house. We were supremely happy.

Then one day a letter from mother revived all the memories of misery I had endured for so many years.

Dear Norma,

I must tell you what has happened. Max and Nellie came to visit us last Sunday afternoon. Pete had been drinking heavily and began immediately to rush at Max shouting, "*How* are you going to kill me?"

He went to the kitchen and got a butcher knife and pushed Max against the wall. He held him that way with the knife at his stomach. He kept saying,"*How* are you going to kill me?'' It was awful! Nellie and I didn't know what to do. Max told us to call the police, so Nellie hurried to get help.

When the police came they dragged Pete away from Max. They had to hold him until Max and Nellie could leave. Oh, Norma, it's a miracle no one was hurt! Max told me he was going as far away from Seattle as he could and would never see his father again. They've moved to New York. They left right away. I feel miserable.

I can't live with Pete any longer. May I come to stay with you? I wouldn't interfere. Maybe I could help you. I'll do anything! Please help me!

Love,
Mom

After Randy had read the letter I asked him, ''What do you think, dear?''

''Your mom's life has always been hard. Where else could she go? Sure, let her come. You know I've always liked Kay.''

''Are you sure you don't mind? It's asking a lot of a man to provide a home for his mother-in-law. Honey, you don't know how much I appreciate this.''

''I'll get along fine with her. Tell her to come on down.''

''Now that dad has no one to argue with except mother, I can imagine how terrible her life is. She always hated arguing. When I was at home I often heard her say, 'Life isn't worth living with this constant arguing and bickering.' ''

I knew mother hated dad. She might have grown to love him if he had been kind and gentle with her and if there had been no drinking. Instead she had developed a strong dislike for him which finally turned to hate. Many a night I had heard her cry, ''Leave me alone, Pete. Don't touch me. I hate you!''

We met mother at the bus depot. As she stepped down from the bus, I could see by her puffy face that she was still drinking. ''Well, Lord,'' I prayed silently, ''help us handle this problem.'' She still looked beautiful. She wore the beige cashmere coat and red silk dress I had sent her for Christmas. It had been so thrilling to buy my parents fine gifts. I had sent dad a good-looking gray suit and overcoat, and had found an alligator violin case that became his dearest possession.

''Welcome, Kay!'' Randy exclaimed lovingly, drawing her to him in his strong arms. She leaned against his broad chest, gratitude glowing in her tear-filled eyes.

''Oh, mom, it's so good to see you!'' I said, taking my turn to hold her close. We made our way to the car, carrying her few possessions in one medium-sized suitcase. ''I can't wait for you to see the house! It's not finished yet, but eventually we'll have a bedroom and bath at one side of the house just for you. It'll give you privacy. It should be ready in a few weeks—but you don't mind roughing it, do you, mom?"

"You know I don't. Just living in peace is all I want."

We drove toward Pasadena, full of animated conversation. Duffy rushed back and forth, licking first a window, then one of us. He wanted to get acquainted with mom, so he kept nuzzling her, yipping for attention. He was such a little character. We adored him and it looked as if mom liked him too.

The bright lights of a tavern were blinking as we stopped for a traffic signal. "Let's stop and I'll buy you a drink!" mom offered.

Randy glanced at me, suddenly serious, then turned and met mom's eyes squarely. "No, Kay," he said. "In fact, even before we go another foot we have to settle something."

I knew what was coming. It had to be said.

"We're happy to have you with us, Kay," Randy went on, "but there's to be absolutely no drinking! If you want to drink, you can go back to Pete right now. I don't want to be cruel, but you've got to realize that we've got a happy home and I won't have it ruined by booze!"

Mother's jaw firmed. I waited tensely.

"All right, Randy," she said. "I'd rather be dead than go back to Pete! I'll quit." She said it with such determination that I believed her.

The next morning, her spirits rose as she walked around our property. With her vivid imagination she seemed to picture everything as we described how we wanted it to become.

Mother overcame her drinking problem. How we admired her as we saw the struggle it was! We loved her and bore with her patiently through those hard months. During the last years of her life she was entirely free of the habit.

CHAPTER TWENTY-TWO

Weeks went by—happy weeks of planning and waiting—then our dreams really came true. The doctor confirmed it: I was pregnant! Elated, Randy kept saying, "I can't believe it! You sure don't show it!"

The house was really taking shape. Our bedroom completed, we purchased an extra-hard king-size bed and for the first time in months, Randy slept comfortably. The army cot had been miserable for his sore back. We moved one of the bunks into the second bedroom upstairs where mother would sleep till her own rooms were finished and we could afford to buy a good bed for her.

It was time for Duffy to have his ears cropped. After his operation we felt sorry for him as he struggled with the contraptions that were taped to his head. His eyes questioned us as he kept trying to shake them off. He seemed listless, perhaps from the ether. We worried that the night would be too cold for him in his little bed in the breakfast room, so we connected an electric space heater to the temporary light pole outside and placed it near his bed.

What a luxury it was for us to stretch out spread-eagle on our big bed! We had been cramped for months. Sleep came swiftly, as we were exhausted.

From a deep sleep, I felt Randy sit bolt upright.

"What's that?" he said, listening intently.

"What's what?" I asked sleepily.

"Waaaah-waaaaaah," came a mournful cry like that of a baby. "Ah-ooooooo-ooooooo."

Randy jumped out of bed and grabbed for his blue jeans. He threw open the door as I was stepping into my slippers. We couldn't see anything for a couple of seconds, then WHOOSH— fire broke through the closed kitchen door like an explosion!

"The house is on fire!" he yelled. "Get out! Wake up your mom! Oh, it's Duffy! He's burning!"

Duffy's yowls were horrible. I ran down the stairs. Randy said, "Your mom! Get your mom! Get out the front door!" He was heading for the kitchen in a low crouch.

From the entry hall where I stood, I saw flames shooting out the windows of the breakfast room.

"The neighbors!" I thought. Their home was just below our bedroom window. Maybe they'd hear me if I called from there. I ran back up the stairs, going first to mom's door. I banged with my fists, yelling, "The house is on fire, mom, are you awake? Mom, do you hear me?"

"Yes, I'm awake," came the shaky reply.

I ran back into our bedroom, closing the door behind me. I rushed to the window. There was a little crank on the steel casement. It moved stiffly. I fought to open it. "Help! Help! FIRE!" I screamed, using my diaphragm as I had never done before. Again and again I screamed, "Help! Fire! Help!"

No lights came on next door. I ran to the door again to go help mother. As I opened it, a blast of hot smoke hit my lungs. Gasping, I fell to the floor. The heat seared my throat and nose. My eyes stung. I tried to creep down the stairs. The heat was too intense.

Crawling on my stomach, I felt my way along the wall beside the steps. Coughing and choking I crawled back to mom's bedroom door. My hand scratched at the panel. "Mom, h-h-help me," I managed to gasp.

The door opened—I crawled through. Coughing wildly and rubbing my eyes, I kicked the door shut behind me. Mother was pacing back and forth wringing her hands. "Oh, no! Norma, what shall we do? What shall we do? Oh, your beautiful home!"

We were on the second story. I ran to the window. The bright glare of the fire reflecting on the yard was all I could see. Where was Randy? Duffy's screams had stopped.

We'll have to crawl out this window, mom," I told her.

"But it's such a drop!" she said fearfully.

"If we hang onto the ledge here, I don't think we'll get hurt. C'mon, we have to hurry!"

My throat ached. My lungs burned. I helped mother climb into the window. Struggling awkwardly, she got stuck. We began to laugh hysterically. Using all the strength I had, I managed to drop her to the soft earth below where heaps of decomposed granite, which had been dug out from around the foundation, formed a sand pile.

I climbed out and also dropped to the ground. Jarred, but unhurt, we hugged each other. I thought of the baby I was carrying. "O Lord, don't let this harm the baby!" I prayed.

We stumbled up the driveway where we stood looking at the hideous sight. Randy's voice came from the other side of the house. Fire trucks wailed their sirens. House lights were popping on throughout the valley.

Sandy Ridland, a neighbor, was running down the driveway in his robe, his hair disheveled.

The blazing shake roof made it almost as light as day. Helpless, mom and I stood like granite statues watching our home crumble before us: her room and bath nearly gone, the roof falling in on the kitchen. The dining room would be next. So far, no fire was licking through the shakes at the entry or bedroom wing.

A fire truck clanged its arrival on the street below the house. The firemen yelled for Randy to help them pull the hose up the steep bank. One fireman connected the hose to a hydrant as another called on the radio for more help. Randy and a third fireman dragged the hose to the breakfast room door. As the man kicked the bottom of the Dutch door in, Randy, in his eagerness to help, pushed too hard with the hose and made the man fall into the burning room, face first. Miraculously, he got up unhurt. The heavy spray of water had kept him from getting burned.

They doused the fire in the breakfast room and kitchen, then headed for the dining room by way of the patio. As they directed the stream of water into the dining room, Randy jerked his bare feet out of the way.

A second fire truck wailed to a stop in front of the house and with amazing speed the firemen played water over the burning mass.

Another neighbor, Tom Dawson, made his way to mother and me, comforting and reassuring us. "You can spend the rest of the night at our house!"

"Thank you, Tommy," I said gratefully.

I stared at the house as the fire sputtered its last. Blackness began to prevail again, and I felt remarkably calm—almost numb. I stood mute until Randy came up the driveway from the other side of the house. We rushed into each other's arms. Then the tears came.

"Just so you and Kay are both all right—that's all that counts," he said, hugging us both at once.

"What about Duffy?" I asked.

"He's gone, honey. I tried to get to him, but it was too late. Poor little guy. What an awful death!"

"Do you realize he saved our lives?" I said, remembering the awful howls.

"Yes, we'd probably have slept till it was to late—to get out."

"Poor little Duffy," mom cried.

Tears stung my eyes. We started walking up the driveway with Tommy.

"My feet!" Randy said. He sat down on the asphalt and lifted one foot to feel it, saying, "I don't know what's wrong with my feet. Tommy, flash your light over here, will you?"

The beams of light on Randy's bare feet revealed huge black blisters from his toes to about one inch from the backs of his heels.

"Golly! That's a mess," Tommy said, scowling.

"*That's* what I felt when that water boiled out of the dining room!" Randy recalled.

Walking on the backs of his heels, as he was to do for weeks, Randy led mom and me to the Dawsons' huge Spanish mansion at the end of Keswick Road. These kind people showed Randy and me to one guest room, then understandingly left us to sorrow by ourselves while they made mother comfortable in another room.

We lay awake all night, holding each other close. How grateful we were to be alive. "We'll just rebuild it!" Randy said with his usual optimism. I marveled at him. His feet blistered, months of hard work gone in an hour, and he could be so undaunted. We mourned the loss of Duffy. But our mourning always turned to praise to God for sparing our lives.

The next morning we went to inspect the damage. As we pushed the front door open, we saw the splendid hand-carved beams Randy had labored over so lovingly. They were severely blistered; it would take many hours to restore them to their former beauty. The kitchen wing was gone—we knew that. Intense heat below had blistered the paint in the bedrooms, but the plaster in the living room, bedrooms, and bath was intact. All of our clothes were smoke damaged. Nearly everything we owned had been stored in the breakfast room. It was all gone. This was where the fire had started. We believed Duffy must have upset the heater, igniting the curtains.

Uncle Adolph helped us get rooms at the Paramount Hotel on Melrose Avenue in Hollywood. Difficult as it was to find accommodations in that postwar era, we were grateful for our two rooms on the third floor.

The very first night we were there, we awoke to see smoke pouring in under our bedroom door. "Oh, no!" Randy yelled. He ran to the window, but a quick look reminded him that we were three stories up! Quickly he called the front desk.

"Nothing to worry about," the clerk said. "It was a small fire in a first-floor bathroom. It's out now. It'll take a little while for the smoke to clear."

Randy rushed to mom's room where he found her crying, sitting on her feet in a little crumpled heap on her bed. He reassured her, and wearily we settled ourselves again to try to get some sleep.

The insurance money helped to rebuild the house. We lived in the dreary hotel rooms until two weeks before Ron was born, a total of six months.

The thrill was still there as we prepared to move back into our home. This time, everything was completed. Mom's room proved to be just the sanctuary she needed. In the nursery, a bassinet with all the dainty trimmings awaited God's greatest gift to us. Physically, I had suffered no harm from the terror and exertions of the night of the fire, and every day we thanked God for his protection through it all.

When Randy wanted to tease me he'd say, "Are you sure you're going to have a baby? Where are you keeping it?"

At six months, I had finally gone into maternity clothes. I worked as before. My doctor, Hildegard Wilkerson, showed some concern toward the end of my pregnancy because the baby wasn't moving into position for birth. I went to see her often the last few weeks and she always told me the same thing, "The baby's head isn't down yet."

On November 13, 1948, at the end of seven hours of labor, I went into the delivery room still hearing that the head hadn't moved into the right position. I went under the anesthesia murmuring, "Is the head right—?"

It was a difficult delivery—a breech birth. When I regained consciousness, the nurse was carrying in our very own precious baby.

"Here's your son!" she said, holding him close to me.

"Oh, he's *so* sweet," was all I could say. He looked so fair, not the red-faced little baby I had been prepared for. "Let me hold him," I said, reaching up to take the tiny form to my breast. He lay sweet and quiet, trying to open his eyes. I couldn't hold back the tears. With joyful thanksgiving I praised God for this miracle. "Oh, let me be a good mother, Lord," I prayed. "Let me guide him; help me train him to make the right decisions. Bless him with health and peace and a saving faith in Jesus Christ. Oh, thank you, God, for this little boy."

We named him Ronald.

Awed by his tiny son, Randy was almost afraid to handle him.

Ronnie was a strong, good baby. He ate and slept, never crying. It began to worry me that he was so quiet. I took him to the pediatrician for a checkup when he was four weeks old. "Is he—all right? He never cries," I explained.

"Is he all right?" he laughed. "Consider yourself fortunate; your baby's fine. Not a thing wrong with him. Just feel that you're blessed, my dear."

We still didn't have very much furniture, and we didn't want to go into debt. But finally we accumulated enough money to shop for a couch. A 50-percent sale was advertised at House of Modern on Wilshire Blvd. When we walked to the entrance, there in the display window was exactly what we wanted! It was a fifteen-foot, three-piece sectional couch, circular in shape, tufted in a nubby fabric—watermelon with a fleck of gold.

"Randy, that would be perfect in our living room!"

He agreed and the couch was delivered the next day.

The manager of the Vivian Apartments offered us an apartment-size (six-foot) grand piano, a Brambach. She was asking only $250 for it so we didn't deliberate very long. Neither of us could play it—my hands never did grow large enough to reach an octave—but we thought the piano would make our living room look elegant. And it did.

We soon found, however, it wasn't the great buy we had thought. After we had spent $500 having it refinished, replacing the felts, having the hammers repaired, and everything else done to it that we could think of, it still sounded more like a harpsichord than a piano. The pedal squeaked and nothing we did could eliminate that tiresome sound. When we asked the former owner what had happened to it, she admitted that at several of her parties guests had spilled cocktails inside. The damage was irreparable. Nevertheless, it was adequate as a practice piano for both our sons when they took lessons. We still use it today in our recreation room.

Landscaping came naturally to Randy. Soon our yard became a show place with many varieties of trees, flowering shrubs, and myriads of flowers. He plotted a free-style dichondra lawn in the front yard. Sixteen-inch-high brick planters in circular flowing forms surrounded the house. I planted beds of snapdragons, zinnias, ageratum, and petunias around the perimeter of the garden. Nightingale lighting ornamented the trees; the most prominent one was an olive tree with long graceful branches. At night we could sit inside and watch wild animals come to nibble our plants and drink from a faucet left dripping. Skunks searched for seeds in the dichondra. Though we were thrilled to have deer visit us, they became pests when they devoured Randy's prize roses!

CHAPTER TWENTY-THREE

These were the golden days of radio and the exciting music of operetta came to life on "The Railroad Hour," a popular broadcast starring Gordon MacRae. Carmen Dragon arranged and conducted the musical presentation, while such famous artists as Rise Stevens and Dorothy Kirsten played the leads opposite Gordon. Norman Luboff was choral director, and it was a real education to work with this talented musician.

This was my kind of music and it was during rehearsals that I came to Mr. Luboff's attention.

"Carmen," Norman said, "you really ought to hear Norma sing. Perhaps you could use her in one of the roles."

"No," Mr. Dragon said, "we need name talent—the sponsor wouldn't go for a chorus singer taking part in the show."

"Well," argued Mr. Luboff, "it's a pity she's not getting a chance to shine—perhaps in some other spot. Keep it in mind."

Carmen Dragon did keep it in mind and a few weeks later he asked me if I would be interested in traveling to San Francisco once a week to tape the Standard School Broadcast. He told me it would give me an opportunity to sing every type of song—from arias to folk tunes.

What a thrilling prospect—to open a world of classical music to American children in their classrooms! This was a weekly program beamed to elementary schools in nine western states, as well as

Alaska and Hawaii.

I rushed home to give the news to Randy.

"Hey, that's swell!" he exclaimed. "That's wonderful!"

Flying! San Francisco! Oh, they dressed up in that city! "Mom, we'll have to go shopping. I need more suitable clothes."

That excited mother. She had always loved pretty things and enjoyed seeing me dress up. So first chance we got we hurried off to some fine stores. Mother helped me select two beautiful suits—one was a gray wool with narrow black piping around the collar and a pleat in the front and back of the skirt for easier walking. The second was a beautiful green—simple, with a buttoned front that could be worn partly open or closed all the way. Now I needed a coat.

"Norm," mother called. "Look at this mink stole! It's on sale— Wow! It's still over $700."

I gasped! "Oh, that would be *perfect* for San Francisco!" My common sense told me it was too extravagant.

"Try it on," she prompted.

"Oh, just for the fun of it," I laughed. I slipped into the natural black mink stole. The lining was smooth satin—the fur at the neck caressed my skin. I walked to the full-length mirror. "Oh, mom," I breathed. "Isn't that gorgeous!"

"Honey, you've got to have it," she said, shaking her head in admiration.

"Randy would never go for it," I sighed.

A saleslady approached. "May I help you?" she purred.

"I'm just looking," came the usual reply.

No doubt she saw the longing in my eyes and immediately diagnosed my financial dilemma.

"You can pay for it on time!" she urged confidently.

Oh, how I wanted that fur! I could just see myself wrapped in mink, waltzing down those San Francisco streets. It would go with *everything*!

"We can make the monthly payments low!"

Mom and I looked at each other. I was working. I could pay for it, I was sure. Oh dear, should I ask Randy? I bit my lip, thinking to myself. "I know I shouldn't do this—but if I ask Randy, he'll probably say no. It's just beautiful—maybe if Randy saw it on me...if I could take it on approval—but if he said no, I'd die—"

On and on I debated with myself.

"Let me see what the payments would come to if you paid over a year's time," the saleslady interrupted my thoughts. She went to the counter and stood figuring.

"What shall I do, mother?"

"It's up to you, honey." Mom was no help.

Quickly, the saleslady returned. "That would come to just a little over $70 a month."

"I'll take it." I signed the contract quickly, before I could change my mind.

The beautiful thing was placed in a large box. I carried it lovingly to the trunk of the car where it would be placed secretly each time I traveled to San Francisco. I couldn't bring myself to admit to Randy what I had done.

The day finally arrived when I could don that queenly garment. I had hidden it on the bottom shelf in a dark closet and obscured it with other boxes. Now I waited until Randy went out, then I hurriedly whisked it out to the car and deposited it, still in the box, in the trunk.

When I got to the airport, I parked the car, opened the trunk, put on the mink, and set forth on my journey to the Bay City. Oh, how elegant I felt! I stifled my conscience with thoughts that I was paying for it myself and why shouldn't I have something special?

Each week I flew to San Francisco, still carrying on my deception about the mink stole.

The first few weeks it had been so much fun to wear it, but as weeks and then months passed, I began to dislike myself more and more. The joy of owning that luxurious wrap gradually faded. I found it hard to meet each payment and I felt so guilty, so selfish, so disloyal to Randy.

At last I made that final detestable payment on the stole. I could keep my secret no longer. I decided to confess to my sensible husband the terrible act I had committed.

I spread the wrap out on the bed and waited for him to discover it.

He came in and went to the bathroom to clean up. My heart was pounding as I went about the kitchen table, straightening knives that needed no straightening and stirring pudding that was already cold.

Then he went into the bedroom. The suspense was unbearable. "What's this?" he called.

I ran to the bedroom door. "Something I bought for the trips to San Francisco," I confessed.

His look was penetrating. "How much did that cost?"

The inevitable question. I had known it would come. I shuddered. "Too much, honey. It was about $700."

"*Seven hundred dollars*! Norma! How could you? Take it back!"

"I can't. I paid for it on time. It's paid for."

Randy looked stricken. He walked out of the room. I followed him, crying.

"I'm sorry, Randy; please forgive me," I begged. "I know I shouldn't have bought it."

"Don't talk to me about it now!" he commanded.

Hours passed before he spoke to me again.

"Don't ever do anything sneaky like that again," he said later that evening. "I'm not mad at you. I'm just hurt that you wouldn't discuss it with me. I'd love to buy you things like that, but we don't even have our house furnished yet."

Even before I had told Randy about the stole, I didn't enjoy wearing it. After seeing his disappointment in me and experiencing all the terrible feelings of guilt and shame, the stole became even more distasteful to me. I continued to wear it for a time. Years later I gave it to mom.

During the years of singing background music on recordings made by stars, I had the opportunity to participate in a few "Million sellers." One of the first was "White Christmas" with Bing Crosby.

Our mutual home state of Washington gave us something in common. Bing loved recalling the unusual Indian names of cities like Walla Walla and Puyallup. It became a game to see who could recall the most. Each time he entered the studio he would call a greeting to me. "Hi, Norma. Walla Walla."

"Hello, Bing. Yakima!"

"Pasco!"

"Wallula!"

"Chewelah!"

"Cle-Elum!"

"Nemah!"

On it would go until we ran out of names. I found him such a kind and friendly man. His happy whistle could always be heard through the hallways as he approached the studios; he constantly practiced his golf strokes in pantomime. I worked in radio, movies, and television with him through many years and prize in my collection a fan letter received from Bing Crosby.

During the long waits around CBS, I would knit ski sweaters for Randy. "When are you going to knit something for me?" Bing often teased.

So to surprise him, I knit a pair of baby blue, pink, and white argyles. This brought the following note from him: "Dear Norma, they are sheer heaven! A perfect fit—and my favorite color—baby blue. You are a dear girl for remembering, and I shall think of you while leaping over the Canadian Crags clad 'a pié' in your handiwork. Thanks, Bing Crosby."

I could not have managed my singing career *and* my home if it had not been for mother. She and I grew very close. Oh, how glad I was that she was with us. Ronnie became *our* baby. She loved him nearly as much as I did, I think.

One of Randy's less favorite dishes and one I'm very fond of is clam chowder. No one could make it like mother. I came home from work one late afternoon hoping she hadn't started dinner yet.

"Mother, I'd love to have some of your clam chowder."

"Of course," she said. "Let's make some for dinner."

"I'll help you," I said. "I want to see exactly how you do it."

Ronnie was sitting in the highchair, scribbling with a red crayon. "Rinso White! Rinso Bright!" he chirped at me, and laughed. He had recognized my voice as I sang that commercial on the radio.

I pulled him out of the highchair and kissed him on his chubby neck. He leaned back giggling and I gave him a tight squeeze before I put him down, and he toddled away to play.

Mother was cutting a half pound of bacon into tiny bits and putting them on the stove to fry. "You can slice those two onions and four stalks of celery," she said. While I wept over the onions, mother peeled the three potatoes she laid on the counter. When I finished the onions, mother tossed them into the pan and sautéed them for just a few minutes. "See, when they're transparent like that—that's all," she cautioned.

I diced the potatoes into tiny cubes. "How much water on the potatoes?" I asked.

"Just enough to cover them. And you add the celery. Now you simmer those together without a cover and let the water almost evaporate."

"Rinso White! Rinso Bright!" We heard Ron singing from the breakfast room.

"He's been doing that all day," mother said. "Ever since he heard it over the radio this morning."

I was doing many commercials on radio in those days. Another of the well remembered ones was the jello commercial. "J-E-LL-O!"

"Now you add a quart of milk to that," mother said, indicating the potatoes and celery, "then the bacon and onions, and a can of creamed corn and the clams—all three cans of clams. Just heat it. It shouldn't cook."

"That just makes my mouth water," I said, setting the table as I kept an eye on the pot.

It was fun working together in our kitchen, and I was making up for lost time, learning the cooking skills father had forbidden me to

Upper: Mom and Dad with their little brood on the farm in Idaho.
Lower left: Sister Kay and I, tucked in the dresser drawer—we were mom's
    little dolls!
Lower right: Playmates in our large yard in Tacoma. I'm the little one,
    front right.

Upper left: Even at seventeen, Kay had a queenly beauty—wavy auburn hair, flawless skin, and large violet-blue eyes like mother's.

Upper right: I worshiped this handsome brother of mine and tagged along wherever he would let me go.

Lower left: Max, Kay, and I with mom, shortly before the three of us started going our separate adult ways.

Lower right: At sixteen, I won a popularity contest in Lake City. This pretty sweater and photograph were my prizes.

Lower center: As Yum Yum in *The Mikado*. Kay designed this costume for the production at Lincoln High School.

Upper left: Randy was one of the most promising young racers in the Northwest when this picture was taken. A broken back kept him from his dream of becoming a contender in the Olympics.

Upper right: How could Randy have given me a second glance in my baggy borrowed ski outfit?

Lower: Our wedding day. The chapel was set up for another wedding later in the day, so we "borrowed" the flowers. The dear friends pictured here are still our skiing buddies. At our right, Jerry Hiatt and Larry Thackwell; at our left, Barbara Thackwell and June Roe.

Upper: The Girl Friends. I was fortunate to be in this fabulous quartet. We spent almost twenty years together, singing in every facet of the industry. Top, Betty Noyes; left, Betty Allan; bottom, Dorothy McCarty—all three still among my dearest friends.

Lower: My short-lived "movie career"—a bit part in the Bing Crosby picture *Mr. Music*. I was pampered and praised for those few days, so I can easily understand why some successful actresses fail to keep their feet on the ground!

Upper: I never tired of hearing my father play his beloved violin. I'm happy he spent his last years near our family, sharing himself and his talents with us.

Lower: I have to say it again: my heart overflowed with love for my mother.

In concert with Carmen Dragon and the Honolulu Symphony in Hawaii.

New Year's Eve, 1960. Lawrence Welk invited me to join his musical family—the beginning of a long and marvelous association with the best boss
a singer could have.

Left: At the top of Kratka Ridge. Randy and I want to enjoy this sport as long as our legs will carry us!
Right: Steady, Norma!

Upper: A scene from a Welk show. Lawrence is a big tease—always full of fun. I'm grateful to be a part of his musical family.

Lower: Peggy, Kathy, Janet, and JoAnn join me in wishing Lawrence another Happy Birthday on camera. Lawrence takes his birthday celebrations very seriously, and each year the cast waits eagerly for a slice of the cake as soon as the show is over.

Upper left: Enjoying a joke on the set with Dick Dale and Jimmy Roberts.
Upper right: Isn't it great to get paid for having this much fun?
Lower: Lawrence featured my art work on a special "Norma" show.

Randy and I flew to Seattle to surprise my dear friend Carl A. Pitzer at his retirement dinner. His wife, Catherine, stands beside him with Jane Dayton, a friend who sang with me in the University Christian Church choir. Next to my parents it was Carl Pitzer who most influenced my life. He was instrumental in leading me to Christ, and gave me my first singing lessons and choral training. I can never thank him enough for the love and kindness he showed me as I grew up.

Left: Bob Ralston accompanies me at a religious rally. It is tremendous to see the Holy Spirit work in these meetings.

Right: During the Sacred Festival of Music in Birmingham, Alabama, Bob Ralston and I rehearse a number for Maestro Amerigo Morino, conductor of the Birmingham Symphony. Years ago I sang for Mr. Morino when he directed the CBS Radio Staff Orchestra.

Left: On the platform during a Billy Graham Crusade, I had a chance to visit with Ethel Waters. What a fantastic person she is!
Right: I praise God for the privilege of being a small part of the Billy Graham Crusades. Randy and I greatly value Dr. Graham's friendship.

Left: With Bev Shea and Dr. Graham on the platform. Even the downpour didn't dampen the spirit in this Crusade—there was hardly an empty seat.
Right: Singing God's praises—the answer to my earnest prayers.

Upper: In 1961 I sang the national anthem for President Kennedy at the Palladium in Hollywood.
Lower: A highlight of my life! President Nixon invited me to participate in Sunday morning worship service at the White House. Mark, Randy, and I found the Nixons to be most gracious hosts.

Upper: Ron beams proudly at Mark's college graduation.
Center left: We were all thrilled when our beautiful daughter-in-law, Candi, completed her nurse's training.
Center right: Ron with Kristen, our "miracle baby."
Lower right: How grateful we are for every day God has spared our little Kristen to us.
Lower left: I'm a typical proud grandmother!

How blessed can a woman be? Randy is one of God's choicest gifts to me, and our love is richer now than when we were first married.

learn from her when I was a youngster.

Watching someone rise from obscurity to a place of prominence in the music world is always a joy to me. Nelson Riddle was a struggling arranger when I first met him. His work was always outstanding and it was no surprise to me that he became so famous.

"If I ever make it big," he'd say, "I'll use your voice on my albums."

He was true to his word, and I did several sessions for him after he became well known. My voice was used in flute-like obbligatos. I thoroughly enjoyed performing these high, lyrical passages. Gradually I was overcoming some of my shyness and becoming more confident of my ability. His Capitol album of *Oklahoma* was the one where he used me most prominently, even giving me name credit on the liner, which was unheard of in those days.

Frank Sinatra used Nelson Riddle on many of his hit records and after hearing Nelson's new *Oklahoma* album, he said, "I have to have that soprano on my records." That led to many jobs with Frank, who was always sweet and thoughtful to me.

On January 19, 1949, the mail brought me a letter that was the first of hundreds to follow: a real fan letter.

Dear Miss 1/5 of the Talking People,

If you'll kindly pardon this somewhat irregular form of a letter I'll tell you the purpose of my writing you.

It's just that ever since I was privileged to see Meredith Willson's program December 29 of last year, I have been completely enthralled by your lovely voice. And I would like to say to you, stick with it—for with a voice like yours, your "break" is bound to come soon, and I sincerely hope it will be a big one!

Though these words come from afar and are from someone whom you do not know, I hope they will be words of encouragement to you for I am sure there are many others who feel the same as I.

With sincere best wishes to a gal who will, someday, really go places,

Janet McKinney(real name)

Others who have "felt the same" have kept up a steady influx of mail ever since, growing heavier as the years go by. Besides the Welk Show viewers, people write to me after seeing the Billy Graham Crusades and the Birmingham Sacred Concerts and the many other appearances I make each year. I love my audiences. I never sing without praying that God will use me to bring them joy.

CHAPTER TWENTY-FOUR

"I want to see my baby." Once again I was waking up in a hospital room. As I came out of the anesthesia I became dimly aware of a lovely brunette in the bed next to mine. "I want to see my baby," I murmured again.

A strong voice answered, "You've got an eight-pound boy! So have I! My name's Shirley De Grey and this is my husband, Dick." He rose to his feet and smiled. They were a handsome couple, about Randy's and my age.

The door opened and the nurse brought in my son—our son. But where was Randy? I took the baby eagerly, wondering why I felt so terribly weak. "Oh, isn't he sweet!" I spoke the very words and felt the same emotions I had had when Ron was brought to me. My heart sang with praise to God. Two sons. How wonderful! When I wondered out loud where Randy was, Shirley told me he had just stepped out. "He's been here constantly, but he just left for a minute. Dick and I have been talking with him, and we've discovered that we're neighbors—we live only a few blocks from you!"

Just then Randy entered the room, looking haggard. His eyes were full of tears as he kissed me. "Hi, sweetheart," he whispered. "You look fine. The baby's perfectly healthy. I've never prayed so much for anything in my life. I've been sitting in the waiting room, praying that you'd be all right—that you'd both live." He struggled for self-control.

I began to realize that something had been very wrong indeed.

"Is...is everything all right now?" I asked.

"Not entirely. The greatest danger is past, but you may not come home right away. But that's nothing compared to—losing you." His voice trembled. "Dr. Wilkerson came out of the delivery room to warn me. She told me, 'Toxemia has set in. Norma's blood pressure is almost 290.' Can you imagine that, honey? She said you and the baby were both in danger and that she had—to—tell me—" Randy could hardly finish. "She had to tell me I might lose you." He leaned over the bed and kissed me again.

The pregnancy had been normal until the last month. Dr. Wilkerson had warned me that my ankles were swelling alarmingly. "Cut out salt," she advised.

Day after day I'd waited for the signal. Ron's delivery had been relatively fast so I knew that this time we'd have to hurry to the hospital as soon as contractions became regular. "O Lord, just give us a healthy baby," I repeated over and over.

The doctor had ordered me to bed. I spent a lot of time reading to three-year-old Ronnie.

"Soon mommie is going to the hospital and then I'll bring you home your own little brother or sister!" I promised.

"I don't want one," he pouted.

Two weeks had passed—then at last, early in the morning, I felt the first labor pains begin. When they were eight minutes apart I had whispered to Randy, "Let's go!"

Sleepily he'd groaned, "Are you sure?"

"Yes! Let's hurry. I'll bet this one's going to come fast."

Mom had my bag all packed. Hurriedly we dressed and woke mother. I went into Ron's room and prayed the kind of little prayer common to mothers when they leave their families to have another child. "Dear Lord, let me come home again to take care of Ronnie and stay with him until he's grown. If it be your will, let me be safely delivered of this little one I'm carrying." Tenderly I kissed his blond head and patted his little seat.

In the hall, mom kissed me and admonished Randy, "Drive carefully!"

The hospital was only twenty minutes away, but the pains were getting closer together. The signing in took more time than necessary, I thought.

"Do you smoke?" the receptionist asked.

"No." *What a funny question,* I thought. "There's not much time," I pleaded. "Please let me go to the OB floor quickly." A feeling of pressure around me heart made me uneasy. "I feel awfully funny," I told Randy.

He took over, making sure I would be taken to the labor room immediately. The nurse gave me an injection as soon as I lay down on the narrow bed. That was all I remembered.

One hour and forty-five minutes after the first warning pain on September 29, 1951, Mark Randal made his way into the world.

Shirley De Grey was a delightful roommate during those days in the hospital. I learned that the receptionist had asked me about smoking because Shirley had requested that only a non-smoker be assigned to share her room. It was only one of many things we had in common. Not only were our sons born just twenty minutes apart, but we were both married on June 5th. She and Dick and Randy and I have been celebrating our anniversaries together ever since.

In spite of all the complications, I recovered satisfactorily and was soon able to take little Mark home. He was a contented baby too, but Ron had a terrible time getting used to sharing our attention with his little brother.

Dr. Wilkerson advised us not to have any more children. I wept for the little girl I'd never have, while I thanked God for our two healthy sons.

CHAPTER TWENTY-FIVE

When Ron was four I had a small part in a Bing Crosby movie, *Mr. Music.*

Larry Crosby, Bing's brother, invited me to his office where he told me, "Paramount wants to sign you to a contract. They will pay you $250 a week, but you have to quit all your other work. They want to send you to all kinds of classes, and you must be free to attend." I thanked them, but declined.

Another agent had heard good reports about my work, and asked me to audition at RKO. I went for an interview wearing a modest crepe dress. The large cigar-smoking gentleman sitting behind the desk looked me over from head to toe and said, "You look like you're pushing thirty!" I turned and left the room, slamming the door.

That ended my movie "career."

About three years before, Randy had gone skiing for a weekend with a group of friends. When he got back on Sunday night he was all excited about a plan being formed by eleven of his buddies, all ski enthusiasts.

"We want to start our own ski area!" he said. He was just bubbling over with the plans they had made. Seldom had I seen him so elated.

The germ soon became a full-grown idea. They scouted the Angeles Crest and decided on a site across from the San Gorgonio Ski Club, sixty miles from downtown Los Angeles.

"We've decided to call it Kratka Ridge Ski Area," Randy reported after their next meeting. "Two brothers named Kratka were sitting on top of the mountain when the government surveyors were mapping the area, so they named the mountain for them!"

Randy was made builder and manager. During those early years of organization and development, he was away for long weekends. The project took a great deal of his attention and energy. First they cleared and fashioned an excellent beginners' slope—then a fine intermediate area. In no time, Randy and the partners had erected a comfortable hut.

By late 1951, Kratka had not only the warming house but three rope tows, an excellent "top of the mountain tow," and the fellows were talking about installing their own chair lift. Two of the partners were engineers and they scouted every area in California that had a chair lift. Noting the best features of each, they set out to design their own.

The nine partners still left on the project cleared the area themselves, working every weekend for almost two years. One of the partners was named Howard Worthing, and all machinery for the lift was machined and completed at his sheet metal shop, including the hull wheel, chairs, pre-fabbed towers, and other parts.

When mother came to live with us, Randy and I gave her a certificate to a modeling school as a Christmas gift. She enjoyed learning to walk gracefully, how to sit and stand properly, and how to wear her makeup and do her hair. She developed poise and confidence. We loved watching her practice the model's stance.

In 1952, she went to New York to visit Max. While she was there she thought she'd investigate the possibility of going into professional modeling. She walked into the office of the Powers Modeling firm. John Powers exclaimed, "*You* are a *beautiful woman*," and hired her on the spot.

Mother found this life exciting for a few months but soon got weary of the long hard hours of standing on sore feet. Eventually she became homesick and returned to us. In her absence I had employed a competent woman, Josephine Carr, to baby-sit when I had to go to work. Now it was a comfort to know that mom was always at home when I was gone. She cooked and cleaned for the family in my absence. The boys were never lonely as she was always eager to talk and play with them. There was a mutual love and understanding among us. She knew we needed and loved her. Often she would tell us, "I've never been happier in all my life."

It was a pleasure to buy her attractive clothes—classic suits and dresses, pretty lingerie, pearls, amber jewelry—all the things she enjoyed and had never had before. She was a perfect size ten, and wore clothes with a model's flair.

A pewter collection was mom's pride and joy. When Randy and I traveled, as we began to do later, we would search lovingly for beautiful vases, plates, dishes, or unusual gifts. How glad we were that at last mom had everything she had ever wanted—both material things and the peace and security her earlier life had not provided.

Mother's sudden success as a model gave Max the idea. For him it became a career. Mother and I loved seeing his face smiling at us from billboards, leading magazines, and the Sears Roebuck catalog.

Ron was always a sturdy, active little boy. "Helping dad" made him feel like a big man and he was so happy when Randy would ask him to bring tools as he worked around the house. Ron learned to recognize the different kinds of wrenches, screw drivers, pliers, and hammers and brought them proudly to Randy on call.

Working in the yard was exciting too. One day Randy was thinning out some brush. He heard Ron's cheerful little voice, "Here, daddy! Lookit, I'm helping."

Randy turned and there came Ron, dragging behind him a precious pine tree which Randy had been nursing for months. Ron's proud upturned face kept his father from crying out in dismay. "Thank you, Ronnie. You're helping daddy all right," Randy groaned as he guided his helper to the brush where he could do no damage.

Ron was usually radiantly healthy, but five times during one winter he had bouts with croup. One chilly night, that familiar hoarse, barking cough startled me out of a sound sleep. I hurried in to comfort him. His breath scraped and rattled in his chest worse than I had ever heard before. Remembering that the De Greys had had a lot of croup problems with their little ones, I called Dick and he hurried over immediately. He instructed me to heat up the bathroom and place Ron in warm blankets in the tub.

When the room was very warm, Dick turned on the hot water in the shower stall to produce steam. He stayed with us for several hours. We debated whether or not we should take Ron to the hospital for a tracheotomy; he was barely able to breathe.

I went to our bedroom and knelt to pray. As always, I felt the reassurance that God was with us, protecting our family.

Ron's breathing finally eased and we walked with Dick to his car, thanking him for rushing to our assistance. I brought Ron into our bed. Randy offered to sleep on the couch the rest of the night.

I lay beside Ronnie, watching and praying. "God," I prayed over and over, "please heal our little son."

Suddenly I noticed a brightness behind me. I looked around. Standing near the bed was a lovely young blonde woman with a white blouse and a dark skirt. I was stunned! I was not sleeping—in fact, I was very wide awake. Transfixed, I watched her for what seemed like thirty seconds. She just stood there with a radiant smile on her face, looking down at Ron. Then she faded away. It was a glorious experience. I felt no fear—just awe. I have always believed that I was permitted to see Ron's guardian angel. It was such a precious, intimate vision that it was some time before I could even share it with Randy.

The next morning Ron felt much better. And that was the last time he ever had the croup.

Little Mark rapidly became a person to be reckoned with in our family. When he was about two years old his favorite pastime was learning to read new words. He liked nothing better than to have me hold him in my lap and point to one object after another, saying its name, then writing it down for him. He'd laugh and giggle with excitement at the game—and he never forgot a new word. By the time he was three he could read more than a hundred words. Later he began to invent little gadgets, stringing wires around the house ("making a telephone"). He took clocks apart, then reassembled them so they worked again.

What exciting and satisfying years those were! How we praised God every day for our dear little boys, so strong and bright, and for our joyful, peaceful home life—all of us bound together in God's great love and care.

CHAPTER TWENTY-SIX

The phone jangled noisily. Picking it up I heard, "Hi, Norma. This is Caroline Boyle. Dave and I want you to come to dinner tonight."

"We'd love to!"

"We're so excited about our trip to Europe! We're going to make it for less than $1,000 apiece. We'll take movies of some of the big ski races. Dave hopes to make a saleable film—"

"How marvelous! How long will you be gone?"

"About two months."

"You lucky people! Can't wait to see you and hear all about it!"

"Dinner at six—OK?"

"Great! We'll see you tonight."

That evening, maps were spread all over the floor. Hours sped by as Dave and Caroline shared the excitement of the impending trip.

"Why don't you go with us?" Dave asked.

In unison we said, "That sounds wonderful!"

At first it seemed impossible. But we had saved a little money. We had no debt on our house. Mother lived with us and could care for the children. I wondered aloud if Arline and her husband, Jim Mature, wouldn't like to move into our house for a few months. They had no children and were living in an apartment; they might like a house complete with family for a change.

We were getting excited about the possibility of going, so we asked Arline and Jim. They agreed to come and help mother take care of Ron and Mark.

We left all the planning for the itinerary up to Dave. We had enough to do to get arrangements made at home to allow us to be gone for two months.

Right after New Year's Day of 1953 we left by car for New York where we would board the *America*. Dave and Caroline were going to fly and meet us at Zurich, Switzerland.

Sally and Lee Sweetland lived in New York now and had invited us to call on them, and to leave our car in their care. Max and Nellie had an apartment in Greenwich Village. We hadn't seen each other for twelve years—not since Max had moved East.

Max had put himself through the Julliard School of Music and was still going to Columbia University where he later got his master's degree. He intended to teach. Meanwhile, he had gone into modeling.

We arrived at their apartment while Max was at work. Nellie greeted us warmly. She looked absolutely beautiful, and charmed us as she gave us a tour of their interesting quarters. She showed us some paintings Max had done, and we were impressed with his work in oils. We met twelve-year-old Diane, a ballet student, and Schuyler, a charming boy of ten.

While Nellie was preparing dinner, I studied one of Max's paintings. In it he depicted a rough sea, on which a Viking ship tossed. A huge serpent was coming out of the water, its jaws open wide, as if attacking the ship. Gripping the side of the boat, cowering and looking fearfully into the hideous face of the serpent was a sailor. That sailor was my father.

Now the front door opened and there stood Max.

"Max!" I ran to greet him. "You look marvelous!"

"Well, well, Norma! You don't look so bad yourself."

We hugged each other, laughing and crying together.

I couldn't believe my eyes. He had on a black coat with a velvet collar and held a derby. I thought he was one of the handsomest men I had ever seen in my life. He and Randy seemed to like each other at once. Before dinner I talked Max into singing an aria, and Nellie, an extraordinary pianist, accompanied him beautifully. What a thrill it was to hear his fine baritone voice again—now so rich and mature.

Nellie served us beef Stroganoff—one of her specialties—and had laid a beautiful table. It was so good to be in their home and to get acquainted with their darling children. Conversation at the table was lively—but I wasn't able to talk. I was chewing. And chewing. The piece of beef I had in my mouth wasn't going to get chewed up. I had to decide whether to swallow it or remove it from my mouth. I decided to swallow it.

It wouldn't go down. The meat was lodged in my throat so that I couldn't breathe or make a sound. I was choking. Things started to whirl around the perimeter of my vision. I clutched my throat, trying to push the meat down. No one was looking at me. I tapped Max's shoulder and started to wave my arms. Everyone noticed me at the same time. I pointed to my throat and they all jumped up, calling out suggestions.

"Get an egg!" Max shouted. Nellie was already on her way to

the refrigerator. I struggled. I was growing faint.

Randy rushed over and half-carried me to the bathroom.

"Put your head back," Max ordered. Randy held me as I obeyed. I felt numb and inwardly I was praying desperately, feeling sure that once again death was near. Max began to pour the slimy, slippery raw egg down my throat. I gagged violently and the meat was dislodged.

My throat ached sharply but it was heavenly to be able to draw deep breaths. The faintness began to pass as my heart slowed down. I swallowed gingerly many times as we returned to the table, but I was afraid to eat any more. It took days for the tenderness to disappear from my throat.

I have made Stroganoff from Nellie's recipe these many years, but I always use pure filet steak without any sinew and I cut it very small. I haven't checked with Nellie, but I have an idea that since that memorable day she's done it the same way!

The next day Max and Nellie accompanied us to the Sweetlands' large home in Hastings on the Hudson. We left our car in their double garage and the six of us drove to the ship. They came aboard and inspected the huge vessel with us, including the tiny third-class stateroom that would be our home for the next six days. At last the call came, "All ashore that's going ashore!" and they hurried down to the dock to watch us sail. We stood at the rail and waved to them and they waved back, yelling, "Good-bye! Good-bye!"

For fifteen minutes, we kept waving, but we weren't leaving! Finally the gangplanks were about to be raised, when we saw the entire crew stomp off the ship. We heard a passenger say, "There's been a strike!" After several more shouts of "Good-bye" between us and our party on the shore, Max yelled up to us, "This is getting silly," and they left, laughing.

The strike was settled about an hour later and we headed for the dining room. We discovered that traveling third class was pretty miserable aboard the *America*. Not only was the food disappointing but the waiters and stewards were rude. The head steward was cross with us because of his own mistake in issuing only one meal ticket for the two of us. So we had to wait in the passageway while everyone else was seated. The waiters made it plain that we were in the way. They'd growl, "You're not supposed to be standing here. Wait back there!" So we'd move and be jostled by other waiters. Finally we were led like cattle to table 9 where nothing we ordered was served, and the food had been ruined both by its poor preparation and by the delay.

The first day out Randy became desperately seasick. The very thought of food nauseated him; he couldn't even keep the dramamine down. My words of sympathy weren't welcome, so I left our stuffy, hot cabin to wander about alone. Clouds drifted low over a gray sea, making it hard to see the horizon. The ocean was too rough to permit sitting on deck.

Randy had complained of a small pain in his stomach before we left New York. The second day out he was no better, so he went to see the ship's doctor, who ordered him back to bed with an ice pack. The diagnosis was appendicitis.

Maybe I have my Scandinavian ancestors to thank for my love of the sea. I thoroughly enjoyed it when the ship was rolling and bucking through the immense waves. I never missed a meal and I felt wonderful.

Randy's condition stayed about the same, with nausea and some pain. The doctor said he thought he'd better remove Randy's appendix. This seemed a bit hasty to us. "How do you decide when it's appendicitis?" Randy asked.

"By the white blood count."

"Well, how do you learn what the blood count is?"

"When we draw blood—"

"You never drew blood from me," Randy said.

The doctor gasped. "Oh," he cried, "I thought you were someone else. We nearly operated on the wrong man!"

The morning of January 16th it was wonderful to see land again, even if we were only letting off passengers at the Emerald Isle.

We traveled across the channel to Le Havre, France, where a joyful Randy bid an eager farewell to the crew. He stepped on solid ground only to find it moving! "Hey, honey," he laughed. "This isn't fair—I'm still rolling." With each step his foot seemed to reach the ground too early. I experienced the same thing. We lurched to a bench and sat laughing at ourselves.

We loaded our luggage onto a train, found a vacant seat, and settled back to enjoy our ride to Paris. It was hard to believe that we were in a foreign country. I kept pinching myself—we were *really* in France! Our eyes were glued to the scene as the train moved out of the station. Old buildings were picturesque; people's clothes were actually different, reminding me of actors I had seen dressed in costumes. Yes, this was a new experience—a grand, exhilarating encounter with the unknown. Gradually we picked up speed. (Randy was so excited that he stood most of the way.) Soon the city gave way to green farmland. Quaint homes with barns attached stood close to the tracks. Old wooden fences surrounded yards where women were hanging clothes. Children waved at the train as if it were an old friend. The smiles on their faces showed they had the same love for trains that our own children felt. Orderly little gardens lined the adjacent strips of land near the tracks. These people utilized every inch of ground.

We splurged by staying one night in a fine hotel in Paris. Lovely antique marbletop tables graced the charming room. The bed was hard, but after the bunk aboard ship it felt marvelous.

We spent three days sightseeing in Paris. Walking down the Champs Elysees to the Arc de Triomphe I worried about the movie Dave wanted to film, showing Randy scrambling eggs over the eternal flame housed in the impressive Arc. I hoped he'd reconsider, as I was sure they'd end up in jail.

The city was astonishingly beautiful with her tree-lined avenues. The stained glass windows in Notre Dame brought tears to our eyes. We walked up the hill to Montmartre with its twisting streets, to see the magnificent view of the city below.

The Louvre was breathtaking and kindled in me the desire to try painting.

We viewed the Eiffel Tower from the base, as we didn't want to pay the fee for the elevator ride to the top.

Reluctantly we left Paris and headed for Zurich. We carried our twelve pieces of luggage without help as much as possible to save money.

In Zurich we stayed at the Maria Theresa Hotel. Upon arriving we hurried to the express office where we were to meet Dave and Caroline. A letter was awaiting us. "Greetings, World Travelers," it read. "We're sorry to tell you we won't be able to make the trip. Dave is ill. Have a wonderful time—we'll be with you in spirit."

Randy and I looked at each other in shock. Dave and Caroline had the itinerary and maps.

"What do we do now? Go home?" Randy looked depressed.

"Well, we've come this far, honey. Why don't we stay for awhile and see how it goes?" I suggested, putting on what I hoped was a cheerful smile.

"OK, but we sure can't lug all this stuff around Europe. Let's wear our ski clothes and carry just what we can fit into the rucksacks."

"It's a deal."

We bought a large map and marked the places we wanted to see. With skis, poles, apples, bread, and cheese, we set out.

March 18, 1953
Zermatt, Switzerland

Dearest Mother,

One of the breathtaking sights of the trip has been the Matterhorn. Oh, how I hope you can see it some day! We stayed at a very poor little hotel.

On the train to Zermatt we had visited with a delightful surgeon of one of the largest hospitals in Europe, at Linz,

105

Austria. He's a back and brain specialist. Do you know that he earns only $80 a month? People in Austria pay 67¢ a month and get full medical coverage. This surgeon works 100 hours or more a week. Says he never had time to be married and have a family.

We arrived in Zermatt after dark, so we got our first glimpse of the mountain when we woke up and walked out onto the balcony. There in the distance was the magnificent Matterhorn. I was so thrilled. I had the strange feeling I'd seen it before. Later we took a tiny slow train to the top of a mountain where we had a perfect view of the Matterhorn and surroundings—huge mountains, glaciers, and snowfields. We took pictures—I'll send them to you soon. Then we nestled among the rocks and ate our apples and cheese. We skied down to the half-way point, to a T-bar lift, and enjoyed the slopes the rest of the day.

That night we had dinner with our surgeon friend in his quarters at the hospital in Zermatt. He was a delightful host. We sat and talked and he produced bread, cake, sausages, and delicious coffee. I sang several songs and he seemed so touched—he actually cried.

We've had some pretty unpleasant experiences along with the pleasant ones. We stayed in a filthy hotel at Ulzio in Italy where we both got diarrhea from the food. The next morning we got on a bus and had a wild ride up a steep mountain road. The driver went so *fast* and there were no guard rails! We passed dingy little towns, and saw women washing clothes in dirty rivers and streams. The children were playing in the streets right among horse and cow manure. Finally we arrived at beautiful Sestriers—and the Grand Hotel Alberg, which was really elegant. Mom, you would have loved it. *At last*—another *bath*, our third since being in Europe! We had some excellent skiing, then we had a big fancy dinner in the hotel and went to bed.

From there we went to the Tyrolean Alps. We're staying in pensiones, where we always have meals with the family. Randy's handling the German language very well; he's able to converse with the people. I'm even picking up a little German myself.

We've had a great time skiing! I'm tan from the neck of my sweater up to my forehead. The rest of me is white. Can you image how I'll look in my gowns back in Hollywood? A two-toned neck! Ugh!

Whenever I see children of Ron's and Mark's ages I get a big lump in my throat and sometimes start to cry. Randy keeps telling me I'm spoiling the trip. But, oh, I miss the boys so much.

We've stayed in so many tiny hotels with only cold water. Some of the trains are rickety, but the beauty that we see from the windows is magnificent! Sweeping valleys, old French towns, ice sculpture on walls of rock beside the track! I love seeing the church spires towering over each little city. Chamonix didn't impress us. The telepheriques (cable cars) at their ski areas looked frightening, so we stayed on the train. Other skiers stayed on too, so we followed them. They turned out to be a group from a *private ski club!* We found a little restaurant where we talked to two ski guides, who invited us to go on a ski tour with them.

So we left our luggage, put the climbing skins on our skis and went with the guides. They said, "We can leave this morning and stop at the top of the mountain to eat and then ski over to Switzerland and take the train back."

We climbed and climbed—a long journey up the mountain. After we stopped to eat, we took the skins off our skis and began our descent over Southern France into Switzerland. It was a twenty-mile run! We were supposed to arrive at a little station at 4:00 to take a train back to Mt. Blanc. The sun had made the snow sticky and I was too light to ski on it. The men managed fine, but I floundered all the way. When we got there the train had left—I had made us miss it—and there were no hotels. So there was nothing to do but walk back to Mt. Blanc. We could walk on roads part of the time. As it grew dark the moonlight was beautiful on the snow. When we could, we skied down hill. It was amazing—skiing in the moonlight.

Our guides knew of a small community with a restaurant. The owner was a friend of theirs. We arrived there at 10 o'clock at night. The guides asked their friend if it would be possible to fix us something to eat.

Mother, you know how much I love cheese fondue. That's what they served us. I've never been so hungry or enjoyed fondue so much. Our guides then said we could walk a few more hours and we'd reach a hotel.

About 3 o'clock in the morning we rapped at a door of an inn at Argenteeres. A sleepy woman with the cutest night cap peeked out. No, she didn't want anyone. She was *closed*. Our guides pleaded, so she opened up and gave Randy and me an ice-cold room without hot water. She handed me some sheets and I made up a bed for us. We slept—oh, so gratefully.

The next day we had breakfast and went back to Mt.

Blanc. We bought Randy the skis he'd been wanting for a long time.

He couldn't wait to use them. My feet were too blistered to ski, but I went with him in a frightening cable car to the half-way point where I sat at an outdoor cafe and drank coffee while Randy boarded a rickety cable tram and sailed 5,000 feet above ground to the top of the ski run. He had a horrid run down over icy slopes that dropped into canyons. Oh, mom, I was so relieved when he came back safely. He's had charley horses every night from straining so hard to keep from falling.

Mother, we're really having a wonderful time. It isn't all cold rooms, cold water, and disappointing breakfasts. Every so often we get a good warm hotel with hot water and a square meal, and I must say the world looks brighter after that.

God bless you and the boys.
Love to all,
Norma

P.S. In Paris I bought you a black and white checked silk umbrella in a black leather case.

Reports of a twelve-mile run from St. Anton to St. Christof in Austria intrigued Randy. I worried that my painstaking style of skiing would hinder his speed, but we prepared to make the exciting run.

I tried to keep up as he sped in front of me, making perfect christies mile after mile. Occasionally he had to stop and wait for me to catch up.

Finally the tiny storybook village of St. Christof lay beneath us, looking like a scene from a Christmas card. A wide-open run made Randy yodel with excitement. I stood and marveled at the grace and ease of his form as he moved swiftly to a clump of trees half a mile away.

Turning to make sure there was no one approaching, I pushed off. Randy stood watching as I skied toward him.

Suddenly, I was struck from behind with terrible force. I went sprawling, then blacked out.

A young woman had skied right into me—she too was knocked unconscious.

We came to at about the same time. Randy, breathless from climbing, knelt beside me, and gently stroked my face with shaking fingers.

"Are you all right?" he asked, his tanned face tense with concern.

"My neck hurts," I whispered. The intensity of the pain forced me to hold my head still.

The young woman stood up, brushing the snow from her jacket. She started hurling angry shouts at me. I recognized French but couldn't understand her abusive volley of words. She skied off. Randy and I were left alone.

"*She* shouldn't be mad; she hit *you!* She was the one coming from behind," Randy said.

He took off his parka and rolled it up to make a brace for my neck. He had studied first aid and I had confidence in him.

It was a struggle to get to my feet and I found it almost impossible to make my way down the mountain.

Randy found a kind couple who were willing to drive us back to St. Anton. We learned there was a medical office nearby, and hastily made our way to the modern building.

Randy explained to the doctor in German that his wife had injured her neck and he was afraid it was broken. He described how it happened and told him that I was in terrible pain.

The doctor led me to an examination room. He guided me to a black stool and made me sit down. Grabbing my head between his hands, he began to twist it violently, whirling my aching head back and forth. Satisfied with his "examination" he declared proudly in a thick accent, "It iss not broken. Dot vill be fifteen dollars, plees!"

I shudder to think what would have happened if my neck *had* been broken.

Painfully we made our way back to Haus Soleder where we had a charming room. I wasn't able to ski for a week but we used the opportunity to visit some excellent galleries in the little village. I was particularly impressed with Rembrandt's work. As I stood there for hours, admiring his paintings, I didn't realize how much art would mean to me later in life.

We traveled on to Innsbruck. The city was full of bombed-out buildings and ragged children, looking too old for their age. The ravages of the war were still in evidence, but we marveled at the brave spirit of the people. They were throwing themselves into the rebuilding of their city. It was beyond our comprehension how they could laugh and sing when they had been so bombed and battered. We saw the elderly with bags of sticks, bearded old men wearing lederhosen, heavy wool socks, tyrolean hats, ski boots, and carrying rugged old sticks as canes.

When at last we turned our faces toward home, we had been gone for two and one-half months. When we arrived in New York we wasted no time getting home. We took turns driving and made it in four days.

Of course I cried when I saw the boys. Ron was delighted to have us home, but Mark studied us as though we were strangers, making me cry all the harder. Mother, Jim, and Arline had only good reports to give us and before long everything returned to normal. We found that we had made the trip for less than $1,000 apiece—and we still had $300 in the bank!

CHAPTER TWENTY-SEVEN

As the years went by, our next-door neighbors Roy and Audrey Utke became our close friends. I loved the beautiful sign Roy had posted in his garage so that he could see it each time he backed out. It read, "Prayer changes things."

Late in the summer, we were having coffee together on our patio one day when Audrey said, "Roy and I are going to take a class in painting at night school next month. Why don't you and Randy join us?"

"That sounds interesting," Randy and I said in unison. We agreed to sign up.

I took four classes in charcoal and perspective, but a new job kept me from continuing. The lessons got me started and were helpful, but just drawing didn't intrigue me.

I bought some oil paints and started using them by the trial and error method. At first I did a still life, then I struggled through a few landscapes. I purchased some Walter Foster art books and found them extremely helpful.

One day while leafing through a magazine on art, I saw the face of an old man. "That's the way I'd like to be able to paint!" I thought. "If only I could capture on canvas the real personality and inner feelings of a subject. I'd love to paint a portrait that would make someone really come alive."

Randy cut a square piece of canvas out of an old work apron. I copied the face of the old man, struggling to get skin tones. It was my first portrait in oil. While I was painting, the hours flew by. I loved it! Once at the easel, I lost all track of time. When mother would tell me, "It's time to start dinner," I couldn't believe it. I would find I had painted all day.

I had been working hard at several singing jobs and as usual when I overdo, my weariness settled in my throat. Leaving the boys with mother, I drove to our family doctor.

"Strep throat," Dr. Watson announced, as he held my tongue down. "I'd better give you a shot of penicillin."

A few minutes later I was on my way home. Suddenly my eye began to sting. I rubbed it, but that only seemed to make it worse. Then my nose began to itch and I felt a strange, tingling sensation in my whole body.

As I drove up the hill toward home, my eyelids puffed up and I began to feel faint. I glanced up into the rear view mirror and stared at what I saw. I almost forgot to drive.

My nose was spreading out across my face. My skin was flame red and coarse. I couldn't recognize myself!

I looked at my arms. The skin was bumpy. My ears were hot. Brushing away my hair with a thick hand I saw in the mirror that my ears had swollen to twice their size.

Thank God I was home! I pulled into the driveway with a screech of brakes and flew up the stairs to the house. Mother met me in the entry and screamed, "Norma, is that you?"

Just then, my heart started to pound at what seemed like twice its normal rate.

Seizing my arm and leading me toward the bedroom, mother said, "Come in and lie down."

I heard her calling the doctor, frantic excitement in her voice. The boys were crawling over the bed, looking with alarm into my awful face. "Mommy, mommy, what's the matter with you?" I couldn't answer them. The pounding of my heart wracked my whole body and I wondered if this was the way I was going to die.

Dr. Watson arrived in ten minutes from his office, which I had always thought was fifteen minutes away. I knew my life depended on how fast he would act.

The boys were crying, "What's the matter with my mommy? Mommy, mommy!"

"Please take the boys out of here," the doctor said firmly to mother. Tearfully and with a longing glance toward me, mother took the boys, screaming, from the bed.

"Reaction to the shot," the doctor murmured.

I knew that could mean death. "O God," I thought. "Is this the way it's going to end?" I hoped if I was going to die looking so terrible my face would return to normal so that people viewing me in the casket would see the Norma Zimmer they recognized—or if I stayed like that I hoped Randy would insist on a closed casket.

Red of face and heavily perspiring, the doctor swiftly injected me twice. By then my heart was racing like a motor, without pause between beats.

My thickened tongue almost filled my mouth; my nose had swollen shut. I could hardly draw a breath.

The doctor stayed near, feeling my pulse, observing me carefully. For a half hour there was no change.

Then I heard him say, "The blisters are starting to go down." He was touching my hands. There was more feeling in them. They were getting softer.

Forty-five minutes after the shots of digitalis and antihistamine, I was breathing more easily and there was some semblance of order to my heartbeat.

It took a couple of hours before I was back to normal. There never were two happier boys than Ron and Mark. They crawled all over the bed kissing me, both of them trying to hug me at once.

"Be sure you never take penicillin again," the doctor warned as he left. "Always tell any doctor who treats you that you can't take penicillin in any form."

He needn't have warned me. A scare like that could never be forgotten.

Mother was badly shaken. I comforted her and the boys and assured them everything would be all right.

Randy had been gone during the entire episode. When he returned late that night and learned what the four of us had been through he almost wept. Over and over he said, "Honey, I'm sorry I wasn't here. I'm so glad you're all right. What a dreadful experience to go through! Thank the Lord you're okay!" The next morning, he called the doctor to thank him for dropping everything at the office and coming to my aid immediately.

The doctor said, "That was the most violent penicillin reaction I have ever seen!"

By the way, the sore throat was gone!

That was the third time in four years I had come close to death.

In late 1954, Kratka Ridge Ski Area had its chair lift, a single device with seventy chairs. Its thirty-foot-high towers are set in concrete and no chair is ever more than eighteen feet off the ground. It can transport approximately 650 skiers from the bottom to the top of the crest in an hour.

Randy believes that the single chair lift is safer because it's much easier to handle only one person at the top of the lift.

If there was ever a time that I felt any threat to our marriage, it was during the time that Randy managed Kratka Ridge. He had to travel there, an hour from our home, every day. He put in such long hours that he would leave home long before the children were up in the morning and return at night after we were all in bed.

Mother and the boys were wonderful companions, but I felt neglected. The mountain was more important to Randy than I was, I felt. Surely he could leave in time to eat dinner with us occasionally! Night after night I'd hug the pillow as I struggled to get to sleep.

112

"Protect Randy, Lord, bring him home safely. Keep him from harm," I'd pray, as I remembered the times he'd finally come home exhausted from struggling through avalanches and freezing icy road conditions. The anxiety was terrible, and the loneliness I felt when I woke to find he wasn't home yet, caused me to cry out to God.

"What's happening to our marriage? This is not the way it should be. O God, help me to accept things the way they are. Help me to be a good wife and mother. Give me patience and strength to cope with my problems."

If sleep didn't come, I'd reach for my Bible and read through one of my favorite books, Proverbs. "Better to live in the desert than with a quarrelsome complaining woman!" (Proverbs 21:19). Then back to Proverbs 21:9, "It is better to live in the corner of an attic than with a crabby wife in a lovely home!"

When Randy would finally come home I kept quiet about my unhappiness till it began to ruin our closeness.

"Randy," I said finally, "this is no way to live—we were meant to be together. We don't have a family life any more. Ron misses you. Mark hardly *knows* you. We never have time to play with the kids; they're in bed when you get home and when you leave. We can't go on like this—please try to find another job. We need you here at home."

"I hate these long hours too, but someone has to keep the area runnning!" he said wearily.

I kept my mouth closed, but my heart ached because he didn't seem to understand. After several years of my pleading, he consented.

Randy was worn out too and could see what was happening to me. He had often talked of a dream to build a beautiful mobile home park. He had used many available days off, weekends, and off-season periods scouting around Los Angeles in search of a suitable piece of property. Now he brought up the idea again. "I just haven't had the time to look—I'd like to buy a few acres and build a park, a nice one—not the usual trailer camp."

I knew. We had talked of it often.

"Randy, why don't you just quit entirely at Kratka Ridge and spend a few weeks looking for property?"

We had saved $25,000 and had no debt on our house; we had paid for it as we were building it.

In 1958, when the tax statement for our home arrived, Randy sat shaking his head in disbelief. "Boy! They've raised us to $700 this year! What a jump from the $150 we started with, honey! I love our home, but we can't stay here if they keep raising our taxes like this. I think we'd better look around for another investment."

"Randy," I said, "with your knowledge of building, you could do most of the work yourself—I mean, if you were to buy property for a mobile home park. Think of what a challenge it would be. You're not afraid of work, that's for sure—why don't we look harder for some property?"

"Yes, I'll get some folders and make a detailed list of all the locations I look at," he said.

So the partners of Kratka hired another manager. Randy had built it up and now all it needed was someone to manage the area during ski season.

Each morning for the next several weeks, Randy scoured the southland for acreage. Prices had skyrocketed to $40,000 an acre in the San Fernando Valley, where we had hoped to locate. He began a search of Orange County. Some place, we knew, the Lord had just what we needed, and we trusted him to show us where it was.

Arline and Jim Mature lived in La Habra, an orange grove community thirty miles south of Los Angeles. "Why don't you look for property here?" they asked. "There's still a lot of good land and it's not too expensive."

Arline is very persuasive and it wasn't long before Randy had searched the area.

Arriving home late one afternoon, he exclaimed, "I've found some acreage on Ocean Avenue and Beach Boulevard."

"Ocean Avenue! I've always wanted to live by the water!"

"Well, it isn't exactly near the water, it's about twenty miles from the ocean," he said in his dry, amused way.

We drove to inspect it and I thought the ten-acre orange grove seemed promising. Randy could already envision the beautiful mobile home park he would create. We walked leisurely over the property. There was a knoll at one side from which we could see Mt. Baldy to the northeast in the San Gabriel Mountains. The view was exquisite. Only a few homes were visible in that uncrowded community.

We got back in the car and drove around the area.

Two blocks east of the site was the city dump. Worse yet, two blocks north there was a railroad track. Our spirits sagged. We inquired and learned that the garbage dump would soon be made into a park. The railroad track, we were assured, was almost dead.

We really wanted the property, but the owners, Mr. and Mrs. Shoebridge, were asking $89,000. Randy said, "It's just impossible for us to pay them $89,000. I could as easily fly to the moon." He thought for a minute. "Tell you what I'll do—I'll make them an offer. I'll make it low enough so maybe we can work something out."

The Shoebridges were absolutely insulted when the realtor told them we had offered $60,000. It seemed this place was not for us. For the time being, we dropped the idea of buying property for a mobile home park and Randy started building a house for someone in our neighborhood.

A month later we got a call from the Shoebridges' realtor. "We'd like to give you a chance to buy the property for $70,000," he said.

Randy's a good business man and he negotiated until the price was $64,000.

We paid the Shoebridges $17,000 down on the property. They agreed to live there and take care of the orange crop until we sold our house.

The following week we were just finishing dinner when the phone rang. It was for Randy. I could tell he was talking about selling our house and seemed excited. He came back to the table. "Well, would you believe that! I went to Eddie Moniot's today for a haircut and said, 'Hey, Eddie, are you and Evelyn in the market for a great buy? We're going to sell our house in Flintridge.' Eddie looked shocked and protested, 'Oh, no! You can't do that. You kids have worked too hard on that house. It's a jewel box of a place and you put so much of yourselves in it.' Just now he called to tell me he's got somebody interested in buying our house."

"Oh, how exciting," I said, though I felt mixed emotions about leaving our home.

"Yeah, this guy sat down in the chair right after me. His name is White. He had no more'n sat down when he said, 'Eddie, there's a freeway coming through my property and I'm going to lose my home.' And Eddie told him, 'I know just the house you should buy in Flintridge!' "

Of course we were delighted. Mr. and Mrs. White came over that very evening, and we could tell from their expressions that they liked our home—all Randy's brick work, the patios, and the place for the swimming pool. When they came inside Mrs. White said, "My husband's favorite hobby is 35 mm slides. I wonder where we could set up his equipment."

This was Randy's shining hour. In his dry, unemotional way he calmly went up to the large picture. He said, "Well, the way we do it is to open up this picture and—presto! a projection room!"

They gasped. Mr. White was practically jumping up and down. "I want it! I want it!" he said.

"And I lower a screen over here," Randy went on, crossing the room.

"That does it! I want it!" The man was like a child in his joy.

They bought our home a few days later. Randy and I were astounded as Mr. White drew out his money clip and counted out the entire amount in cash!

We hated to leave our beautiful home, but were even sadder to leave the Utkes and the De Greys.

During the thirty days that it took for our deal to go through, we had several opportunities to get to know Mr. and Mrs. Shoebridge and their sons, who had farmed the orange grove with them. When they visited us in Flintridge, Mrs. Shoebridge fell in love with our place and said they feared it would be a comedown for us to move into the little ranch house. "I don't see how you can stand to leave this house. Oh, Norma, I can't see you moving into that little ranch house." Her sons grew a little irritated with her. "After all, mother, we grew up there and we loved it, so why shouldn't they?"

We moved out to the 900-square-foot ranch house. The property had its own well. A tall storage tank stood near the house, supplying the water with five pounds of pressure. Daylight could be seen between the walls where the boys' bedroom had been added on and the house had settled.

Before we moved in, Jim and Randy painted the entire inside of the house. The living room had a high, domed ceiling; using huge paint rollers, they started at one end and painted an arc all the way across and down to the other side, over and over. In an hour the room was completed.

The first night we were there we learned that the railroad wasn't quite dead. A train whistled through just as we were going to sleep. The next morning at daylight we were awakened by another train. But I suppose that compared to the railroad yards in Los Angeles this was practically a dead track.

We had sold our king-size bed, as our tiny bedroom could only accommodate a queen size. No wall in our living room was large enough for our three-sectional davenport, so we split the sections, using one for a chair. This was the watermelon couch we had coveted and bought so proudly when we moved to Flintridge, but now I was becoming a little tired of it. I determined to choose more subdued colors thereafter. How we ever got our apartment grand piano into that house remains a mystery, but there it stood in all its elegance. There was just enough space left for the television set.

Mice rollicked through the rooms night and day. The grove was a haven for squirrels, mice, and crickets.

The boys had the largest room in the place. They had a great time deciding what to put on their plywood walls.

"We're going to tear this down and build ourselves something better anyway," Randy laughed, "so let them pound nails."

The house was white with brown trim, but somehow it seemed to me it should be yellow. "Randy, please paint it yellow with white trim," I pleaded. "I think it would be so lovely with that huge bougainvillea between it and the garage."

He fixed those clear hazel eyes on me and I knew that once more common sense would prevail. "Paint a house that's going to be torn down?" he asked as though not sure he had heard right. "In the first place I can't spare the time, and besides, we've got to save every penny, so we have something to build this park with." I knew he was right. I bought some white priscilla curtains for the dining-living room. I had some silk-screen prints and I grouped some colorful plates on the wall. Oh, how lovely it was! I adored this little ranch house. If Mrs. Shoebridge had known about my childhood and had realized all the shacks I had lived in, she would have considered this a mansion, as I did.

The first year we lived there, we had an orange crop worth $600. But of course we hadn't bought the grove to raise oranges. Randy went ahead to map out plans for the mobile home park—his dream come true.

We had trouble convincing the city fathers that the area should be rezoned to include our mobile home park. We couldn't afford an architect, but Randy, who is good at everything, drew up his own plans with the help of a friend, Bob Williamson, who was an engineer.

We really started economizing now. Our diet consisted of beans one night and split pea soup the next, with a leg of lamb or a roast about once a week. Fortunately, we all loved fruits and vegetables which were always plentiful. Our conversation, of necessity, centered largely around managing to build the park with our limited finances. The extent of our frugality became evident to me when Ronnie asked me very seriously one day, "Mommie, are we *poor?*"

The girls in the quartet were teasing me because I wore the same clothes all the time. In two years, the only new piece of clothing I bought for myself was a pair of hose.

Randy got up at 4:00 every morning. Later, Jim would join him and sometimes pop would come down for a while and help work on the place. They pulled the trees, leveled the ground, dug the trenches, poured 3,800 yards of concrete at $10 a yard. They installed all the electricity themselves, laying the electrical wires in cement underground. They put in the streets, the sewer, the water, the gas.

The first building Randy put up consisted of an office, a pool room, which was also to be used at first for a recreation hall, bathrooms, a laundry with washers and dryers. He had completed thirty-seven spaces for mobile homes at a cost of $42,000. This used up all our capital. Fortunately, I was working eight and nine shows a week with the Girl Friends Quartet and making good money.

As Randy completed each space and put in beautiful dichondra lawns, awaiting the mobile homes folks would place on each rented space, I prayed that God would bring us just the right tenants. I wanted them to be people who would love our little park and be happy there. Little did I know as I stood praying at one space after another, how wonderfully God would answer my prayers. There would come a time when I would bless God for a good number of these fine folks.

Our monthly payments for two years were $300 a month and after that they jumped to $500 a month. Randy worked seven days a week, never taking even a day off for skiing, as he didn't want to risk an injury. Slowly our thirty-seven spaces were being filled with eager renters who brought in attractive mobile homes. We fell in love with each couple. We regarded each of them as an answer to a specific prayer.

Now our park needed a swimming pool but we didn't have the money. The Anthony Pool Company made arrangements for us to go to a bank in La Habra for the loan. When we went to sign the papers, the bank manager became very obnoxious.

"A trailer camp? I wouldn't lend you any money unless I had the first mortgage on it. You can't attract anything but second-class citizens to a place like that—poor risk." He was so insulting I left in tears. We deeply resented his generalities about trailer parks. We had worked so hard and were proud of our park and our tenants.

When we returned to Park La Habra we hurried to mother's mobile home for a much-needed cup of coffee.

Mother had grown very lovely in her happiness with us. Randy made her the manager of the park and put her on a salary. Besides doing the office work, maintaining the buildings, and cooking for our family, she took care of all the dichondra lawns and mulched around all the trees. She took great pride in keeping everything spotless. She interviewed prospective tenants and had an instinct for sizing people up. She knew just whom to accept. Mother collected the rents and together she and I planned social activities for our residents.

Who should be sitting there on her step but the salesman from the pool company. We told him our sad story.

"Don't you worry about it," he said. "We'll get another bank. That's funny, though. I've never heard of them turning down a loan on a pool. Well, I'll fix you up with a bank in Pasadena."

We did get the loan. Randy and Jim put a red brick deck around the pool and our people were thrilled with it.

We were ready for the next twenty spaces.

As Randy and Jim worked on the park, Ron and Mark would rush home from school to change clothes so they could "help dad." Randy believed in giving boys responsibility at an early age.

We have pictures of Ron driving a tractor when he was eight years old.

Loren and Crystal Smith moved into our growing community, and Crystal, a high school teacher, endeared herself to us by her interest in our boys' education. Whenever they had difficulty with any subject, she volunteered to tutor them. We accepted her unselfish offer and all through the years she spent many evenings assisting them in their studies.

Randy always found time to play ball with the boys and I enjoyed running races, wrestling, and roughhousing with our growing sons. Every evening there was a time of prayer as I tucked them into bed.

CHAPTER TWENTY-EIGHT

In 1958 a crowd of 17,000 people came to Hollywood Bowl to see and hear the sixth annual Family Night produced by Walt Disney— and I had been asked to sing!

The workday sun took its time fading over the famous green shell. Many times Randy and I had strolled those walks and climbed those steps to the highest point. Now *I* sat on the stage, heart pounding, looking over the vast audience. My rented gown was elegant. I had gone to Western Costume just the day before to select a hoop-skirted aqua satin gown. It was perfect for the evening. I had never sung before a crowd like this. There were many children—countless eyes, new-button-bright with excitement, little bodies wriggling under the supervision of fond, watchful parents. It was overwhelming to watch thousands of helium-filled balloons being released into the velvet darkness, floodlights following their ascent.

As I sat on stage waiting for my cue, I admired the performance before me—dancers from Scotland, Austria, Japan, Poland, ending with a troupe of our own American square dancers.

Next came "The Mouseketeers." Little did I know that one of them, Bobby Burgess, would become a dear friend.

I was next!

George Bruns, the conductor, nodded for me to take my place at a microphone at center stage. The chorus behind me was directed by Dr. Charles Hirt. As I sang a beautiful selection from the classic "Sleeping Beauty," with Tschaikowsky's limpid, emotional music, my heart sang along. If only dad could be here! But mom sat in the audience with Randy and the boys as I sang with all my heart. My voice soared—I felt borne along by more than my own power. It was a supreme moment and I praised God for his goodness.

All too soon it was over. I took my seat and watched Zorro appear like lightning. Caped and armed, he plummeted from the topmost point of the Bowl's great shell. Ron and Mark would be gasping, I knew. They adored this fearless midnight-cloaked friend of the friendless—sworn foe of all bad guys! To top off the whole enchanted evening, Tinkerbell slid from the highest point on the hill, across the entire crowd to the stage to the strains of "When You Wish upon a Star."

My family came to congratulate me, buzzing about the whole performance. From out of the crowd came my dear friend Betty Allan of the Girl Friends and her fine husband, John. Tears streamed down her face as she told me how thrilled she was at this great opportunity I had been given.

One evening that fall I drove into our park right at 6 o'clock. It had been an exhausting day and I was anxious to see my family. They would all be at the rec hall for our weekly potluck. I would just bring my things in the house, wash up a bit, and then join them. I knew mother would have cooked something good to contribute to the dinner.

I got out of the car and started to walk briskly in the darkness toward the ranch house. Suddenly, is was as though God said, "Don't go any farther!"

My heart turned to ice and I swung around and ran to the recreation hall. I felt as though something terrible was behind me. Breathless, I pushed open the heavy oak door and stood inside, panting.

It didn't seem like the sort of thing to tell everyone about, or to proceed to investigate. Now that I was safe inside the hall, the terror out there seemed less real.

After dinner, when Randy, mother, and the boys and I went back to the house, I walked into the bedroom and turned on the light.

The bed! It was all messed up. There were footprints on the spread and the pillows were rumpled.

Randy quickly checked all around the house with a flashlight. he and the boys carefully searched all over the park, flashing light among the trees and homes. Randy called the police and they offered to come over.

Randy said, "I just thought maybe you were looking for somebody. If you are, they've been in our house, but they're gone now."

Mother and I felt very uneasy to think that our house had been entered during our short absence.

The next day we read in the *La Habra Star* that the county sheriff had chased a rapist for five blocks and lost him right across the street from our ranch house. They had searched but had not found him. Later the man was found only a few blocks from our park.

I shall always be convinced that God warned me not to go into the house.

We finally had enough money to buy a mobile home for our family. After shopping carefully we decided on a Paramount. It measured 45 by 10 feet, half the size of the tiny ranch house, but with spirits high we moved into Space 1. The tiny dwelling was charming. We felt as if we were playing house. We moved the piano into the recreation hall where it has been useful ever since.

Now we were ready to tear down the ranch house so we could start bulldozing. Eight feet of dirt had to be taken off the top of the hill before we could build.

We had all the plans but we were short of money. The bank was willing to lend us the amount we needed but the interest had jumped from 6 to 8%, which would bring our monthly payments up to $800. We felt that was more than we could handle at the same time we were building the park.

In trying to juggle funds and find sufficient money, we went to the Shoebridges. We explained that we were borrowing money and felt they should know we'd be paying them off for their earlier loan. As we drove away, I asked Randy, "Why didn't you ask them if they could lend us some money?"

Randy looked at me patiently. "Oh, I wouldn't do that; they've been so good to us already."

The next morning, the phone rang at 8 o'clock. It was Mr. Shoebridge. "Would $17,000 now help you?" he asked. "And $20,000 more in a few months?"

Randy was ecstatic!

"Pay the interest, 7%, but you don't have to pay anything on the principal for five years," he said.

God was so good; how beautifully he was answering our prayers!

Randy began working on twenty more spaces and soon got the $20,000 from the Shoebridges. Nine more months went by. Now we had seventy-seven spaces ready and mother began showing them to prospective renters.

Again I stood before every empty space as Randy was completing it and prayed that the Lord would send us the right folks. We had been warned not to live in the park, but we have never regretted it. It's been like an extended family. In all the years we've operated Park La Habra there have been only two residents we've asked to leave. One woman for drunkenness, and a couple who found fault with everyone and everything! They were creating unhappiness for others, so we reminded them they were on wheels.

Now Randy designed a whole new recreation room. The building would have a card room, a big kitchen, a hydraulic stage in a 30-by-60-foot recreation room, a projection room, and ample storage space.

One of our tenants, Barney Rudd, approached Randy. "I don't know how you're managing this," he said, "but Lola and I have a little money in the bank. How about letting us lend you some?"

"Boy, this is really fantastic!" Randy exclaimed when he told me about it. He was even more excited a little later when another tenant, Sno Brown, said, "I told Barney Rudd I had some money to invest and he said, 'Lend it to the kids. They'll give you 7%, I'm sure.'" So Sno and Helen Brown also made loans to us. Randy put that $20,000 in savings and had enough to build the last thirty spaces after the rec hall was done, giving us a total of 107 spaces.

When it was all finished and was filling up, it was paid for, except for the $27,000 which was due a few years later. Randy and Jim and our boys continued to work on the park. I maintained a schedule singing with the quartet. Arline's and Jim's daughter, Marline, a sweet, happy child, came by often to play with Mark. They were good buddies, and through the years, as Marline has matured into a beautiful young woman, they have remained great friends.

For six years, without missing a day, Randy had worked from before dawn until dark. At night he would do the office work that required his special attention.

It's hard to describe the feeling of assurance we have as we dwell in our mobile home park—surrounded by lovely people. They're fun-loving, active, thoughtful folks.

After mother, Randy, and I established a routine of activities, the members of the community took over. Committees were formed. Now monthly chairmen direct social events. Our park family love getting together. One Sunday evening potluck a month wasn't enough—Wednesday evenings were added where delicious dishes are brought piping hot to the large tables. There's no need to be lonely—there's always someone interested in playing pool, swimming, walking, or bicycling.

Classes are held for painting, sewing, or crafts. Slides and movies are shared with neighbors. Thursday afternoon Bible study classes are well attended. The men share their cooking skills by shopping for and preparing a marvelous Sunday breakfast once a month. Every Saturday morning there is a friendship hour where a hearty brunch is served.

Luaus that give competition to the Islands are held once a year.

122

Professional acts thrill the audience with sword dances, fire juggling, hulas, and Tahitian dances.

When illness strikes, neighbors run in with homemade soups and offers to clean the house, do the laundry, and shop for one another. It's like living in a small town, though privacy is respected.

One day Randy bounded into the trailer. He rushed to the refrigerator and poured himself some carrot juice, then checked through the morning's mail. "*Trailer News* has some nice things to say about our park. Look at this, honey," he said, holding it out to me.

I looked where Randy was pointing, and read:

This was originally a 77-space park but another thirty spaces have been added. These are all forty feet wide by seventy feet long. Practically all construction was done by Randy Zimmer, who on this day was so covered with splashed concrete and paint that he wouldn't stop to have his picture taken.

All utilities are underground and the park has a pleasant contoured look, like a gentleman's country estate. Every space is landscaped and immaculately kept.

Here is none of that squared-off look so prevalent in mass-produced housing. Pool, patio, and building, set back beyond the curving entrance way, keep a rustic air of simplicity and belie their efficient use of interior space.

Outdoor recreation areas, including shuffleboard courts, are estimated to be in excess of 4,000 square feet. Clubhouse area under roof is almost 5,000 square feet and centers around a dance and assembly hall, complete with space for a new movie projector soon to be installed, and a hydraulically controlled stage, which lets down flush with the floor or rises to any desired heights.

Across a covered concrete walkway is the office; adjoining this is a men's billiard room, perhaps the most popular spot in the park and always occupied.

Behind the dance floor is an elaborately furnished kitchen. Here coffee is always on and a heaping plate of cookies keeps guests wandering kitchenward. A card room with space for five tables is down a hallway with a view overlooking the pool.

The top of the clubhouse is in part devoted to a patio with new furnishings.

About 50 percent of the guests are retired. They have five potlucks a month, card games nightly and sometimes days, a sewing bee on Wednesday, art classes on Tuesday, shuffleboard tournaments, slide shows, and movies to come shortly. Practically no one moves out of Park La Habra!

CHAPTER TWENTY-NINE

For seventeen years I had been working with the Girl Friends, doing background singing for many stars—Frank Sinatra, Bing Crosby, Dean Martin, Nelson Eddy, Eddie Fisher, Mario Lanza, Nat King Cole, Dinah Shore, Doris Day, Pat Boone, George Beverly Shea. We had also sung on many Lawrence Welk albums. I did top soprano work for many fine choral groups like the voices of Walter Schumann, Ralph Carmichael, Johnny Mann Singers, Pete King Chorale, Jud Conlin and the Rhythmaires, Ken Darby, Jeff Alexander, Charlie Henderson, and Lynn Murray.

My voice was used in dozens of moving picture scores. I seldom remembered the name of the film; I just sang the music and went on my way. Regular places of employment were Paramount, MGM, Universal, Warner Bros., RKO, and Walt Disney Studios. Many of those recording sessions produced material that is still being used at Disneyland, in attractions such as Alice in Wonderland, America the Beautiful, It's a Small World, The Tiki Room, and Mr. Lincoln.

For years I sang on eight weekly radio programs: Bing Crosby, Jack Benny, Lucille Ball, Phil Harris, Edgar Bergen, Tony Martin, Frank Sinatra, and Nelson Eddy.

Sandwiched in among all these jobs came literally hundreds of commercials: "Rinso White, Rinso Bright! Happy little washday song!"; "J-E-LL-O!"; Texaco, Signal Gasoline ("Signal, Signal, Signal gasoline—Your car will go far with go-farther gasoline"); Post cereals ("Most any cereal is fine with me, as long as you spell it P-O-S-T"); Max Factor ("Mr. Max Factor of Hollywood has something special for you"). And so on and on!

As a concert soprano, I was traveling the country with Carmen Dragon and the Standard School Broadcast, radio's oldest network musical and educational program. It was designed to give children a greater appreciation of the classics. They first broadcast in 1928. And while I was with them in later years, they were on more than a hundred stations in ten western states, the East Coast, Alaska, and Hawaii, bringing the program to 1,750,000 students who listened in 7,000 schools.

We were doing as many as seventy jobs a month. We worked constantly and sometimes I really felt the strain. One night as I was driving home very late, completely exhausted, I prayed, "O God, I want to be using my voice to glorify *you*. If you can use me in some way, please show me what it is."

One of the records we had done with Mr. Welk was a Thanksgiving album in which I had a one-line solo. Together we sang, "Be thankful, be thankful, for sweet things in life he is sharing. Be thankful, be thankful, when trees you have planted are bearing. Be grateful, be grateful *to know he will always be caring*. Be thankful, be thankful and you'll be repaid with his love." The italicized phrase was my tiny solo on this record.

One morning that November of 1959, I was answering my mail when the telephone rang. I answered. It was a warm, musical voice—with a familiar cadence.

"Hello-o. This is Lawrence Welk. Is this Norma Zimmer?"

I almost fainted.

He said, "You did such a lovely job of that solo on my Thanksgiving album that I would like to have you come and do it on my show. Would you have time?"

"Oh, yes, Mr. Welk. I'd love to." I couldn't believe it. What a thrill! "Thank you, Lord," I murmured as I hung up.

In a state of excitement, I drove to the studio at the appointed time. I hadn't done much solo work on television.

Mr. Welk greeted me cordially as I entered the studio. He made me feel that I was special to him. As I observed the warmth and magnetism of his personality, I began to understand why he is so well loved by everyone.

I had worked with the Lennon sisters on their albums and today they ran to hug me. They were always so loving and full of fun. George Cates, the musical supervisor, came to greet me, smiling broadly. "Glad to see you here, Norma. I've been urging Lawrence to use you on our program. I certainly did enjoy working with you on the 'Moonglow' recordings." From the start, I felt accepted by everyone on the stage. It was an unusually friendly group. We rehearsed "Be Thankful."

Joe Feeney had been fighting laryngitis, and during that day he lost his voice. Mr. Welk asked if I could add another song. Of course, I was glad to, and I sang "Smoke Gets in Your Eyes."

That had been one of the most exciting nights of my career and I was so thankful for the opportunity. I assumed that it was a one-time thing—a nice job—and I went on working with the Girl Friends Quartet.

The following week, Mr. Welk called me again. "Well, well, I had *many* phone calls after your appearance. Would you come back and do another show with us?"

Naturally, I accepted with great delight. I had a large repertoire of songs that Mr. Welk liked. Week after week he asked me back. Fan mail came in from many places, asking for more of Norma Zimmer. I was so grateful. Tears still often come to my eyes when I think of the wonderfully kind audience we have and the way people take time to write of their appreciation.

The folks in our Park La Habra were happy for me—most of them are Lawrence Welk fans. Our weekly potlucks buzzed with excitement.

On the New Year's Eve show, in front of the camera, Lawrence Welk invited me to become a member of his musical family. I felt the look of shock come into my face. The audience, seeing that look of amazement, asked later if it had been rehearsed because it seemed exaggerated. But it wasn't; it was entirely spontaneous. I can still feel the total surprise of that moment. I accepted on the spot.

I became a regular on the Lawrence Welk Show and was still a member of the Quartet. Now I *was* one busy girl!

The Lawrence Welk people are friendly and warm—both the crew and the cast on stage. The Lennon sisters, Jo Ann Castle, and Barbara Boylan were with the show in those days and we became dear friends. I love them and we still see one another when we can. But just as old friends are precious, new ones quickly become so—and the girls who have joined the show in recent years are so charming and talented. I love them all—Tanya, Cissy, Ralna, Gail, Sandi, Mary Lou, Anacani, Ava, and Charlotte—each one a top-notch musician and warm friend to me.

The girls on the show share a dressing room and this is where friendships begin and grow. We have so much fun in those tension-filled moments between numbers when we're all making costume changes. I'm afraid we leave the room in absolute disarray for our patient wardrobe girls, Joann De Longpre, Jackie Eifert, Ann Marie Harrel, and Hazel Dewey!

Jim Hobson has been our director since I started with the show. He's extremely talented—and so handsome that I think he should be on the other side of the camera! My makeup man from the first show to this present day has been Duane Fulcher. The camera men, Herm Falk, Jimmy Angel, and Jim Baldwin, still work on the Welk show and have been wonderful to me with their constructive suggestions. Once when I was absent with a case of flu, these three nice fellows sent me two dozen red roses.

The art director, Chuck Koon, and the costumer, Rose Weiss, are still the same helpful, kind people they were then. Roselle Friedland is hairdresser for all the girls and never fails to cheer me with her direct honesty. Everyone loves her.

For about six years I bought my own gowns. Much of my earnings went for clothes. Now, however, many of the gowns are purchased by Rose Weiss with a budget from the show. Rose does the buying for all the performers, both men and women; she's a genius at costuming.

We do repeat the dresses after some time has elapsed—perhaps a year or two. But our wardrobe people are very clever about redesigning clothes so they look different. Our seamstress, Gertrude Spangler, is an artist at this.

Being on the Welk show opened up many doors for me. I began to get invitations to do concerts all over the United States. It was because of the recordings and shows I did for Mr. Welk that Cliff Barrows of the Billy Graham team heard and liked my singing. It's very possible that if I had never sung for Lawrence Welk I would still be doing background singing in Hollywood.

Mr. Welk's first telephone call occurred only three days after my prayer that night on the freeway when I said, "God, if you can use my voice in some way, please show me."

In 1962, Mr. Welk officially named me his "Champagne Lady." I had some reservations about that title, but he told me this was the highest compliment he could give a female vocalist. "It means only an effervescent, bubbling personality and music," he explained.

I had known for years that the Welk style of music was called "champagne music"—not to promote champagne, as Mr. Welk is very much opposed to liquor, but because a listener had said, "Your music just bubbles—like champagne." Now Mr. Welk persuaded me that it was an honor. I accepted it gratefully.

Not all the listeners have approved of my title on the show. They have questioned, as I originally did, why I, a Christian, should be willing to be called by such a questionable name. I can only reply that after I became aware of how Mr. Welk feels about liquor and its devastating results, and how highly he means to honor me, I have complete peace about it.

Some of my letters have criticized me for singing love songs with Jimmy Roberts.

When I first sang on the Welk show, I seldom looked at Jimmy during our duets but kept my eyes on the camera throughout the song. Then fans would write in and say, "Why don't you look at Jimmy when you sing? You're singing *to* someone, you should *look* at him."

Jim Hobson thought too that in show business we should acknowledge each other. "It's just a performance," he said. So we started singing love songs to each other, looking from the camera into each other's eyes.

That offended some others of the viewers. "Why do you sing love songs to each other, when you're both married?" they would ask. By this time, we had all decided that it was a performance and had nothing at all to do with our private lives. When two actors in a film, even a Christian film, speak the words, "I love you," they look at each other, not at the camera. I feel the same is true in song.

Not all of our duets require us to gaze at each other. I recall the day we sang "Far Away Places." A huge balloon, like the one used in *Around the World in Eighty Days,* was hung from the grids on a carpenter pipe. This allowed the contraption to swing freely in a motion similar to a boat on moving water. During our rehearsal, I noticed Jimmy's color changing from his usual healthy glow to a ghastly pallor. He was getting seasick! A hurried call to the studio nurse produced dramamine in time for the show.

Occasionally I get a hate letter. These are usually anonymous. One read, "Why don't you get off that Welk show, you old bag? It's plain to see that you're not young. If you'd step aside, some younger person could have your job. You know you don't use Geritol every day like you say you do. You're a liar."

But I *do* use Geritol and I use all the products I advertise. I wouldn't advertise anything I didn't use. Fortunately, letters of that kind are few.

Most of my correspondence is encouraging. Just last year, I received a precious letter enclosing a cartoon. The letter said, "My husband is in love with you, but I don't mind. He's seventy-nine and I'm seventy-eight."

The cartoon showed a woman singing on television. My fan had labeled her "Norma." Directly in front of the screen sat an elderly man leaning forward with animated interest. His wife sat beside him with a sour look on her face. She was saying, "Would you like me to leave so you can be alone with her?"

Frances Young of Allentown, Pennsylvania, heads up a fan club for me. An amazing woman, she not only stays in close touch with me but with most of the members of the club as well. She sends bulletins to hundreds of members about four times a year, giving them information about my appearances, and personal data such as family joys and sorrows. Randy and I have visited her and she has been to California to see us many times.

CHAPTER THIRTY

There's a letter from your dad," Randy said. He had been out working around the park since 6 o'clock. I was getting ready for work now at 9:00.

"Dear Norma," dad wrote. "It's cold and damp here in Seattle all the time and it seems to bother me more as I get older. It's pretty lonely here too. I really don't have much to stay for. I have quite a few pupils but I've been wondering if you could find any for me down there. I'd come in a minute if I could find some. I could help some around the park, too, if you need it. I miss your mother. I still love her, but she doesn't want to come back to me."

Randy and I knew mother would never live with dad again, but Randy agreed that we should let him come down. So I called music stores and found two that said they would like to have him teach violin through their stores in Whittier and La Habra.

I wrote dad and said, "Sure, come on down. Why not give it a try?"

We rented a small apartment for him in Fullerton, four miles from La Habra, and I fixed it up so he would be comfortable. I still loved dad and hoped to help him find some happiness too in his old age.

Dad drove down and began his new life. Mornings he helped around the park and afternoons he taught violin. He became a familiar sight going around Park La Habra with his broom and dustpan, sweeping up leaves and dust that always flew and blew around. The people in the park enjoyed him, and he began teaching violin to Ron and Mark. I never saw him again in the drunken condition I remembered from my early years. Dad still nipped a little but was always able to keep students and support himself.

His arrival on the scene did bring with it some tension. Mother refused to speak a word to him; she wouldn't even look at him. To me she would say, "Norma, if I die first, don't let dad live in my mobile home. If you do, I'll haunt you!" She remained stony toward him and as far as I know they never spoke once in the two and a half years dad worked around the park.

The Lennon sisters offered to sing at our first luau at Park La Habra and Jo Ann Castle told us she'd be happy to play the piano. Their coming triggered a great flurry of excitement among our residents. Ron and Mark were greatly impressed by this prospect. Ron had a crush on Janet Lennon. He kept asking me if it was possible for a boy to date a girl older than himself. I told him I thought so, but he never got up the courage to ask her out.

We had our little home shining. My latest portraits were hanging on the paneled walls. The girls arrived in their usual high spirits. To them, our mobile home was like a doll house, and they moved from one room to another, admiring the completeness of the tiny place. Everything a person needed!

"Did you paint these pictures, Norma?" Kathy inquired.

I admitted that I had.

"Mr. Welk should see these!" Peggy said.

They went back and told Mr. Welk about them. As a result, he made plans to feature me on a broadcast in 1964. I was amazed when he asked me to bring some of my art work to use on the set.

Mom, Randy, and the boys participated in the show. Specialty numbers were arranged—a dance with Bobbie Burgess and Barbara Boylan; a chance to direct the orchestra; a tag dance with Ron, Mark, and Randy. Bob Lido and Aladdin sang a comedy routine with me. I sang "Whistle While You Work," as the camera panned over all the portraits and landscapes I had painted.

It was a special evening. I'm still grateful to Mr. Welk for featuring me that night.

After that I had a number of requests from viewers who wanted to buy paintings from me. But I can't sell my pieces yet. It would be like selling a child. I give them to my family and good friends. I have had my work appraised and have been encouraged. Many of my paintings went on tour with the Celebrity Art Exhibit.

I have no fear of growing old and retiring from singing. If my voice becomes old and cracked, I'll be happy—painting portraits!

CHAPTER THIRTY-ONE

Three days a week are usually required to produce a Lawrence Welk show. Thursday at ten finds all the singers assembled at the Annex studios in Hollywood to rehearse the group songs. George Cates wants a real performance with each run-through, so after one or two hours we're all warmed up. Newcomers soon find their sightreading ability improving with the training they receive each week in these sessions. Lunch is called and a short walk around the corner to Lou's Quickie Grill provides the most generous and delicious sandwiches one can find in Hollywood. Tuna melt is my favorite, but it's so huge I sometimes carry half of it back to the studio to share with George Thow. George helps write "intros" and other continuity, including Lawrence's announcements, plus many other jobs, and never has time to go out for meals. Members of the cast who are fellow-Christians often group together for good fellowship at lunch or other breaks. Tom Netherton, Johnny Zell, Ava Barber, Anacani, Gail Farrell and I frequently enjoy times of sharing with one another.

Group numbers are recorded first, then one by one the solos are rehearsed and taped to make sure they're polished enough to be presented on the show. It's usually my luck to finish at four o'clock and I enter the freeway network during peak traffic.

Thirty miles to go at a snail's pace—but it's a good time to meditate and pray. Some of my best conversations with the Lord take place during those solitary journeys!

Mondays are spent camera blocking and learning dance routines. Jack Imel is our clever choreographer and his movements are all aimed at giving the camera men ample opportunities for close-ups, considered a *must* by Mr. Welk.

Fittings come next and there's a scramble into the tiny work room where Gertrude Spangler patiently fits nine impatient girls into the beautiful sets of costumes Rose Weiss has selected. On occasional trips to the wholesale house, we all troop from one showroom to another. "That's a Norma dress," or "That's a Ralna dress," is shouted in unison when a particular style is shown.

Rose Weiss must be given the credit for teaching me to dress. "Frumpy" is the only description for the way I looked when I joined the show. Patiently Rose has advised how to select things that look best on my figure.

Tuesday is the big day! Upon arriving at Studio E at ABC, I always head for Mr. Welk's dressing room to greet him. He's jolly and full of mischief with an ever-present twinkle in his eye. But when run-through begins, his genius comes forth. He has an uncanny talent for knowing which songs are right for every performer, the tempo at which each song should be sung, or each instrumental number should be played. It's evident in his personal appearances especially that he's a man of talent and charisma as he has the audience in his hand at once.

Mr. Welk sits glued to his monitor during the entire run-through. If anything displeases him, he rushes on stage to correct the problem. No one argues with him—everyone admits he's *The Boss*! Lawrence has a way of making people feel that they are important to him. He's quick to give encouragement, but if he feels a performer isn't working up to his or her ability, a scolding is forthcoming. Many times he has approached me after my number on the show with tears in his eyes. "That was perfection," he'd say. I've seen him compliment several others the same way.

Dress rehearsal is performed in front of a live audience. Sometimes it's more fun than the real broadcast, because Lawrence is relaxed. He chats and visits with the people, answering questions.

We break for dinner, then rush back. Electricity fills the air as the seconds are counted: five, four, three, two, ONE! The Lawrence Welk Show!

In *one* hour—just as if it were being beamed live to the millions watching, the show is taped without stopping! If there is a goof, you see it! Some other one-hour programs take twenty-four hours to tape. Not so with ours.

I'm so grateful to be part of Lawrence's musical family! Several times he has offered to play his accordion and entertain our folks at Park La Habra's annual Christmas party. Needless to say, this causes great excitement in our park family.

Hymns are popular on the Welk show and all the singers want to do them. Through the exposure I'd received singing inspirational selections, RCA Victor hired me to make three sacred albums.

For years I had watched and admired Billy Graham on television. Sipping coffee with mother one afternoon, I got a telephone call. I could hardly believe what I heard. It was Cliff Barrows. He told me he had heard me sing "Until Tomorrow," by Irene Atkinson, on one of my records. "We'd like you to come and sing it in the Portland Crusade," he said.

I can't explain how astounded I was. A warm feeling of gratitude filled my heart for this great privilege. I was happy to have the opportunity to stand before the world and proclaim Jesus Christ as my own personal Savior. I accepted eagerly and flew to Portland to join the team.

I was seated next to Billy on the platform. I told him how much I had always been encouraged by the telecast and I said, "Oh, Dr. Graham, the world needs more men like you."

I will never forget what he said. "No, Norma, the world needs God."

I was only slightly rebuked. I sensed that this godly man believes this with all his heart and that constant reiteration of that theme keeps him the humble man he is. By always turning the glory back to God, he has remained small in his own eyes. But not in mine. I consider him probably the greatest man in this century.

After I started singing in the Billy Graham Crusades, I received a few letters saying, "Why are you serving both God and the secular world?" They said I should give up the Welk show and sing only the sacred concerts. But I felt it was through the exposure on the Welk show that I received my opportunities to sing in the Billy Graham Crusades and all the sacred concerts I have done.

In 1965, Randy and I traveled to Stockholm, Sweden, where I was to do an album of duets with Jimmy Roberts for Word Records.

Randy had always been fascinated by East Germany, so when Jimmy and I were finished with our recording sessions, Randy suggested that he and I drive through Denmark to Gedser, a small town located at the southernmost tip of that sweet, clean country. From there we could board a ferry to Wanamunda, East Germany.

When we arrived in Gedser late in the afternoon we found that the next boat wouldn't leave till six in the morning. Strolling around the quiet little village we became uneasy as we saw figures peeking at us from heavily draped windows. There were no flowers surrounding the cottages—unusual for Denmark, we thought. In other cities we had passed through, blossoms cascaded in profusion over thatched roof dwellings.

"There's a hotel," I said to Randy. We hurried to it. A friendly clerk led us to the second story, room No. 7. "Dies ist Ihr Zimmer," he said smiling and bowing. He raised the shade. Smiling once more he said, "Das Abendessen Kann bis 9 uhr eingenomen werden."

Randy thanked him. As the man left he said, "Ich wunsche Ihnen auch einen angenehmen Tag."

The restaurant was crowded with uniformed men as we seated ourselves at a table near the door. Our desk clerk, acting now as a waiter, placed menus in front of us. Randy gave the order in German. With a look of fear, the same man who had spoken German so beautifully only a few moments earlier now shook his head and protested that he didn't speak the language. His glances at the uniformed men made us realize the situation. This was the city of Denmark nearest to East Germany. Many people had escaped here by boat or other means. Intrigue was in the air—uneasiness could be felt. Some of these soldiers were border guards.

We gulped down a fair dinner, then returned to our dimly-lit room, where we slept fitfully.

The next morning we drove onto the white vessel which was to ferry us to Germany. Passengers were few in number, poorly dressed, and unfriendly.

A bleak area containing long white wooden benches and tables was designated as the coffee shop. A long counter held baskets of rolls, coffee service, sausages, and cheeses. How I longed for a good old American breakfast of scrambled eggs, bacon, and whole wheat toast!

Randy stood in line to get the visa. He had to answer many questions.

The channel between the two countries had to be dredged constantly to keep open a lane for the ships. Just after sighting East Germany we felt our boat shudder sharply. We had hit bottom and torn a hole in the hull, but we were able to limp into Wanamunda.

The beaches were crowded with swimmers. A few bright umbrellas gave a holiday atmosphere to the otherwise somber scene. The dock and buildings surrounding it were dirty and run-down. Everything looked old and dilapidated as we drove off the ship. A border guard at the side of the road motioned us to stop. Randy parked the car and disappeared into the guard station.

I sat and observed the surrounding landscape. Somehow the grass didn't look as green as it did at home. A sad pall hung heavy in the air. A strange feeling came over me. Here I was sitting alone in a communist country. I began to think of couples who had been held against their will. Randy was staying away so long I became uneasy. Then I saw him jumping down the stairs, taking two at a time.

Wearing a broad smile, he slid in beside me.

I asked, "Did you get insurance and East German marks?"

"No, they told me to just go ahead," he said with confidence.

"No insurance! Honey, that's dangerous! No German money?"

"No, but we'll drive right to Berlin. We won't need any money."

"How come you didn't get the insurance?" I nagged.

"Well, there was a long line in front of me and the people were all complaining about the wait. I felt sorry for the workers. You should've heard the way those people were mouthing off. Finally I said to them—the others waiting in line—'This wait is nothing compared to what we went through in New York last week.' In no time two guards came up to me and grabbed me by the arm and told me to go along. I'd have been scared but they didn't look fierce. They said I was a good guy. I think they were so happy to hear a kind word they just let me go through. So here I am."

I handed him the map and we studied it together. Randy said, "I'd like to enter East Berlin from East Germany. It looks like we go right there," he said, pointing to a spot on the map.

"I think we ought to head for West Berlin," I protested.

We headed for Berlin, 300 miles away, driving through tiny towns where there were no cars, only a few bikes. Disrepair was in evidence everywhere. We went miles without passing or meeting cars. Occasionally an army truck would share the road. Horses pulled hay wagons—we even saw a large dog pulling a cart. Men strained to haul huge loads on wheeled trailers.

We parked in one of the small cities and got out of the car to take pictures of a pathetic hardware store which showed wares that looked like a movie set depicting the 1800s. As we focused the camera an elderly gentleman started to shake his fist at us. It surprised me, as I thought we appeared to be one of them, driving our little VW. But Randy reminded me that we had a U.S. license plate. A scowling crowd started to gather. We scampered back into our little car and sped away.

Signs saying "West Berlin" began to appear. No amount of nagging could keep Randy from heading toward East Berlin. At last we saw trucks ahead of us entering the zig-zag maze of railroad ties that led to the city of East Berlin. It was like a slalom course. Barricades for several hundred feet were placed so that cars had to slow down to make direct turns past tanks. Machine guns were trained on the passing vehicle.

"I didn't think that they had guards at the East Berlin entrance from East Germany," Randy said nervously.

"I don't like this," I whispered.

Police dogs ran beside the road, their collars attached to long wires. "Those dogs look like killers!" I murmured.

The truck just in front of us was allowed through the gate. Randy kept moving right behind him. Suddenly, whistles started blowing, the gate crashed before us, and two armed guards rushed to our open windows. We each had a machine gun at our throats. "Passport, bitte," barked the guard on Randy's side.

He fumbled in his breast pocket. His hands shook as he passed the document to the soldier. After studying the only passport we had between us the guard said, "Das ist nicht deine Frau."

"This certainly *is* my wife," Randy replied with dignity.

My heart stopped. I could feel the blood draining from my head. "O Lord, what if they keep me here?" I prayed silently.

The guard at Randy's side of the car asked if I had any identification, while the guard at my side held the gun to my head. Beads of perspiration trickled down my forehead. With trembling fingers I fumbled with the clasp of my purse. I almost burst into a hysterical laugh at the sight of my thumb shaking uncontrollably. Then the laugh in my throat turned to a sob at the realization of what was happening. My purse was now open, but I couldn't focus my tear-filled eyes to find my wallet. I wiped my eyes and struggled to compose myself. I drew out the wallet and opened it to my identification cards. The California license had my description. I handed it to the guard, who stomped off and disappeared into an office. After what seemed an interminable wait, he came out and returned my license to me. It had satisfied the guards. They told us to go back and enter Berlin from the other side.

Forty miles to go and the gas gauge was bobbing on "empty"!

That was the longest ride I can remember. We passed the inspection at the border without further incident, and entered West Berlin. It was like Christmas—lights, activity, people laughing and talking and walking with their heads high.

Our VW drank its fill of petrol—I'm sure we had driven on fumes and a prayer those last miles. We thanked God that we were safe in the free zone.

CHAPTER THIRTY-TWO

Kay and her husband, Dr. William Sloan, lived in Seattle where he had established a medical practice. Kay's health had never been good, but in the mid-'60s she became acutely ill with a liver condition.

She called mother almost every day just to have someone to talk to. She had many personal problems and she suffered from depression. I learned that when Kay would watch me singing on the Welk show she would sit and weep.

On one of our visits to their home, her husband asked us to take Kay home with us for a little change for her. We had her in our home for two months and she did show some improvement. We put her on a diet of fresh vegetable juices and natural foods. We tried hard to make her happy. But her condition deteriorated soon after she returned home. I have since wondered if perhaps she absorbed too much arsenic as a child, as I had.

I was with mother in her little mobile home when the call came that Kay had died. It was the day before Christmas. Mother and I both felt a mixture of grief and relief that Kay had been delivered from her suffering.

Randy, mother, and I flew to Seattle to be with her husband and their three sons, Steven, John (J.P.), and Michael. Even as she lay in the casket, I noticed her beautiful hands. She was still so lovely. Like mother, she had turned gray very young and did not color her hair. She seemed at peace at last, her violet eyes forever closed. Even harder to believe was the fact that her gentle voice had been stilled. I mentioned this to her husband and he said, "Kay's voice would soothe a wild beast." I thought he was speaking figuratively, but he said, "I've seen it happen. One time when we took the boys to the zoo, there was a lion roaring and pacing as though he wanted to burst out of the cage and attack us. Kay started talking gently to him and before long he had stopped roaring and was rubbing his mane against the bars."

We held the funeral in a beautiful chapel in Seattle. She was buried at Washelli cemetery and after the service we walked over icy snow to the grave site. A nurse who had taken care of Kay came to my side as I stood shivering, looking at the casket. "I wanted you to know that Kay told me, 'I'm at peace with God. I'm ready to go.' " I had thought she was, but this testimony reassured me even further and took much of the sadness out of that bleak winter day.

After two years of working with both the Girl Friends and the Welk show, I realized I couldn't keep up the pace, so I resigned from the quartet. This was a painful separation; we had worked together for nineteen years and were very fond of each other. The girls have been my foremost cheering squad. I have no fans more loyal than Betty Allan, Betty Noyes, Dorothy McCarty, and Dorothy Morton.

I used my extra time to help around the park. I love to work and be active physically. There's always much to be done and Randy welcomes the help.

One July afternoon in 1966 I set out with my bucket and scrub brush. I met Randy at the recreation hall. "Your dad didn't show up today," he said.

"That's strange. Did you call his apartment?"

"Not yet. I wouldn't want him to think we're checking up on him."

We went our separate ways, not too concerned about dad. But when he failed to show up the next day and didn't answer his telephone, Randy said, "I'm going to get into the car and drive around. Maybe I'll see his car somewhere."

I decided to work outside again. It was a beautiful day and I can't stay in unless indoor work is of great urgency. So while Randy was gone, I got into some old jeans and tied a brown silk scarf around my head. I sallied forth with rags and brushes to mop out the garbage area.

This is a walled-in partly-enclosed area near the recreation hall. As I was sweeping up a pile of dirt outside the building, a car drove slowly up to our entrance and turned in. I didn't recognize it, but I looked up and waved, assuming they had come to see someone who lived in our park.

The car stopped next to me.

A window rolled down and an elderly lady called out, "Is this the mobile home park that Norma Zimmer owns?"

"Yes, it is," I answered.

"Could we—does she ever come here? Could we ever see her?"

"Oh, yes, she's here," I replied with a smile.

As I smiled they recognized me. "Are—are *you* Norma Zimmer?"

"Yes, I am."

There was a slight pause, an embarrassed silence. Then the woman blurted, "Couldn't you afford to hire that done?"

I was almost too startled by the lady's question to give a sensible answer. People wonder why I work as hard as I do. The answer is simple. I like to work. I love giving concerts and being on the Lawrence Welk Show but I would really miss it if I could never don jeans and scarf and do physical work. I love to garden. Every year I plant vegetables around the studio where I do my painting. Randy and I both prefer natural foods, so I use organic fertilizers and always have a good garden.

I eagerly await the Jack La Lanne exercise program every morning. For years I have done a half-hour of calisthenics every day.

"I suppose so," I said to the lady. "But I enjoy doing it."

I have wondered since whether she thought all I ever do is sing—like the pampered lady in the nursery rhyme who "sits on a cushion and sews a fine seam and feeds upon strawberries, sugar, and cream."

I was still smiling and thinking about this when Randy drove up. He had been gone more than an hour. His face was serious.

"What's happened, Randy? Did you find him?"

Sadly Randy replied, "Yes, honey. I found him."

"Where is he?" I asked.

"I found him slumped over the steering wheel in his car. He was parked in the lot at Ralph's, a bag of groceries next to him."

"Is he—?"

"He's dead."

I was devastated. What a terrible way to die—alone, perhaps in pain. I went to my room and threw myself on the bed, sobbing. If only I could have been with him.

I learned that dad had probably been there a day and a half. He had been dead more than twenty-four hours. How he could have been there that long without being noticed remains a mystery. He had had a heart attack.

Mother accepted the news without a trace of emotion. No tears, no trembling of the jaw. She did say, "What a shame that he had to die like that." I felt she was glad he was out of her life.

Mother didn't want to go to the funeral. She finally went to please me. I tried to hold back the tears because I knew if I started to sob I wouldn't be able to stop. When a few tears squeezed past my swollen lids and trickled down my cheeks, mother leaned over and whispered to me, "I should have brought a towel," referring to the many times she had gone into her bathroom to get me a towel when she knew I was going to cry. Then she would toss it in my lap and say, "Now cry."

But mother shed no tears of her own for dad. She sat dry-eyed and hard-lipped through the service.

We buried him at Memory Gardens in La Habra. As I stood looking at the grave I hoped dad was in heaven. Since coming to California, he had become a student of the Bible. He had never told me he knew the Lord but I believed he did.

Mother made me promise her that when she died we wouldn't bury her in the same cemetery with dad.

Randy's mother died the same year. She had had a growth on her neck for many years and finally her friends had talked her into having it removed. It was malignant. The surgeon wasn't able to get all the cancer and it took her life. She had waited too long. Berdie had always been such a strong woman—it was hard to see her go that way.

Once again we returned to Washelli Cemetery to say good-bye to a loved one. Pop asked me to sing at the funeral. With great difficulty I sang "The Lord's Prayer." I have learned to hold back my emotions while singing. Then later, when I'm alone, I can let the tears come.

The years had healed many wounds. Berdie had finally accepted me, although I never felt she loved me as pop did. Many of her friends were great fans of Lawrence Welk and when I became the Champagne Lady, they were so excited that Berdie got excited too and was, I believe, even proud that I was a member of her family.

After dad's drunken tirade the night of that party, she had been cool to all of us for a long time. Yet the last years dad lived in Seattle, he had frequently visited Randy's folks, enjoying long discussions with Berdie about books. I think they grew to like each other.

I had forgiven Randy's mother for wanting pop to come to California to have our marriage annulled. I could understand how she felt. I not only had an alcoholic father and was very poor, but she was shocked that I was working in a nightclub at the time. She couldn't know that I was never comfortable in that environment and was working there only until I could get something better.

And dad and Randy had gotten along famously the last years. As they worked together around the park they grew quite fond of each other.

Christmas of 1966 we spent skiing in Aspen, Colorado. We took with us a small artificial tree which we set up in our rustic living room at the lodge. We skied every day for two weeks. Our gift to the boys that Christmas was a tiny portable TV and in the evenings all four of us huddled around that tiny four-by-five-inch screen. It was a novelty to us because we had gotten rid of our television set four years earlier. The boys had been watching it too much and didn't heed our warnings to limit themselves. The penalty had been as hard on Randy as on the boys, which seems often to be the case:

parents have to sacrifice to discipline their children!

Ron was now eighteen and Mark fifteen. Ron's interests had turned to girls. While before he had always hurried out to find Randy and see how he might be of help, now he would telephone after school from the home of a girl friend and let me know where he was and when he would be home.

I was a rather strict mother. I insisted on knowing where they were and with whom. When the drug problem became alarming in California, Ron was in senior high and Mark in junior high school. One day I sat down with the boys and told them I'd almost rather see them dead than to become addicted to drugs. I warned them that it was dangerous to experiment with any kind of drugs. Our boys obeyed and stayed clear of drugs, including alcohol and tobacco. A few times they would tell me about their acquaintances who used drugs. "Their folks don't even seem to care," they observed.

Both boys have thanked us for being strict parents.

CHAPTER THIRTY-THREE

Randy had had an increasing amount of trouble with his back ever since we had come to California and occasionally had chiropractic treatments.

One day Randy was doing some cement work in one of the patios in our park. He stretched out across the cement, his weight on his feet and his left hand while he worked the trowel with his right. In this awkward position, he pinched a nerve in his neck which bothered him for a long time.

On a lovely summer day, a lawyer friend and a few other buddies from La Habra invited Randy to go water skiing. He enjoyed the sport. In fact, he loves all sports. So he accepted, even though he hadn't had a great deal of experience on water skis.

The driver of the boat, seeing how well Randy was skiing and thinking he was more experienced than he really was, put the boat into a tight spin which sent Randy off at the end of the rope at an extremely high speed, maybe sixty miles an hour. Randy tensed up and fell, bouncing along on the surface of the water for several seconds, bruising his body as if the water had been asphalt.

Between the cement work and that fall, he developed terrific pain in his neck and right arm. The pain became worse and he lost the use of his arm. It became so difficult for him to walk that he ended up in bed. The muscles were atrophying in the right arm. He struggled to a neurosurgeon to be examined.

"We must operate immediately or you're going to lose the use of that arm," the doctor said.

Randy has never liked to take the opinion of only one doctor, so we went to a university medical center where they gave him an electric myelogram. They gave us their opinion, "Definitely, you're going to have to have your discs trimmed."

They made a leather brace for Randy that reached from the top of his head down to his waist. It took several weeks to have it made and when it was completed, Randy wore it for a few hours at a time. It gave him some relief but I knew he could never become reconciled to wearing a brace the rest of his life.

The doctor said, "Now, Randy, I want to operate and do to your back what the brace is doing for you. But it will leave you with only 20 percent movement of the neck."

Randy winced. That would mean no more sports—the end of his water-and snow-skiing. He wouldn't be able to do his work around the park. "Oh, I don't want to have that done," he said. "I want to think about it."

The doctor consented and Randy came home, dejected.

Perhaps it was the tension of having Randy in such pain. It may have been the restless nights I spent wondering what to do for him. After one of those sleepless nights, I wearily started to stretch. My entire right side was numb! I touched my right cheek with my left hand, but I could feel nothing. I was terrified.

I made my way to the mirror. Staring at myself, I poked at my face and body. I felt as if large doses of novocaine had been injected into the right side of my face, arms, side, and leg. Awkwardly, I dressed to go to work. I kept waiting for the numbness to leave, but it remained day after day. I didn't want to worry Randy, so I didn't mention it to him.

Rose Weiss kept scolding me. "Go to a doctor!" But I was sure it would leave. It was just the tension and worry over Randy, I reasoned. I didn't have time to go to a hospital—they'd probably put me in traction. I gave it to God and prayed constantly.

Finally, when it showed no improvement, I confessed my trouble to Randy. He sent me packing to our family doctor that same day. He could find nothing wrong. After a thorough examination, he gave me some tranquilizers and told me to get more rest.

I brought the pills home, looked at them for a moment and decided I didn't want to go that route. I put them away in the cupboard and continued to pray, claiming God's promises to those who place their trust in him.

We were having a Sunday morning breakfast at the park recreation hall and one of our guests approached me. "I'd like to visit with Randy. I think he can be helped." I took him to where Randy was lying, gray with pain. "Randy, I was telling my doctor about you this week. He's a chiropractor," he said.

Randy replied, "Well, they haven't been able to help me this time. I've been to three different chiropractors."

"Dr. Antonson would like to come up and take a look at you. He uses the Palmer method. He's really helped a lot of tough cases."

We let Dr. Antonson come to see Randy. The doctor was a quiet and unassuming person. His wife, Lee, who came with him, was one of the sweetest women I'd ever talked with. He urged Randy to come to see him in his office at Long Beach.

"Let's try it, honey," I urged. "You can't go on like this." I took Randy in the next day. It was a clean, modest little office—as humble as the doctor.

Sitting still for the series of x-rays was excruciating for Randy. After he finished, Dr. Antonson patted Randy's shoulder and said, "Well, how do you feel now?"

"What do you mean 'How do I feel now?' Not so good!"

The doctor laughed and said he'd have the x-rays developed and then take another set after we'd had some lunch.

An hour later Randy had more x-rays. "I'll have to study these," the doctor said. "So if you want to come back tomorrow, I'll give you an adjustment."

I wrote him a check for the $100 fee.

As we drove home, Randy said, "Oh, I don't know if I want to go back tomorrow. I don't know about this doctor. He doesn't seem to be too confident."

"But, Randy," I argued, "I've already paid him for the x-rays. You really might as well get the adjustment. Try it, honey."

The next day Dr. Antonson showed us the x-rays. "You can see that the atlas is squeezed from one side. The atlas and axis are at the top of your spine and if everything's in place there the rest of the spine can operate."

He put Randy on a little table. Carefully he adjusted him. "Bang!" The pain left Randy's body! He got up and was absolutely free of that problem from that day on.

I never touched the pills the doctor had given me for my numbness. When Randy received such astounding results from Dr. Antonson, I too went through the x-ray routine. After two adjustments the numbness completely left me. Now we go each month for treatments.

Strength was gradually coming back into Randy's arm. When-

ever he got a slight twinge, he went back immediately for an adjustment.

Praise God for directing us to the right man.

CHAPTER THIRTY-FOUR

Since singing in the Portland Crusade I've been invited to appear in practically all of the Graham crusades that have been held in the United States. Dortmund, Germany, is the only crusade overseas that I have participated in. It was beamed into ten different countries. There were interpreters in small booths near the platform. Huge Eidophor screens measuring sixty by seventy-five feet were set up in large auditoriums in each of these ten countries. As the crusade was being televised live in Dortmund, vast audiences in other countries could observe the proceedings by watching the Eidophors. The interpreters' voices were fed in on loudspeakers.

They had one of the huge screens set up in Trondheim, Norway, my father's ancestral home. When I was introduced it was explained that my father's family came from Trondheim. I was told the people there stood up and applauded. Every night when I got up to sing, the people in Norway gave me a standing ovation.

My singing style shocked the staid Germans. They protested to Billy, "She smiles when she sings. She shouldn't smile—"

Billy later told me, "I said, 'That's Norma. That's her style. If she didn't smile and use her hands she couldn't sing. She should be allowed to sing naturally.' "

When Billy told me of this he added, "I told them that I was going to preach my way too. They'd been telling me how to preach and I told them I'll be preaching the way I always have."

I have never gotten used to the thrill of seeing people—especially the young people—come forward at a crusade. I can't keep back the tears as they stream forward to inquire or make their decisions for Christ.

When Randy and I were invited to Dortmund, we asked Ron if he would like to go ahead for six weeks of skiing. Our friend Jan Branger owned a ski resort in Davos, Switzerland, where Ron could visit. He accepted with an excited, "Yippee!"

We ordered a Volkswagen, which he could pick up when he arrived. He would drive to several ski areas, then join us in Dortmund.

Ron came for the last nights of the crusade. He had never looked happier. His body was muscular and hard after the weeks of strenuous activity. He was greeted enthusiastically by the Billy Graham Team members; we had great times of fellowship over meals.

Randy and Ron took turns driving the light blue VW south through France to Spain. We enjoyed our closeness and listened to Ron describe the thrilling experiences he had encountered on his long skiing adventure.

Whenever we cautioned Ron as he was growing up, his constant reply would be, "Don't worry about it!" Here on the trip we heard the familiar refrain again and again as Randy cautioned him to, "Be careful of that car," "Watch out for the traffic circle," "Don't pass here," "How's the gas?" To each remark or question Ron would reply, "*Don't worry* about it."

Tiring of cool weather, we chose to visit the Isle of Majorca. Pop had mentioned Palma hundreds of times, so we were looking forward to a relaxing warm time in the sun. From Barcelona, a magnificent rambling city, we took an overnight ship to Palma. We tried to share pop's enthusiasm for this city, but it was too crowded. People swarmed on the sidewalks. Streets were crammed with honking cars and buses. We were jostled about as we stopped to eat in a sidewalk cafe crowded with people.

"Let's drive to the other side of the island," Randy suggested.

"Fine with me!" Ron agreed.

It was like traveling through southern California as we drove to the east coast through orange groves, vineyards, and palm-lined roads.

We found an impressive hotel at Cala Ratjada. Each of the spacious rooms had balconies overlooking the Mediterranean Sea. We opened the carved doors of our room to gasp at the dark, hand-carved furniture, tile floors, hand-woven bedspreads, and colorful throw rugs. These rooms with three delicious meals a day cost only $4.25 each!

We spent a week basking on the warm sands, sightseeing and touring along the winding seacoast. Randy and I were to drive back to Frankfurt to ship the car home, and Ron was to leave from the modern airport at Palma.

At the beginning of the trip we had given Ron a generous amount and had told him to budget himself because that was *all* he would get! But now his finances were at a low ebb. As we checked him in at the baggage counter he said, "I don't want to be bothered carrying one thing on with me."

"You'll be over weight, Ron. It'll cost you," Randy cautioned.

"I don't care—I'm going to send it all."

"OK—you go ahead," Randy said, taking my arm and leading me away to admire the exhibits located several hundred feet away.

We stood looking at model cars and local artifacts for some time.

"*Mom*!" came a familiar voice.

We looked back at the baggage counter to see Ron beckoning urgently to us. We started back—and as we approached he called, "I need $12 for overweight!"

Randy stopped short, turned on his heels, and called back over his shoulder, "*Don't worry about it*!"

CHAPTER THIRTY-FIVE

On my way to work one morning, I stopped at the park office to see the mail. Mother was collecting rents. The tenants—or our park family, as they prefer to be called—would be coming in to pay their rents and have the donuts and coffee we provided each month.

Today mother greeted me with, "Tessa asked me to go along to Escondido tomorrow."

"To see Lawrence Welk's park?"

"Yes."

"Oh, mother, that's marvelous."

"I don't really want to go."

"You don't? Oh, mom, it will do you good. You stick so close to the park all the time—"

I had opened one of the letters and was most interested in something a woman had written, "You do something on television I have never seen anyone else do! When the camera takes a close-up of you, you are actually looking very lovingly at me! That sounds a bit far out—whoever listens and watches as you sing must get the feeling you are singing for that person only, and it is delightful. Who are you actually looking at that can bring that beautiful expression to your eyes? Don't ever stop, as I think it is one of your many charms."

"Mother, read this," I said, handing it to her. "It's interesting she should say that."

Mother read it, then looked up. "You've always said that you feel you are looking right into the eyes of each person in your audience."

"Yes. And praying, 'God bless you, God bless you.' "

"Isn't it nice to get a letter like that and know that's just the way it comes across."

"It certainly is! Well, I've got to go to work. Mother, I do think you should go to Escondido. You need a day off."

Mother went with five ladies. I soon regretted it.

The woman who drove made an illegal left turn onto Highway 395 in the center of Escondido. A car coming at fifty miles an hour crashed into them, and the woman sitting next to mother was thrown against her, crushing mother against the left side of the car. All of the women had to be carried out of the car except mother, who stepped out by herself, saying, "I'm all right. I can walk."

Instead of putting her in the ambulance, they took her to the hospital in the police car. From the hospital, mother called me, assuring me she was all right. "I could have come right home," she said. "I could have walked home, Norma."

Later she didn't even remember that call, as she went into shock. We learned that she had broken her pelvis and bruised her heart.

I drove the hundred miles to Escondido every day except show day. Usually Randy was able to go with me.

After two months, mother came home but she never regained her strength. I nursed her, and did her cooking and cleaning, but she gradually went downhill.

The doctor told us she wouldn't live long; there were too many internal injuries. She always believed she would get well, and she fought bravely.

Ever since dad's death, mother had been trying to prepare me for the time when she, too, would die. "Now, Norma," she would say, "when I die, don't mourn for me like you did for your father. I'm ready to go. You've given me many years of happiness. I've had a good life since I came here. Be happy for me when I go." But I loved her too much. I couldn't bear the thought of losing her.

One of the high points of my life is the Sacred Music Festival in Birmingham, Alabama, at which I have been invited to sing many times.

For four nights at Thanksgiving time, thousands gather to sing the old familiar hymns to the accompaniment of the Birmingham Symphony Orchestra conducted by a dear friend, Amerigo Morino, with whom I worked years ago at CBS studios in Hollywood. The Birmingham Civic Chorus, directed by Hugh Thomas, stirs the souls of the audience with their special numbers. Bill Mann, a superlative singer and song leader, acts as master of ceremonies. When those thousands raise their voices in songs they learned at their mothers' knees, one really feels the presence of the Spirit.

One great experience I had in Birmingham was to visit the Third Presbyterian Church. It was built by a pastor named Brother Bryan, for whom the city has erected a statue high on a hill at a place called Prayer Point. This is intended for those who want a place to meditate. Brother Bryan, I have read, walked the streets, looking for anyone in need. He would stop street fights by kneeling down to pray. If he found someone in need of a coat, he gave him his. He visited the sick, the flop houses, and jails. He had a large family to provide for and preached to a faithful congregation for years. Everyone in town knew him and loved him.

I had wanted to visit there and I made a point of saying so in an interview in the *Birmingham News* in 1970. An invitation followed swiftly. The next Sunday I went to the church to sing a couple of songs and then listen to the sermon. But when the minister introduced me he said, "Now here is Norma to sing for you and I'm not going to preach a sermon. Today, I'll let *her* give the sermon!"

I was shocked! I had only recently been the shyest person you might ever meet and I am still a woman of few words. Randy had helped me overcome my shyness to some extent—as had my audiences who have received me so kindly—but to give a *sermon*!

As I stepped forward to the pulpit I caught the expression of pure shock that was still on Randy's face. If anyone knew how unqualified I was for that instant sermon, Randy did. But here I was—on the spot!

First I sang a few songs as I prayed for words to say in my "sermon." Randy really gaped at me as I "preached." Only the Lord knows what I said, because I gave him my voice and told him to take over. I got through it and was surprisingly calm.

God really does answer prayer when you want to serve him.

CHAPTER THIRTY-SIX

For years we have taken our vacations and free days to rush to Soap Lake in Washington, where we own an apartment complex which formerly belonged to pop.

The work Randy has put into that place is overwhelming. He put a new roof over the "L"-shaped one-story building, adding a ranch-style porch that gives blessed shade in summer. Every old wooden window has been replaced with aluminum storm windows. Two coats of stucco in a warm shade of adobe cover the exterior. Every apartment has been remodeled—new bathrooms, new sinks and counters in the kitchens. He's torn out old walls, refinished ceilings, painted, re-plastered. Dirty hard work!

We keep one of the apartments for ourselves. To this he added a beautiful living room, with beamed ceiling, rich paneling, and a large used-brick fireplace which he and Jim built.

My contribution was to antique all the furniture, dozens of pieces. It's a miracle, the transformation that takes place when a coat of paint and antiquing gloss is applied to a drab chest or desk. I don't sew, but I struggle to reupholster chairs.

Randy tore out all the old planting, put new rich earth in the yard, and landscaped the entire place to look like something out of a gardener's magazine.

Each time we go there we promise ourselves we'll take two hours each afternoon for swimming and skiing, but if we get two hours a week we're lucky.

We love the people there. Randy's father homesteaded at Soap Lake many years ago. Most of the friends we have there have been friends of the Zimmers for two generations.

We're members of the Evangelicial Free Church in Soap Lake. Our pastor, Robert DeViney, and his wife, Esther, are loving and understanding people. Pastor Bob has a beautiful singing voice. One year as I gave a concert to raise money for our kitchen fund, Pastor joined me in a duet. It was the hit of the evening!

Ever since we bought the building, a sweet smiling lady, Mrs. Schragg, has lived next door to our unit. "Doc" York lives with his wife, Esta, in one of the redecorated apartments. He's a masseur and has an office as part of the health spa. After a hot Soap Lake bath, "Doc" gives a fantastic massage—the best I've ever had. Mr. and Mrs. Sullivan are always on hand to greet us when we arrive.

Bob and Delores Nacke live only a few hundred feet from us and have two precious children, Robin and Robert. Often they call us over to share a barbecue on their gorgeous, tree-filled lawn with its magnificent view of the lake. Bob's hobby is gardening. Daily they bring armloads of produce to share with us.

Next to our apartments stands the house where Arline was born. It is now occupied by dear friends, Pearl and Grace Woollard. Their daughter-in-law, Lil Nelson, and her son Wayne come to visit us each time we're there.

Among our dear friends at Soap Lake were Russell and Mary Beth Thomas. Russell had gone there twenty years earlier to treat his Buerger's disease in the mineral waters of the lake, and had later become county sheriff. Mary Beth is the postmistress. Through them we met Joe and Gladys Theusen, two of the warmest people we've ever known. Both Joe and Russell used to come around to help Randy when he was working on the apartments.

The three of them often talked of taking a trip up the Columbia River—Russell was especially persistent about bringing up the subject.

We finally decided the year had come to do it. Each couple had a boat. Ours was a nineteen-foot California with a 150-horse merc. cruiser, which we brought up to Soap Lake each year for water-skiing. It was white with turquoise leather interior. Russell and Mary Beth had a twenty-foot boat and Joe and Gladys owned a twenty-one-footer. The Theusens invited their friend Amber Lingenfelter to come along. She's been a friend of the Zimmer family for years.

Russell wasn't feeling well that summer. He suffered from stomach cramps. "Are you sure you can do it?" we asked him.

"Positive! Even if it kills me trying," he said.

Early in the morning we put our boats on the river just above the Grand Coulee Dam in Roosevelt Lake. For a hundred miles or so in that huge reservoir we traveled through beautiful desert country. No trees, just sagebrush, hills and wheat fields, with farmhouses in the distance. Sometimes cliffs of lava rock rose abruptly at the edge of the water.

At noon we went ashore and ate the first of our many sumptuous meals. We girls had baked hams and turkeys in advance and had them on ice. Now we brought out our delicious breads and cheeses, carrots, celery, fresh fruits, and fruit juices and spread all the delicious food out for a lakeside picnic. Afterwards, Randy and I slipped into the shallow warm water for a refreshing swim.

That afternoon we hit white water. Joe Theusen had worked on the river a great deal as a patrol and he knew just how the water would fall over the rocks and where to take our boats. Going up the river was treacherous. We went mile after mile in the tumbling white water, following Joe closely. We longed to take pictures, but when it was calm there was really nothing exciting to photograph, and when it was rough we were too busy to take pictures! The trip was thrilling but risky.

At times it was difficult to make headway in the rushing torrent. Often the boats nearly came to a standstill even though we were gunning the engines. We were grateful when we would move ahead, yard by yard. That night, we picnicked on the banks of the river, enjoying the wonderful fellowship of these dear friends. We sang hymns as we watched the sun go down over the water. Exhausted, we fell asleep on our comfortable boats.

After a hearty breakfast on the shore we proceeded up the river. Smoke began to permeate the air. We were in a forested area and some folks coming downstream warned us, "There are forest fires ahead. It's pretty bad up there." We began to wonder if we'd be able to find a place to camp, but we prayed that the Lord would let us complete this trip which we had dreamed of for so long.

We came to a dock where a little sea plane was parked. A sign said, "Castlegar." Hoping to gas up, we stopped. No one was in sight, but we found a sign which read, "Go up these stairs, turn right, go two blocks, and you'll see a house with a picket fence and a rose arbor—"

It was easy to find the house. A friendly gentleman greeted us and walked back to the station with us. "You've been up the river before, haven't you?" he asked, peering closely at me and glancing at the others in our party.

"No, this is the first time," Randy answered.

The man looked at me again, so I echoed what Randy had said. "No, this is our first time. It's something we've always wanted to do, though."

"You sure look familiar," he said. Then, looking back and forth between my face and the gas can, he said, "You aren't on television, by any chance, are you?"

"Yes," I smiled.

"You're Norma Zimmer!"

"Yes, I am, but I don't know how in the world you recognized me, looking like this!"

"Well, I'll be darned! I was thinking all along that I had seen you somewhere. Well, well, you'll have to come up to the house to meet my wife." He set down the can. "I'm Art Anderson; you come on back to the house and be our guests."

Art not only introduced us to his wife, Maggie, but he telephoned his entire family to come and meet us. We had a good meal together while cameras were kept busy snapping photos.

"You've got some rough rapids ahead of you now for a piece," Art said. "There's a big dam, and then the forest fires. You won't be able to camp along the river, I'm sure. Tell you what—Maggie and I will go ahead and open up our summer home. We'll take our car and drive up to meet you above the dam; then you can follow us to our place by boat." So they closed up their business and drove up to meet us.

It was very exciting going through the locks. The dam was a sixty-foot drop. Tangles of driftwood and debris had accumulated in the locks, causing our boats to be bumped around. We worried about their being damaged. We had to hang onto ropes attached to the high cement sidings in order to keep the boats still.

When the water had reached the level of the lake above, the gate opened and we met the Andersons just outside the locks. Forming a procession, with Randy and me at the rear, we skimmed over the blue water and soon arrived at Art's and Maggie's summer home.

At one time it had been high on a hill overlooking the Columbia River, but when the lake was formed it rose and became their front yard. We all tied up at their dock. The house had been built of timbers from some old bridges that had torn apart on the river. It was a charming home, artistically furnished with antiques. There was a huge fireplace. A small guest house stood nearby. They prepared a marvelous barbecued dinner and insisted on giving Randy and me their bed. When we objected they said, "No, we want to be able to say, 'Norma Zimmer slept here.' "

They gave Russell and Mary Beth the second bedroom in the cabin and Joe, Gladys, and Amber the guest house. The Andersons slept on a hide-a-bed couch in the living room.

Next morning we learned that Russell hadn't been able to sleep. Mary Beth had been up with him most of the night, trying to make him comfortable. He was subdued and quiet and we were concerned about him. This was the trip of his dreams but he wasn't able to enjoy it fully.

We took leave of the Andersons and navigated more white water until we got to Nacusp, where we docked and purchased gas from another friendly Canadian, named Brown. Mary Beth told him she needed to take her sick husband up the hill to the hospital. Mr. Brown obligingly offered to drive them. Randy had to buy shoes, so he and I walked through the small, neat town in search of a men's store. He had left his shoes on a log after stopping for lunch and had been going barefoot ever since.

The Thomases came smiling happily. The doctor had said he couldn't find anything seriously wrong. He had given Russell some tranquilizers and stomach medicine and already Russ was feeling some relief. "Ever onward," he said cheerfully. "Let's move on toward Rebelstoke this afternoon."

In high spirits we headed north until the sinking sun cast a golden glow over the wooded countryside. Joe led the way to a sheltered cove, a perfect campsite, where we prepared our evening meal. Russell stayed aboard his boat, assuring us he wasn't hungry. After we had finished dinner Mary Beth left to console her husband, but returned immediately, her pretty face tense with concern. "We've got to go back to the hospital," she urged. "Russ's pain is unbearable."

Hurriedly we packed and returned to Nacusp. Mr. Brown again came to our aid by whisking the Thomases to the hospital.

As we tried to sleep that night, a rap against the side of the boat brought us out of our sleeping bags.

"They've ordered an ambulance to take Russ back to Spokane," Mary Beth told us quickly. "They're afraid it's a twisted intestine. I'm going with him. We'll just have to leave our boat here."

"God be with you," Randy said, putting his arms around her, trying to comfort her. We all hugged each other and said good-bye.

We didn't sleep the rest of the night. Nights had always been so friendly, but now we were all fearful and tense.

Dawn came at last and we stood around the beach with the Theusens, talking about what we should do. "If we leave Russell's boat here, it will mean we'll have to drive up to get it, 600 miles round trip."

As I listened, I asked the Lord for guidance. "I haven't had much experience on a boat, Lord. Could I make this trip?" I knew it was dangerous, and all the experience I had had driving a boat was when Randy skied.

As I stood there praying, I received assurance that I could do it, so I announced to the others, "I'll take the boat back."

"Oh, honey," Randy frowned, "that's too dangerous."

Joe agreed. "Norma, it will be more dangerous going back than coming up. Remember the river is flowing seventeen miles an hour and you're going forty, so you'll be going down the rapids sixty to sixty-five miles an hour on that treacherous water."

My own heart was so quiet, so still. I assured them that I believed God would protect me and Randy finally gave his consent. "You always end up at home," he laughed. This was a little private joke between us, and we smiled at each other as we recalled the first time Randy had said those words to me. It was a night when I came from work in Hollywood very late in a thick fog. Visibility was almost zero in the low places. I crawled along trying to follow the car just ahead of me. Sometimes the fog was so thick I couldn't even see the taillights. It was impossible to see the road so I'd slow almost to a stop, praying that no one would crash into me. At one time I followed a car right up into a private driveway and had to find my way back onto the street again. When after hours on the road I finally got home, I hurried into the house expecting Randy to be pacing the floor. He had gone to bed and was fast asleep!

"Oh, Randy!" I cried, "You haven't even been worrying about me! I was in *terrible* danger and here you are asleep!"

He opened his eyes and grinned, then murmured sleepily, "Oh, honey, you always end up at home."

It was 300 miles back to Soap Lake. Randy insisted we wear wet suits under our clothes—"Just in case we get dumped in the river," he said.

"Now you stay at least 200 feet behind me," Joe warned. He would go first, and I would follow him. We decided since I knew our boat better than Thomases' I would take it and Randy would come behind me with Russell's boat. "Stay back far enough so that if I have any trouble you won't crash into me," Joe warned. "And be sure to stay to the far left when we come out of the locks. The water is flowing over the dam at full capacity and it could easily crush you or plunge you into the rocks at the bottom of the dam."

We started out. I kept my eyes glued on Joe. When he made a turn, I'd try to follow him exactly. We arrived at the dam and entered the locks. It was a frightening experience. Driftwood bumped and banged into our boats. Whirlpools of water churned under us making it hard to hang onto the ropes. It seemed to take an eternity for the water to lower. Then as the huge doors opened, we moved out of the locks, the water churning wildly, creating vast sprays. I followed Joe out as closely as I dared, then looked around to see if Randy was coming.

He was leaning over the back of the boat, apparently struggling with the propeller. He began to run back and forth between the steering wheel and the back of the boat. I could see that the boiling water seemed to be pulling him over toward the dam. Bobbing crazily and moving steadily toward the huge swirling waves of water as they headed for the rocks at the bottom of the dam, Randy's boat was being pulled into the maelstrom.

"What's wrong? O God, help him!" I prayed, desperately afraid. If he capsized, it would be impossible to reach him. I screamed to Joe, but he had already sized up the situation and had started back. I tried to gun my motor, and the prow of our boat went into the air. In my excitement I had pushed the button that controlled the inboard-outboard engine, causing the prop to rise out of the water. I had no control of the boat. For a moment I panicked as I felt the current drawing me too toward the rocks. The spray in my face made it hard to see. I forced myself to think calmly: I must check the button that regulated the pitch of the engines. Relief swept over me as I felt the buzz of the propeller being moved back down into the water. Once more I was in control of my boat.

Suddenly Randy ran back to the driver's seat. Ever so slowly, his boat began to move toward us, away from the danger. "Thank you, Lord!" I found I was sobbing it aloud, over and over.

Joe swung near us, beckoning us to follow him out of the treacherous water. We went a short distance before we came to a sandy beach with shade trees. With shaky knees I climbed out of the boat and stumbled onto the beach. Randy arrived, soaking wet and shivering. I clung to him as I thanked God for helping us through that terrible experience.

"What happened back there, Randy? Oh, honey, I was so worried about you."

"I had a four-foot branch caught in the prop. It's just lucky I had Russ's boat or I'da been a goner. He has a lock on the wheel so I could lock it and go to the back and try to work that thing loose from the prop."

"I saw you running back and forth."

"It seemed like a mile from one end of the boat to the other!"

Joe joined us. "Say, you were really in trouble back there, man!"

Again, Randy explained about the propeller and we rejoiced together that the frightening episode was over and we were all safe.

Joe smiled at me, "Norma, you're getting to be quite a river rat. You piloted that little boat like an old sailor."

"Well, I just followed you, Joe."

"You sure did," Randy laughed. "When Joe would jerk his wheel, you'd jerk yours. When he'd do like this, you'd do like this." He pantomimed my performance. We were all laughing now, free of the tensions of the last few hours.

I said, "Quite seriously, I could feel God in that boat with me, his hand on my hands. It was like the painting of Jesus standing behind the pilot. The only time I was scared was when Randy was in trouble."

After that, nothing on the river could frighten me.

At Castlegar, we informed Maggie and Art of Russell's illness. They suggested we call Spokane. Gratefully we made connections with the army hospital only to be told that Russell had died. Later, an autopsy revealed it had been his gall bladder. We realized now what terrible agony our dear friend had suffered.

Sadly we returned to Soap Lake. Mary Beth asked me to sing Russell's favorite song, "How Great Thou Art," at his funeral. She reminded us that Russ had died doing something he had dreamed of for years. And now he was with God.

Through the years all the Zimmers have been grateful that in 1936 pop sponsored Lielo Rennebaum, a German girl. She came to live with the Zimmer family and helped Randy and Arline with their vegetable juice business in the Seattle Public Market. They had a cheerful booth with bar stools where customers could order a variety of juices. Later, a fire destroyed the market and with it Randy's and Arline's business; Lielo returned to Germany to make plans to stay in America. While there, she joined the Red Cross and fell in love with a German soldier. They married and had a child, then her husband was killed in World War II. When she returned to this country she brought her little son, Fritz, with her.

Lielo moved to Soap Lake where she went to work at Don's, an excellent restaurant that has seafoods shipped in by air and serves the most wonderful Crab Louis and lobster. This eatery is the pride of the little town. Lielo bought a home overlooking the lake and worked hard to support herself and raise her fine son. She was always available and ready to help any of the Zimmers in times of illness and sorrow.

Lielo love pop like her own father. When pop was seventy-five years old he began to develop an alfalfa ranch high on the hills overlooking Soap Lake. He bought a rock picker and tractor, and did all the work himself. Often Lielo would cook delicious German meals to bring to him while he labored long hours. I believe Lielo is the most thoughtful and generous woman I've ever known.

Part of the time pop lived in an apartment in Seattle.

Early one morning in 1969, Randy got a frantic call from the manager of the apartment house where pop lived. "We found your father unconscious this morning. He was lying in front of an open window. It was raining in and he was soaked."

Randy flew up to be with him. Lielo came from Soap Lake to help and suggested they bring him there. "He'll get well quicker east of the mountains," she insisted.

They took him by ambulance, still unconscious, over the mountains. As he entered the clear desert air of eastern Washington, pop regained consciousness. He perked up so rapidly that in two weeks he made a trip to New York.

Shortly after his return from the East, he had a slight stroke. He was eighty-seven at this time and we felt we should move him closer to us. So we purchased a mobile home for him and he came to live with us in Park La Habra.

He walked about the park with a cane, always reminding me of a little Hummel figure. When he tired of his walks, he paused to visit on the patios of the other tenants. He was always full of fun and everyone loved him. He had a wealth of funny stories and jokes and I never once heard him repeat himself. Probably because he was bald, pop always wore a jaunty little straw hat with a colored band. On cool days, he would wear a poplin jacket, seldom bothering to put the collar down. He always wore bright cotton shirts and nicely pressed slacks.

CHAPTER THIRTY-SEVEN

It was August 14, 1970, Ron's wedding day. Ron was being married to Candice Mathews, a beautiful, charming girl, and six hundred friends and relatives gathered in the First United Methodist Church of Costa Mesa to witness the beautiful ceremony. Mark was Ron's best man and Randy and I felt proud of our tall, handsome sons as they stood together at the altar in their black tuxes. They were surrounded by Candi's attendants, in gowns of lavender taffeta overlaid by white net. Candi's white satin wedding gown glowed with pearl embroidery and her veil was held in place by a crown of pearls. Her beauty was truly breathtaking.

The wedding had been saddened by a terrible tragedy two days earlier. Kristine Thomas, Candi's maid of honor, had been in a car accident. Candi placed a huge bouquet of yellow roses near the altar in her friend's memory. No one took her place.

As I listened to Ron and Candi taking their vows, I prayed very hard for them. I prayed too that I would be a good mother-in-law. I welcomed having a daughter, and I loved Candi and hoped she and I would always be good friends.

Knowing that Randy's mother had felt I wasn't good enough for him had cast a shadow across my relationship with her. Now I was the mother-in-law. I vowed that nothing I would ever do would come between Candi and me. How thankful I was that they had gone foward hand in hand to confess Christ at the Billy Graham Crusade in Anaheim in 1969. I prayed that God would bless them, guide them, and give them his peace.

Because Ron was troubled with psoriasis—so badly, in fact, that it had prevented him from being in the armed services—Randy and I offered them the opportunity to live at Soap Lake in our cozy little apartment. They agreed and spent the first year of their marriage there. Ron worked in the post office and as a volunteer fireman and Candi commuted to Big Bend College in Moses Lake where she took nurse's training. Every day Ron took advantage of the mud and water of Soap Lake and soaked up a lot of sun. In a few months his psoriasis had cleared up and has never returned.

About a year later Randy and I loaned our home as a honeymoon hideaway to Paul MacLeod and his bride Kathy Bowlin, friends from Soap Lake. The phone rang one day, as they sat enjoying a cup of coffee in our living room. Kathy jumped up to answer.

From the other end came a woman's pleasant voice.

"This is Debbie Sloan from the White House."

Kathy laughed, "The White House! Who are you kidding? Who is this?"

"This is the White House calling for Norma Zimmer. Is she there?"

Kathy suddenly realized it was for real.

"A-a-no, but I'll have her call you. May I have your phone number, please?"

She was given all the information, and immediately got the message to me.

At first I thought *she* was kidding. Why would I be getting a call from the White House?

I dialed the number, feeling a sensation of unreality as I heard the buzz I knew was sounding in an office at our president's home.

When they answered I asked to speak to Debbie Sloan. She informed me that President Nixon wanted me to sing for a Sunday-morning worship service. Randy and Mark were also invited. Someone must have investigated us, as they knew that Mark was still living at home. We would be the President's guests at the Hay Adams Hotel and would be met at the airport by an official limousine.

I stuttered an acceptance and placed the phone back in its cradle. I sat there in shock, trying to grasp the importance of the invitation. Me—the Larsen family runt—being asked to sing for President Nixon! I shook my head; this couldn't be happening to me. How did they know me? Did President and Mrs. Nixon watch the Lawrence Welk Show? Maybe it was through Billy Graham? What an honor! Oh, I had to run to tell mom, Randy, and Mark.

I couldn't find Randy. Mark was working at Disneyland. I bounded up mom's steps. She was sitting on her couch paging through a new home magazine. I told her the news. Her shocked face made me burst into my famous, not-so-ladylike laugh. We sat together chattering as fast as we could about what I would wear, what song to sing, how would it feel, what a privilege and honor it was. I couldn't wait to tell Randy and Mark.

They finally came home and their smiles showed how thrilled they were!

"I'll wear my navy suit—with a red, white, and blue tie!" Mark exclaimed.

"Guess I'll wear the dark brown suit," Randy decided. My choice was a pink silk suit with matching shoes, a delicate scarf, and a pearl necklace. I decided to sing my favorite song, "The Lord's Prayer," and the beautiful old hymn "Only Believe."

We began to count the days until the appointed time in September. As a rule I sleep like a log, but the excitement and anticipation made me awaken several times each night. I began to worry that the loss of sleep would affect my voice and cause bags under my eyes. I prayed for rest and a calm heart.

The big day arrived! Mom stood proudly on her front porch, waving good-bye as we drove out of the park. Usually she hated to see us leave, but not this time. She was just as pleased as we were.

A White House limousine was waiting to pick us up at Dulles Airport. The chauffeur graciously gave us a tour of the Washington Monument, the Pentagon, the Lincoln Memorial, and the Capitol. Mark was impressed especially with the Lincoln Memorial. The huge sculptured figure of Mr. Lincoln seemed to be alive, the expression on the face had such patience and understanding. "It's eerie," Mark whispered. "He seems to be looking at us."

Reservations had been made for us at the Hay Adams Hotel across the park from the White House. We arrived at sunset and were shown to our elegant rooms. They were glowing in the reddish rays of the sun. Heavy draperies hung at the immense, high rounded window that looked out across the park to the lighted White House. We stood at the window transfixed—the sight would be indelibly recorded in our memory.

"Let's go for a walk," Randy suggested.

"Swell," Mark said. "I can't wait to walk around the famous memorials and see the sights."

I wanted to stay in our room and meditate. I had brought my dogeared Bible, and was anxious to read and pray to prepare myself for this wonderful experience. Performing always gives me butterflies and already my stomach felt a bit shaky. The realization that I would be singing for the President of the United States kept overwhelming me. I knelt to pray—imploring God to let my singing glorify him—not myself.

That night I was too excited to sleep. We got up early and went to breakfast in the hotel restaurant. While we were at the table I said to Randy, "Oh, honey, you need a shave."

"I know," he said, rubbing his chin. "I'll shave when I get upstairs."

We were going to be called for in one of the White House cars. I went upstairs and got into my pink silk suit, put on my makeup, and got my hair just right. I was so excited I could hardly stand it.

We were running a little late. The limousine was due and we should have been down in the lobby. I gave one final pat to my hair and we scurried down and were driven to the back entrance of the White House. A guard at the gate asked for our identification, and while we were waiting to be given our clearance, I glanced at Randy. He had forgotten to shave! Here we were, guests of President and Mrs. Richard Nixon, and in the excitement Randy had come with a day's growth of stubby beard.

I didn't say anything. What could he do now? I felt it would only embarrass him and make him miserable to call it to his attention. It was too late—there was nothing we could do.

Just as we drove up to the door of the White House, Randy's hand flew to his face, and with a look of shock he groaned, "Oh, no! Norma, I forgot to shave!"

I said, "I know, honey. I just noticed it but wasn't going to say anything. I didn't want to upset you."

We were met by Debbie Sloan. She seemed so kind that we told her our problem and she assured us, "We'll take care of that." She took Randy up to a little room used by the Secret Service. There he was given a small black shaving kit.

He returned a few minutes later, ruddy and smiling. He reminded me that not too long ago someone had tried to bomb the White House. "When I was coming downstairs just now with that little black package I felt like shouting all the way, 'It's just a shaver. It's just a shaver!' "

We were invited to look around the first floor. It was exciting to see the famous rooms I'd read about. I practiced in the East Room where I would be singing. After the rehearsal we were all brought up to the Oval Room. We were greeted warmly by Ruth and Billy Graham, who were there with two of their children, and Billy's mother. Dr. Ben Haden, who was to give the message, was there with his wife.

Soon President and Mrs. Nixon entered. Mrs. Nixon came over and put her arms around me, saying, "Norma, I've always wanted to meet you. I've admired you so much all these years. We enjoy the Lawrence Welk Show."

President Nixon was gracious and cordial. "You're from my old stomping grounds—La Habra and Whittier," he reminded us. He talked to Mark about Fullerton College where he was enrolled. The Nixons' friendly manner put us all at ease.

A delicious brunch was served—fruit juice, scrambled eggs, rolls, and coffee. As the time drew near for the service to begin, the President said, "I know you would like some pictures. We'll send for the photographer." Our family posed with the Nixons—then it was time for the worship service.

I sang with all my heart—while looking out prayerfully over the audience which included many officials who carried great burdens of responsibility in government. How I wanted to minister faith and encouragement to them all.

Of all the honors I have ever received, this was the highest. I'm happy that mother lived to see me invited to the White House. She had never expressed much pride in my accomplishments. Her attitude was one of disinterest in my career—perhaps it was a reaction to dad's pressuring us to "make something of ourselves." But this invitation to sing for President Nixon made mother extremely proud and happy. She would sit in her little mobile home with tears in her eyes and say, "I have to pinch myself to see if I'm dreaming. My own daughter sang for a president in the White House!"

CHAPTER THIRTY-EIGHT

Randy and I had enjoyed our regular morning cup of coffee with mother. As we left her little home, he to work about the park, and I to answer fan mail, I said, "Mother didn't look at all well this morning. Did you notice how her mouth drooped? I thought her eyes looked strange, didn't you? So much larger."

A few days later, Randy admitted that he had promised mother not to tell me that he had found her slumped over at her sink the afternoon before I had noticed a change in her.

"Oh, Randy," I said. "We mustn't lose any time getting mother to Dr. Kraushaar." Pop had been greatly helped by medication for thinning the blood, and I felt if mother was starting to have little strokes we shouldn't delay getting help for her.

Mother didn't object to seeing the doctor but when he said, "Mrs. Larsen, I'd like to put you in the hospital for tests. It would be only a few days," mother looked at me with the most troubled expression on her face. "Oh," she said, "I don't want to go to the hospital."

"Mom," I said, "it's only for some tests. Don't you think you should help the doctor try to learn what he can about your condition?" Finally I persuaded her to enter the hospital four miles from our house.

I visited her every day except the day I was taping the Welk show. Randy adored mother and we often drove up together to visit her.

Mother looked so beautiful when we'd come to see her. She always wore a little makeup and one of her pretty bedjackets. She would brush through her shiny gray hair and let it lie gleaming softly against the pillows. When we would come in, her violet eyes would brighten a bit. The nurses enjoyed her and often took their breaks in her room so they could chat with her. She was always good company.

Seven days went by and it seemed mother was growing weaker. She admitted that the tests were hard on her and made her tired. On the day I had to tape the Welk show I didn't plan to go see mother, so I telephoned her room early in the morning. There was no answer, so I waited a few minutes and tried again. This time a nurse answered.

I said, "This is Mrs. Larsen's daughter, Norma. I was just calling to see how mother is and I didn't get an answer."

"No, well, she became ill during the night."

A shock went through my body.

The day nurse didn't know much about it, so I decided to call Dr. Kraushaar. My fingers trembled as I dialed.

He said, "Your mother became unconscious during the night,

and when I left her she had not regained consciousness. We don't know yet what the trouble is."

I hung up and threw myself on the bed. "O God, why didn't they call me?" Fear and rage and sorrow boiled together in my heart. And I felt so guilty. I had talked mother into going into the hospital when she really didn't want to go. I wondered if the tests had been too much for her.

I called the studio to say I couldn't come and rushed to the hospital.

Mother was in the intensive care unit. A monitor recorded her heartbeat. Even as a layman I could see it was dangerously irregular. I moved to her side. Her beautiful hands lay across her chest. Gently I slipped mine into hers.

"Mom, can you hear me?" I whispered. Her lids fluttered. I bent down to kiss her cheek.

"Mom, it's Norma." I fought to hold back the tears. I mustn't let my voice quaver—I had to make her feel secure.

"Mom, I'm here—you're going to be fine. Can you hear me mother?"

Her fingers pressed mine.

"Hi, sweetheart—oh, I love you. I'm so glad you can hear me," I whispered into her ear.

Again she gripped my hand. Then she withdrew her right hand and lovingly patted mine. A slight smile showed on her lips.

I was encouraged.

"I love you, mother. You're going to be all right; I'll take care of you."

I couldn't hold the tears back.

"I'll be right back," I assured her, as I hurried out of the room to find Dr. Kraushaar.

"I want to have mother moved to the La Habra Hospital," I told him. "It's only two minutes from our home; that way I could spend more time with her."

He finally consented and we moved mom by ambulance to the La Habra intensive care unit.

Five minutes out of every hour was all that the family members could be with her. We took turns every hour for two days. She squeezed my hand only once again. Before my eyes, I could see her failing. I took her in my arms, kissed her and said, "Mother, I commit you to the Lord."

I had just arrived home when I was called back. Mother had gone to her heavenly home.

I was heartbroken. She had been my mainstay for the many years she had lived with us. She had helped Randy and me raise our family. She was always sympathetic and loving. I had lost the best friend I have ever had.

Mom was gone but my mind couldn't comprehend it. Many mornings Randy and I automatically headed for her mobile home for our cup of coffee, a habit formed over many years. Then grief would wash over me again at the realization that she wasn't there! If we had not had God to lean on, it would have been much harder to get through those weeks of adjustment.

Two months had passed since she had left us. It was unbelievable that she was gone. We had enjoyed her company in our home for nearly twenty-five years.

I had a deep longing to return to the farm in Idaho.

"Randy," I said one night. "Let's drive up to Idaho." I had two precious weeks off.

Randy looked at me, waiting for a reason.

"I would like to walk around the farm where mom lived so many years—and wouldn't it be nice to visit some of the relatives—"

"And ski Schweitzer Basin," Randy suggested.

"Aunt Vi and mom's brother, Uncle Bill, and his son—"

"Bill, Jr.—"

"Yes. He and Doreen—we can have such Christian fellowship with them. We've never seen their children."

"Let's see. Bill's got girls, hasn't he? Two of 'em?"

"Yes. And Uncle Bill is postmaster at Mullan—"

"How about your Larsen relatives? Wouldn't you like to see Bill and Nancy in Selah, Washington?"

"I'd love it! Let's make this a visiting trip," I bubbled. "I'd like to stop the first night and stay with Eva, Iver, and Cousin Karen—they're always so much fun to be with."

How long will it take you to get—"

"I'm ready."

"OK. Let's pack the car and go."

We drove leisurely north through California on Highway 99, then east on 97. Mt. Shasta loomed up like a monstrous ice cream sundae, visible for miles, ever-changing as we approached and then passed it.

Oregon highways are straight swaths cut through the abundant pine groves. We drove in silence as we so often do, overwhelmed once again by the beauty of God's wonderful world.

The sign "Entering Washington" was the only clue that we were leaving Oregon. In Spokane we visited with cousin Elma and her husband Ralph Sacco. They owned a busy printing shop. We accepted their hospitality for a night in their comfortable home.

The next morning, we went into Idaho. Highway 10 went through Coeur D'Alene, a beautiful city situated on a huge lake surrounded by verdant hills. A few miles farther the despoiled countryside illustrated the tragic results of the pollutants emitted from the mines and smelters.

I read the signs of towns I had heard of all my life: Kellogg, Wallace, and then *Mullan*. Here mom had walked to school or skied in winter. She had spoken of a horse-drawn wagon or a school bus that transported the children from the little community of Larson where grandfather's dairy had been. The train ran in front of the farm, and a water tank in the green valley was about the only existing structure other than a group of farmhouses. There was no city, not even a hamlet, but three miles east of Mullan, on a signpost placed beside the track, in big black letters it said "LARSON." This was all that remained to show where I was born.

When we drove up the valley on a narrow asphalt road, I noticed the mountains rising gently behind the meadows. Just off the road ahead was a huge barn—and a small log cabin!

"That's it, honey," I cried.

"Yup! Just like Bill said," Randy agreed.

We pulled off the road. I sat silently viewing the farmland. Blades of green were shooting up where heavy snows had covered the earth only a short time before. Already buttercups peeped at us. Various tiny wild flowers grew in profusion everywhere. A small creek gurgled aimlessly through the acreage.

I slid out of the car and stood breathing in the fresh spring air. "Mom might have stood right here," I mused. "She looked at these mountains and hiked right up there."

I studied the hills. Memories of her girlhood, as she had related them, came back to me. "She raced the new autos atop her frisky mare on this very road. She waded over these gray and white stones on the creekbed."

The log cabin now stood at a slight tilt—weathered wood, with windows only about two feet square—dusty from years of neglect.

Randy went toward the barn and I moved toward the quaint little cabin. I crossed the threshold and stared at the interior. The faded paper on the walls was intact. There was an old stove, small and rusty. I pictured a bed, curtains, rag rugs, and flowers—yes, mother could have made this into a cozy home.

Suddenly I wasn't alone. Through a doorway ambled a chestnut mare! I walked toward the curious visitor. My log cabin had been converted into a stable!

Randy was calling to me. "This old barn could still be used!" he said.

I hurried across the barnyard and joined him.

"Grampa was so proud of his big cattle barn," I reminisced.

"The farmhouse must have been here," Randy said, pointing to a foundation. The big family home had burned down.

"Let's go inside the barn, honey," I coaxed. "Mom and her friends used to have contests in here to see who could stand the smell the longest. She always won because she loved the earthy smells of the cows," I laughed.

The interior was splendid. Hay was scattered everywhere. A sturdy ladder led to the hayloft. I climbed up and sat in the soft fragrant hay. Sun filtered through holes in the roof. I could imagine children and teen-agers of mother's day playing up here—perhaps having programs and vaudeville acts.

Randy said, "That would make a good picture," and he brought out the Leica. I posed for two photos, then made my way down the ladder and out of the huge building.

We spent a couple of hours strolling around the property. Somehow I felt nearer to mom here than I had anywhere since her death. As we pulled away from mom's childhood home and my own birthplace, I couldn't hold back the tears. But they were healing tears. I had been in touch with my roots and that touch helped to wipe away the bitterness of separation and bereavement.

CHAPTER THIRTY-NINE

It became steadily more difficult for pop to walk or get in and out of a car, so I began to stay at home and watch television with him on Sunday mornings.

We watched the Hour of Power with Dr. Robert Schuller of Garden Grove, California. One Sunday, Dr. Schuller began to describe how wonderful it was to have Christ in your life. I was deeply moved and as Dr. Schuller went on telling of the peace and joy one receives when he accepts Christ as his own personal Savior, I stole a glance at pop. Tears were streaming down his face.

He sat that way for some time, his chest heaving with sobs. Then he turned to me and said joyfully, "I found the Lord. I found the Lord."

That week, I wrote to Dr. Schuller. "My father-in-law, who is ninety years old, received Christ last Sunday as a result of your invitation. Thank you, Dr. Schuller, for presenting such a beautiful Christ-centered service for the television audience."

Immediately there came back a letter of appreciation for my note and with it an invitation to sing at a fund-raising banquet they were having at the Disneyland Hotel.

I accepted gladly. Shortly after that Dr. Schuller's wife, Arvella, called me to ask if I would sing on an "Hour of Power" broadcast. Happily, I agreed. When I arrived at 9 o'clock for makeup I was pleased to find Charlie Blackman there as makeup man. We have worked together on the Billy Graham telecasts for years. The organist, Richard Unfried, was an excellent accompanist and it thrilled my soul to sit and listen to the choir. Dr. Schuller's message was exciting and after the service he invited me to his study for coffee. He asked if I could sing every week for the telecast but I had to refuse his invitation because of my many other weekend concerts all over the United States. But I agreed to sing on the "Hour of Power" one Sunday a month and have done so now for five years.

We had buried mother in the Forest Lawn Cemetery in Cypress in January. At Easter I was invited to sing at the Forest Lawn-Cypress Sunrise Service.

Through the years I have been able to keep rigid control over my emotions while singing for an audience. I knew this day would be the supreme test of that discipline.

Randy and I arrived in the darkness and made our way forward to the seats reserved for us. After bowing my head for prayer, I looked at the program. The top part of the front cover was dark purple in the shape of clouds. The bottom inch showed a hill with three crosses in the background and in the foreground Christ stood with his arms extended.

I opened it and began to read. Bob Ralston, a good friend from the Lawrence Welk Show, was the organist. He nodded to us now from the organ where he sat.

Promptly at 5:30, Bob started to play. Then the Western High School a capella choir of Anaheim sang "Sanctus," by Norden.

By now it was starting to get light. I'll never forget how my scalp prickled when five hundred doves were released to circle the amphitheater. They circled three times then flew off into the east. It seemed to me they did indeed symbolize the Holy Spirit, for at that moment the presence of God became very real in that place.

The congregation and choir burst into the great hymn "Christ the Lord Is Risen Today. Alleluia!" followed by the invocation and choral response.

It was getting quite light when I rose to sing. I had chosen "In the End of the Sabbath," by Oley Speaks. Bob accompanied me. I prayed that God would still my emotions and help me to sing for his glory. I looked into the eyes of my audience and prayed, "God bless you; God bless you." Peace came into my own heart and I felt quite calm. I started softly:

> In the end of the Sabbath,
> As it began to dawn,
> Came Mary Magdalena and the other Mary

To see the sepulchre...
To see the sepulchre...
As it began to dawn.

I was singing as quietly as I could. My audience seemed hushed and moved. Together we stood at Christ's grave as it began to dawn in Cypress. The volume grew slightly:

And behold there was a great earthquake.
And behold there was a great earthquake,
For the angel of the Lord descended from heaven
And came and rolled back the stone from the door
and sat upon it.
His countenance was like lightning
And his raiment white as snow;
And for fear of him the keepers did shake
And became as dead men.
And the angel answered
And said unto the women,
"Fear not ye, fear not ye,
For I know that ye seek Jesus,
Which was crucified.
Fear not ye, fear not ye,
For I know that ye seek Jesus,
Which was crucified.
He is not here, for he is risen.
He is not here, he is not here."

With a great fortissimo, I reiterated the angel's words:

"Fear not ye, fear not ye,
For he is risen, is risen. Fear *not*!"

I held that note. The sun was coming up. I put all I had into that last line, and with all my heart I rang out the message, "*He is risen*!"

On that high, loud cry of victory the sun burst over the horizon in full splendor. I tingled with the conviction of that greatest truth in all the world. Never had words I sang ministered so powerfully to my own heart.

I stood in my own personal triumph over Christ's grave—and mother's.

CHAPTER FORTY

Sacred concerts have become the most satisfying segment of my career. Phyllis Chetakian, a vivacious blonde pianist whom I met through the Garden Grove Community Church, works and travels with me occasionally as my accompanist. She and her husband, Ed, and their daughters Pam and Lori joined Randy and me in Colorado one summer in the early '70s to perform for the POW and MIA families, who were invited by James Irwin to a mountain retreat. Randy and Ed enjoyed talking to some of the men about the means of communication they used in their prison cells—tapping out Morse code messages to one another, learning each other's names, sharing memorized passages of Scripture.

Many of my concerts are arranged for me by Cy Jackson, a dear Christian friend and a representative of Word Records. It was through a concert set up by Cy at Mount Hermon in central California that we met two people who were to become our very dear friends, Everett and Marcy Tigner. I first saw Everett standing near a display of my albums. He held one in his hand, saying to the people milling about, "Get your records now! They're going fast—get 'em while they last."

His voice had a chuckling quality of joy and the smile on his handsome face was one of the warmest I've ever seen.

After the concert, Cy and his wife, Vera, introduced us to the Tigners. Everett's wife, Marcy, possessed a gorgeous smile too and when she spoke she had a pixie, childlike, lyrical voice. It was no surprise to learn she was Marcy of "Little Marcy" Christian records for children. Everett, we learned, was a salesman for Tyndale House. He lost no time in presenting Randy and me with a copy of *The Living Bible.* Our friendship blossomed from our first meeting. Cy and Vera and Everett and Marcy all live only a few miles from us, in one of Randy's new mobile home developments, Lake Park La Habra, so we enjoy frequent times of fellowship.

After a year in Soap Lake, Ron and Candi moved to Park La Habra and Ron took over as manager.

It was a blessing for me to have them in the park, for while they were living there, pop became very sick. Candi, Ron, Randy, and I nursed him by turns day and night. I thought it was so good of them to share the responsibility of nursing him through those long nights.

One of pop's best friends, with whom he had chatted many a sunny afternoon as he had paused to rest on her patio, was Tina Thomsen, a tiny Danish lady who had a gift of loving everyone with tenderness and understanding. As pop weakened, she spent much time preparing his meals, visiting with him, and helping us care for him whenever she could.

Finally, pop got to the place where we couldn't take care of him any more. He needed constant attention as his mind suffered from the many years of hardening of the arteries. Sadly, we took him to the Basler Convalescent Hospital in Fullerton. There he received excellent care.

One morning two months later, he called to his favorite nurse. His eyes were dancing with anticipation. With a lovely smile on his face he said, "I'm going home. Today I'm going away." And then he died.

We had services for him at a local mortuary, then drove up to Seattle for the burial. We laid him beside Berdie at Washelli on his ninety-first birthday.

Now all four of our parents were dead—and all who have lost their parents will understand that no matter how "grown-up" and independent we are, the loss of father and mother leaves an empty place that stubbornly refuses to be filled.

CHAPTER FORTY-ONE

Life in the park became too confining for Ron and Candi. There were too many rules for a young couple—no pets, no loud noise after ten, quiet until 8 A.M. They had done a fine job, but they wanted freedom to have cats and dogs and play loud music on their beautiful new stereo.

We were happy for them when they found a small, comfortable house in Yucca Valley, although we missed them. From the large windows they had a magnificent view of beautiful Mount San Gorgonio and behind their house were expanses of scenic trails where they could ride their trail bikes to their hearts' content. Since childhood Ron had dreamed of becoming a fireman and he was excited when he got a job with the fire department in Yucca Valley.

I remember the day they told us we were going to be grandparents. Randy and I were both excited. I recalled that when our children were born Randy's parents didn't want to be called grandma and grandpa, so I was delighted that Randy was awaiting our grandchild with as much excitement as I was.

I was deeply touched when the Lennon sisters, Tanya Welk, and Ralna Hovis gave Candi the most delightful shower I've ever attended. They had invited all my friends from the Welk show as well as Candi's relatives and friends. The girls served a delicious luncheon in Tanya's garden, which had been specially decorated in a yellow and white motif. A unique feature of this shower was that the hostesses gave me a special "grandma's gift"—a playpen and high chair!

I hoped the baby would be a girl. I felt the same hunger for a little girl that had caused me to weep when the doctor had advised us not to have any more children after Mark was born.

Candi was to go to Palm Springs to the hospital when the baby was due. On July 16, Ron called. "Well, you have your granddaughter!"

A shout went up from both Randy and me because at last we were going to have a sweet feminine little darling with pink skirts and ruffled pinafores.

I had to go to work that day, so I didn't get to see Candi and our little granddaughter until her second day. I was so excited that it took me a long time to find the entrance to the maternity section. When I did get inside, I had to wait for several minutes at the information desk. Finally I just went up to a nurse and said, "Help me! I want to see my grandchild and daughter-in-law!"

Candi heard my voice and came quickly down the hall to meet me. "Oh, hi, Norma." She looked marvelous. She took me at once to the window to see the baby, whom they had decided to name Kristen Leigh.

There she was—way back in a corner—my own little granddaughter. She was so sweet, but still somewhat shriveled. I couldn't see any resemblance to our boys or to any members of our families— with the exception of pop. Yes, she resembled Randy's father.

How do you describe the feelings that flood over you as you stand and look at your grandchild? The emotion is almost indescribable. The love that flows to that tiny bit of humanity! I stood there and just thanked the Lord that he gave us a sweet little girl, so perfectly formed. Every tiny limb and feature was there and in place. She seemed to be in perfect condition. We were so grateful to God.

As I stood looking at her I wondered what path the Lord would choose for her and I thought, "How can I help to bring her to an early knowledge of Jesus?" I wanted to be sure that she would find Christ early in her life and not have to wade through years of loneliness as I had. I wanted to impart to her the same love for Christ that gives warmth and direction to my life.

I was working regularly, so the next time I saw Kristen she was a week old and at home with her parents. I drove to Yucca Valley, taking with me Lielo Rennebaum and my Aunt Eva and Uncle Ivar, who had come to live in our park, much to our delight.

Candi had made a lovely nursery for Kristen, all in yellow. The needlepoint picture of a tea party which I had labored to make hung above her bed. I could see plenty of evidence that Kristen's other grandparents, Joyce and Leigh, were also delighted to have this precious grandchild. Already little Kristen's shelves were lined with stuffed toys and dolls.

We took turns holding the baby and Candi let me give her a bottle. I was overwhelmed with joy. I noticed that her head was a little larger than seemed normal, but even that reminded me of pop. I didn't mention it to Candi, for fear she would think I was criticizing anything about Kristen.

But Candi, having had nurse's training, and being naturally a very sharp person, had also noticed, and was watching the head for growth. The fontanelle—the soft spot—had begun to show a slight bulge.

When Kristen was two and a half weeks old Candi took her to the doctor and called me the same day.

"Dr. Edalatpour says there's definitely fluid on the brain and they have to operate."

I kept myself from crying out in my anxiety. I wanted to be sure to catch every word Candi was saying.

She went on, "It's dangerous. She'll have to wear a shunt from her head to her stomach to drain off the fluid—"

The thought of this tiny baby being put through this ordeal made me shut my eyes and shake my head. O dear God, why did this have to happen? Two perfectly healthy young people, such perfect specimens—Ron whose nutrition has always been so carefully planned—and vivacious, healthy Candi. Neither of them had ever experienced ill health. Why, God, *why*? My cheeks were wet with tears.

Then I checked my frightened thoughts, and prayed, "Lord, you promise in your Word that you will keep in perfect peace the person whose mind is stayed on you. Please keep my mind—our minds—on you, Lord. I put our little girl in your hands, Father. I know your will is best."

For a moment I considered all that "his will" might involve for our baby. We might lose her.

Candi was saying, "They said she might...be retarded."

I marveled at Candi. She was being so brave, so mature. Everything in me rebelled at the thought of Kristen's being retarded. No! I fought against it. Then the Lord's comforting words came to me from 1 Peter 4:12, "Dear friends, don't be bewildered or surprised when you go through the fiery trials ahead, for this is no strange unusual thing that is going to happen to you." My soul responded, "God, you can work miracles. Help this baby to overcome this problem. Give us the strength to go through it."

I learned from Candi that Kristen would have the operation as soon as possible.

We encouraged each other and said good-bye. I let the tears flow for a while, then raised my head high and squared my shoulders. "Well," I thought, "we can ride out this storm too. God doesn't promise us all ease." Then right on top of that I thought, "But why a tiny baby? Why couldn't he test us some other way than in this newborn child?" So I argued with myself and God.

They took Kristen to Hogue Memorial Hospital in Costa Mesa, anticipating surgery right away. On the days we weren't able to drive there to see her, Candi informed us by phone of what was being done.

"They aren't able to shunt her because of a significant amount of blood in the spinal fluid which would plug up the shunt," she said. This condition prevented them from performing this operation until Kristen was eight and a half weeks old. Then they finally shunted her out of desperation, fearful of brain damage.

We were all so thankful when that frightening surgery had been done. Afterwards, the doctors again warned Ron and Candi that Kristen might be retarded. "They said perhaps we should put her in an institution where we wouldn't get so attached to her because it would get more difficult as the years go by to keep her at home," Candi told us. "But I said, 'Absolutely not! If God hadn't thought we could handle this child he wouldn't have given her to us.' "

Ron said, "We'll take her home and love her."

The doctors said they would have to live within minutes of the hospital if they were to take her home, because if the shunt clogged up she would have to have immediate attention. So, while Kristen was in the hospital, Ron and Candi broke up housekeeping in Yucca Valley. Ron quit his job as fireman there and they moved to an apartment within walking distance of the hospital where Kristen became the darling of all the hospital staff.

Ron and Candi brought her home to their apartment after a few weeks, but it was not to be for long.

At five and a half months Kristen was a smiling, happy baby. The shunt appeared to be working well. She showed absolutely no signs of retardation, for which we were all grateful.

Then one day Candi noticed a swelling in Kristen's little tummy. Her heart fell at the sight and feel of that lump. She rushed Kristen to her pediatrician, Dr. David Kagnoff, and called us the same day. "He says there's definitely a growth there. They're going to operate."

Surgery was done the same day. It was found to be a malignant mass within the kidney, a Wilm's tumor, primarily found in children. They had to remove the kidney.

For the next six months Kristen was examined every few weeks by three doctors: Kagnoff, pediatrician; Edalatpour, neurosurgeon; and Sheehy, cancer specialist.

Kristen had her first birthday. No more lumps had appeared to indicate the presence of malignant masses. We were rejoicing once more over answered prayer.

Ron and Candi went on vacation and when they returned they took Kristen in for a checkup. In August another mass showed up.

On the eighth of August, Kristen once again submitted to surgery. This time they couldn't remove the mass. "It's infiltrated the other organs and tissues around it—it's no longer encapsulated. It's metastasized," Candi and Ron were told.

Chemotherapy was begun right away. Radiation started in September. One day when I called Candi she said the doctors didn't know what had happened. "She had an ultra-sound—" she paused to explain. "You know the sonar they use—on battleships?"

"Ye-es," I answered, not sure what it was, but having a vague idea.

"Well, the ultra-sound is much the same. Anyway, she had an ultra-sound done and it showed up several masses."

The doctors now believed Kristen to be full of cancer. They stopped the therapy as her platelets had dropped to 10,000. Candi said 50,000 was the point where the doctors became watchful; normal was around 100,000 to 150,000.

The platelets, Candi told me, are the clotting factor in the blood. Kristen's were so low that she could have a massive hemorrhage at any moment. The slightest blow on her head, for example, could kill her.

Kristen's abdomen became severely distended. The doctors believed she had cancer throughout her body. Thirty blood transfusions over a period of a few months failed to bring up her platelet count.

CHAPTER FORTY-TWO

In September 1974, when Kristen was fourteen months old, I sang for a religious broadcasters' banquet. Clinton Fowler, president of KGER, which I listen to a great deal, invited me to sing at the banquet at the International Hotel at Inglewood, a gathering of 400 people. Between numbers I shared with the group about Kristen's condition, and asked for their prayers.

The next day Mr. Fowler called me. "We were all touched by your account of Kristen's illness—her struggle. I would like to start a prayer chain for her around the world."

I was overwhelmed. Mr. Fowler taped a half-hour interview with me in which we talked about Kristen and in between he played sacred songs taken from my albums. He made a cassette tape of the interview and songs, which he sent to broadcasters around the world, asking for prayer for my little grandchild.

Letters began to pour in from far and wide, saying, "We're praying for Kristen."

Thanksgiving was approaching. How we were praying for our little granddaughter. One day Candi called. "Kristen's abdomen is starting to go down." It went down steadily. When it was normal, Dr. Sheehy couldn't feel any masses at all. "That doesn't mean there aren't any," he explained. "There could be masses in, or floating free behind, organs where I can't feel them."

Candi called me when the doctors agreed they could take Kristen home. Her platelets had not come back up. They hoped she would live to go home as the doctors didn't believe she would live to see the next year. "They say it will be easier on us and on her if she can die at home," Candi told me.

Candi was terrified of the responsibility. She had an active one-year-old whose blood platelets were so low she could die at any moment from a bump. The doctors called Kristen a tiger, as her natural vitality never left her for long.

For her first sixteen months, Kristen had spent much of her time in the hospital. Fortunately Ron had taken out health insurance which covered a great deal of the expense, and the Crippled Children's Society had helped. We're so thankful for the good work of that organization.

Through all the surgery and poking and probing, Kristen maintained the most wonderful disposition. I thanked God for every day we might have her.

The first of the year came and Kristen was still with us. She began to improve.

I believe God had a different plan and I really do believe it was the power of prayer that brought Kristen through. Thousands of people must have prayed for her and I believe God prolonged her life.

She is a delightfully happy little girl—superbly adjusted in spite of all the pain and suffering she has endured. The doctors had warned that she would be retarded, yet she is an unusually intelligent child, with understanding that constantly amazes all of us. I sometimes wonder what she might have been if Ron and Candi had heeded the doctors' advice to put her in an institution—if they hadn't listened to their hearts. No doubt institutionalization is the right course for some invalid children, but we are convinced that Kristen belonged in her own home, with her own parents. I'm grateful to God for his grace to us—and grateful to medical science too. All over the country there have been praying friends who have interceded with the Lord for Kristen, and we want to use the pages of this book as a way to thank all of those who have prayed for her.

Chemotherapy has a tendency to take away Kristen's natural resistance to disease. It's difficult to have her around other children, because if they're carrying any germs, Kristen is susceptible to them. It's hard to give her a normal life. Here, Candi and Ron just apply good common sense and try to find a happy balance. If her friends appear free of colds or illness, Candi lets Kristen play with them as normally as possible. Although strenuous play has been discouraged, because of danger to the shunt, it is nearly impossible to prevent this lively little toddler from the running, climbing, and other boisterous activities all three-year-olds enjoy. One of her favorite toys is her hobby horse, which she rides vigorously.

Candi considers herself honored to have been trusted with Kristen's fragile little life. At first she brooded about the possibility of losing her, but now she thinks more about Kristen's living than dying. She has continued her nurse's training, preparing herself for a useful profession, so that if she should lose Kristen she will have an ongoing life. She says she hopes she will be able to help others who suffer. She's learning compassion and patience which will make it possible for her to comfort others in times of sickness and death.

Kristen's illness hasn't made her any less likely to get into scrapes than any other child of her age. One day Candi called me on the telephone to report on Kristen's latest escapade. Between giggles, she described the scene, "She just gave the cat a shower! No kidding—she held the poor cat under the shower and turned the water on."

I chuckled. "Did she take her own clothes off?"

"Oh, no, no, no. She said she was giving the kitty a shower and she was taking one too. There was water from one end of the bathroom to the other. She hadn't closed the shower door, of course... Sometimes I don't know about her!" Then her voice grew tender and proud. "She's such a neat little kid. So fantastic. We may not always have her—I know statistics for her chances of recovery are very bad. We just have to be prepared to let God have her. But then, she was on loan anyway. If he wants to take her back..."

A good reminder for all of us. This little one, like all of our children, is on loan from God—to be held lightly, and committed to his wise and loving care.

CHAPTER FORTY-THREE

In the summer of 1974, Randy and I were in Milwaukee, where at Bob and Jane Henley's request I had done a concert at a huge religious rally.

Randy and I love to hike. The home we stayed in was in a pleasant neighborhood with winding streets, so we decided to take a walk. I guess we had walked for about five miles when we had to stop because Randy's foot began to hurt—most unusual for that active sportsman.

When we returned to the house Randy remarked that his right big toe was becoming very sore and that he thought his shoe sole had buckled. We examined the shoe but found nothing wrong. The next day his toe was worse and he felt as though there were lumps in his foot.

Our time in Milwaukee was over, so we went on to Soap Lake for a little vacation while Randy made some repairs to our property there. The pain had now spread into his right knee. Each day it continued to spread further—into his other foot and knee, then into his hands and wrists, hips, shoulders, and neck. Randy consulted a doctor in Soap Lake who told him he had gout and prescribed butazolidin. He continued to work around our place, but his condition worsened so much that we decided to return to La Habra for further medical attention.

By the time he arrived home he was barely recognizable. His face was gray and drawn with pain, and he could hardly climb the stairs to our house. It had been only two weeks since the onset of the illness, but it was as if he had aged ten years. He insisted on trying to work around the park, hoping that any day he would begin to feel better, but the pain was too severe.

Our park manager, Mike Hurd, was concerned, and urged us to consult his father-in-law, Dr. Rutherford. We followed his suggestion and Dr. Rutherford put Randy in the La Habra Hospital, where he underwent tests and x-rays. Other doctors were called in for consultation. The tentative diagnosis was rheumatoid arthritis. After two weeks they sent Randy home on crutches, barely able to walk. In just a month, this strong, athletic man had been reduced to an invalid, almost entirely unable to care for himself.

The pain was relentless, never letting up night or day. He could no longer sleep on the mattress nor stand the weight of even a sheet on his feet. I had to pull him to the bathroom on a large towel, and he helped as much as he could. He would try to sleep on the couch, but usually he'd be awake through the night watching television. As we talked with other arthritics during these terrible months, we learned that this inability to get sleep at night is one of the most trying circumstances of arthritis.

Life as well as show business must go on. Randy was at home in great pain and I was driving the Pomona Freeway on my way to the ABC Studios to rehearse and tape the Lawrence Welk Show, a regular Tuesday activity. I was to sing Irving Berlin's "Always" in that performance. How would I ever get through that song without breaking down?

As the words went through my mind, the tears welled up in my eyes and my throat thickened. Morning traffic was slowing down on the freeway. As I pulled slowly along, one car length at a time, I meditated and prayed. My mind went to all the wonderful people I work with: the band members, the singers, the art director and stage managers, the director and cameramen, the conductors and backstage people. As they paraded through my thoughts I asked God to bless each one. I asked him to help me be a blessing to them as we worked together.

But I was praying mostly for Randy and that I would be able to get through the day.

The night before, I had prepared fruits, vegetables, and yogurt for Randy's lunch. A container of drinking water was right next to the couch where he lay in the living room. Mark had put a long cord on the phone so Randy could reach it easily.

But no physical activity was easy for Randy. Every move he made brought perspiration to his face. One day when he tried to move the pain had made him faint.

Traffic was moving right along now as I drove to work. I turned off on Silver Lake Boulevard and drove through city streets to Prospect and Talmadge. I turned right and drove to the parking lot. The guard at the gate called out a cheery, "Good morning, Norma."

I parked and ran into the studio. Before anything else I called Randy. No matter how much pain he had, Randy was always cheerful. "Oh, I'm getting along just fine. Don't worry about me."

But I did worry. From my little dressing room, I ran down to Mr. Welk's office. His secretary, Lois Lamont, gave me her usual friendly smile. Mr. Welk stood up when I entered. "Good morning, Norma. How are you today?" He put a fatherly arm around me. Looking searchingly into my eyes, he questioned me gently, "How's Randy this morning?"

He was the first of many concerned people that day to ask me that question. Over and over I had to tell of how Randy was suffering. Each time, the knife in my own heart seemed to go a little deeper. How I wished I could stay with him. That day I had to sing, "Days may not be fair, always. That's when I'll be there, always." But Randy needed me today and I *wasn't* there.

When he first got sick we hadn't imagined it would last this long or get this bad. Now I was seriously thinking of trying to get some time off from the Welk show. Thankfully, I remembered the wonderful people who lived in our mobile home park, women like Helen Benton, Helen Hunt, and Nettie Prater, our neighbors, who looked in on Randy and helped him when he needed it.

I raced downstairs. It was 9:55 and rehearsal was to start at 10:00. I nodded to Chuck Koon, the art director. "You did it again, Chuck. That's lovely. I still marvel at the beautiful sets you create out of a few shrubs and painted boards."

"How's Randy?"

"Oh, Chuck, he's in so much pain."

Jack Immel explained the routines we would be doing and we ran through the first number.

An hour had gone by and Randy was so much on my mind I just had to call him again. "Honey? Do you wish I'd quit bothering you?"

"Oh, no. That's all right. I'm glad you called."

"I hope you weren't sleeping, but I just had to call you. Have you everything you need?"

"Sure. Mark brought me some apple juice before he left for work. I might be able to catch a little sleep now."

"All right, sweetheart. I won't bother you until lunch break. Are the pain pills helping you?"

"Some. Yes, I think I'll be able to sleep a while now."

"You didn't get much rest last night."

"You didn't either."

"No, but I'm fine, really. I'll call you at lunch time."

"Just let it ring. It may take me a while."

"I know."

I went to the dressing room. Rose Weiss was at her desk, supervising the wardrobe. I slipped into the peach chiffon and satin gown she held out to me. Gertrude Spangler was right there measuring for possible alterations. "You've lost weight since last week," she chided gently.

"I tend to skip meals when Randy's in so much pain."

She gave me a gentle frown.

On my way to the dressing room Charlotte Harris and I shared, I bumped into Jim Hobson, our producer-director. He asked about Randy and again I felt close to tears as I described Randy's painful maneuvering. We had sailed on the ocean with Jim and his wife, Elsie. He knew how active Randy had always been—skiiing, sailing, hiking. "I just can't picture Randy that way," he said.

Jim went back up to the studio from which he directed. I got into my costume and went out on stage to rehearse my number. The stage managers, Woody and "Pinky," know where and when each of us should be on stage. I went up to Woody to look at the drawing of the set where he has everyone's routine marked. He said, "Start at the top of the steps and on the Intro, walk down the stairs and stop at your mark. When you sing, 'always, always,' move to the next mark."

I went to the top of the steps and on the introduction walked down the stairs and stopped at my mark. "I'll be loving you, always," I sang.

"With a love that's true, always." My voice broke a little.

Woody used his microphone. "Hold it," he said to the director. He came up to me and put a sympathetic hand on my shoulder. "Are you going to be all right?"

"Yes, I'll be all right." But my chin had started to tremble.

"Wait a minute," Woody said over the microphone.

I fought for composure and went on.

We went through it several times and then broke for lunch.

Roselle came upstairs to my dressing room. "You're going to have lunch with us today, aren't you, Norma?"

"Well, maybe I will. Just let me call Randy first. I'll join you in the cafeteria."

"It will do you good. You won't be able to help Randy if you get sick too!"

The people I work with are so wonderful. These little extra gestures while Randy was so sick endeared them to my heart forever.

I'll never forget how thrilled and touched we were one day during Randy's illness when a huge bouquet of yellow roses and spider mums arrived. On the card we read, "We're thinking of you! We love you!" It was signed by Gail, Ralna, Tanya, Mary Lou, Sandi, Cissy, Ava, Anacani, and Charlotte. This is so typical of the thoughtful and loving things they do.

After lunch the place is a madhouse. Fifteen girls have to have their makeup applied by four makeup men and their hair done by one hairdresser.

I raced up the stairs. I sat down in the chair of Roselle Friedland, the hairdresser. She looked sharply at me and commented, "You look terrible." Not for Roselle the sympathetic, "Oh, you poor thing," approach. She went on, "Why do you get so upset? Why

178

do you worry so much? Everything's going to be all right." Roselle is a German immigrant and has endeared herself to every person on the show with her frank comments. "You need a few rollers," she observed.

"I know. I don't want my ears to show. I know you'll fix it up, Rosie."

Fifteen minutes later she was finished. Duane Fulcher beckoned me to his chair for makeup. As he applied the foundation and the powder I meditated and prayed, but my thoughts kept turning to Randy. By the time Duane had finished my powder, tiny rivulets of tears had found their way down my cheeks. I had been weeping without realizing it. I apologized as he repaired my makeup.

Roselle said, "Now, Norma, you quit your crying. You're going to look terrible on camera!"

The afternoon passed in practice and dress rehearsal. I even remembered to look at the certain exit sign as cameraman Herm Falk had instructed me, to avoid getting a dark shadow on my nose. Herm has always been thoughtful, teaching me how to get the best effect on camera. "If you'll swing your body just a little more to the right when you sit down, Norma, it will make a prettier picture," he might say. I'm grateful for his helpful suggestions.

I skipped supper and went to my dressing room. "O God," I prayed, "help me to put aside my own problems and think only of the people in my audience tonight. Just give me that peace you've always let me have before I go on. Help us to bring joy to our audience."

Once more I pestered Randy to see how he was doing. I could tell he was wincing even though he assured me he was fine.

It was 7:45. At 8:00 we were to tape the telecast before a live audience. Excitement was at its usual high pitch.

Our group number went well and I was encouraged. Everyone seemed in a top mood. Lawrence was reading his cue card about Rose Milk. Bobby and Cissy were dancing and I was next. George Thow, who writes the intros, always says such kind things about me and that night was no exception. It warmed my heart.

I stood at the top of the steps and the camera was on me. The introduction started. Walking down the steps, I sang, "I'll be loving you, always." My voice held steady. "With a love that's true, always."

> When the things you've planned,
> Need a helping hand,
> I will understand, always, always.

I moved to the mark in front of the couch. "Days may not be fair, always." The next line was going to be hard. I forced my thoughts away from Randy. I remembered my audience and looked right into the camera with a prayer that my song would bring joy to someone.

That's when I'll be there, always.
Not for just an hour,
Not for just a day,
Not for just a year, but always.

God had answered my prayer. He helped me forget my own grief by thinking of others.

CHAPTER FORTY-FOUR

During Randy's long illness I thanked God many times for the wonderful people in our park, not the least of whom were Mike Hurd and his dear wife Stephanie.

When Randy was in the La Habra Hospital, Mike and Steph had Mark and me over for meals, as we were both working besides spending many hours a day with Randy.

When Mike was twelve years old he had started delivering the *La Habra Star* to the people in our park. His cheery, round face smiled very readily. He has always had a gift for brightening our days.

One day, as he was biking around our park delivering papers, he asked Randy, "Could you use a little help around the park?"

Randy, who has a real talent for recognizing good help, said, "Sure, we always have work for a good man." So Mike began to help Randy with the work.

Years later, when Ron and Candi moved away from the park, leaving open the position of manager, Mike asked if Randy would give him a chance at the job. Randy said, "OK!" When he and Steph got married they moved into the little mobile home Ron and Candi had left. In December, 1975, their son, Patrick Michael, was born.

Randy wasn't getting any better. Rather, his pain got worse and the use of his right hand was gone. In desperation, I called Dr. Dom Addonzio again. He and his wife, Alice, have been our close friends for many years. Dom repeated his opinion that we just had to get Randy into the UCLA Medical Center. Randy still objected. "They wanted to operate on my spine in 1964. If I had listened to them, I'd have only 20 percent movement of my neck today."

"Well, Randy, then go to Scripps or Loma Linda. You've got to get some help."

We finally decided on Loma Linda Medical School and Hospital.

We thought that because of the Seventh Day Adventists' emphasis on good health habits, their hospital might provide a nutritious, health-building diet along with their diagnosis and treatment. We were to be disappointed on that score. The diet was singular only in its absence of meat. Each meal included a lot of sweets and white bread.

Once more Randy had a complete set of x-rays. "They're going to kill me with x-ray poisoning," Randy said, wryly. They put him through a battery of tests and used him to explain to classes the progress this disease would have.

One day a class surrounded Randy's bed and the doctor threw back the sheet which lay over a bar across Randy's feet, as he couldn't stand the weight of the sheet on his toes.

"First of all," the doctor said, "this foot is going to curl up. The knee joints will deteriorate. He'll walk like this." He walked around Randy's bed in sort of an ape-like fashion.

I saw Randy's reaction. His jaws squared, his eyes took on a steely glint. "I *will* lick this!" he said firmly.

The doctor looked him straight in the eye and said, "The last fellow who said that is now a complete cripple in a wheelchair."

It seemed so easy for the doctor to accept this grim diagnosis. Not so for me—or Randy. This was the only time that Randy got depressed. Some of the decisions he made at that time reflected his depression. For instance, he sold his boat because the doctor said he would never water ski again.

They started Randy on fifty aspirin a day. "When your ears start ringing, let us know and we'll reduce the number until we see how many you can tolerate."

When Randy's ears started to ring they reduced the aspirin gradually until they were down to twenty-five a day. He was also on cortisone and butazolidin.

Then one day a ray of hope came into our day. Our dentist friend, Dr. Harold Stone, sent us a sheet advertising an arthritis clinic in Hot Springs, California, operated by Dr. Bernard Bellew and Dr. Robert Bingham. Dr. Stone's wife, Alberta, called me on the telephone and said, "I really wish you'd take Randy to this clinic. I know you're nutrition-minded and they treat arthritis with nutrition there. One of them—Dr. Bingham—is an orthopedic surgeon. Dr. Bellew has retired from an eye, ear, nose, and throat practice in Beverly Hills to take up a study of nutrition and has found he is able to help arthritis sufferers."

I called immediately to make an appointment with Dr. Bingham. He was so busy that our date was set up for six weeks later. Friends told me the mineral waters there at Desert Hot Springs were good for arthritis, so I decided to take Randy there right away to wait for his appointment.

We got a room in the Ponce de Leon Motel, which was owned by beautiful Christian people, Mr. and Mrs. Fox. Each room had a private patio with a hot jacuzzi of mineral waters. We had a pleasant room with a kitchen, so I was able to cook hot soups for Randy and make fresh vegetable juices every day. We went on a liquid diet for an entire week. Randy improved a bit. He could walk a little without his crutches. We were encouraged, although often Randy's pain was so great that perspiration poured from his body. Still he always had that big smile. "I'm going to lick this," he'd say.

One day we got a telephone call from Dr. Ross La Lansky who had been our dentist when we lived in Flintridge. He said, "I talked to Mark and he told me where you were. I want you to see Dr. Bingham and Dr. Bellew while you're there."

I said, "Thank you! We have an appointment with him next month."

He said, "Well, since you're at Desert Hot Springs now, you go right to the clinic and tell them you want to see them *today*. You go there now!"

Randy and I agreed that we just couldn't barge in and demand instant attention. We much preferred to wait for our appointment.

Finally the day came, and we sat together in Dr. Bellew's office. The first thing Dr. Bellew asked him was, "Have you had an insect bite or puncture wound lately?"

Randy had, as a matter of fact, tried to tell several doctors about a puncture wound he had while working around the park. A lady had spied a big empty wire spool on Randy's truck and she wanted it right away. Randy, always accommodating, promptly climbed into the truck to lift it down for her. While he was trying to move it to the tail-gate, a piece of metal sprang loose like a whip, and a nail pierced the back of Randy's knee. He had come home that day and said, "Honey, I've got a puncture wound here. It hurts like the dickens but it didn't bleed at all." It had been sore and discolored for several days. He didn't get a tetanus shot. "I had one a couple of years ago," he said. "That should still be good."

The other doctors had said that the wound wouldn't have anything to do with the arthritic condition Randy was in now. But Dr. Bellew thought differently. "Arthritis is caused by a virus which could have been introduced into your body by that puncture wound. The 'bug' is around. You can get it from bee stings or cuts or wounds or from infections in your body." He went on to explain that he knew of no other cure than his method of vaccine.

He asked Randy to make arrangements to take the treatment at the clinic, so we packed up and moved to a motel closer to the clinic. We met other patients who were being treated. They were in various stages of arthritis. One man from Texas arrived a helpless cripple in great pain. He could move about only on crutches. He couldn't get into the pools by himself, so they lowered him in with a hoist. He was only thirty-five years old.

A woman had come all the way from the East Coast in hopes of being relieved of pain in one finger. Others walking about were telling of their progress, "You should have seen me two weeks ago," one man said. "I'm going home today." We began to feel sure there was hope for Randy and our spirits really improved.

At last the day came when he was to begin treatment. "We're going to give you a shot of vaccine today. Your white blood count is way up there—18,400—and your sed rate is 54. If the vaccine series doesn't help you, we will give you gout medicine because your uric acid is high too. But we don't treat for two things at once, or we won't know what's happening."

Dr. Bellew took time to explain that he had developed his method in 1946 to prevent flu, colds, and pneumonia, and had then applied it to treating arthritis because he knew it would help. The medical profession for the most part had forgotten about vaccines in arthritis therapy, although it had long been proven safe and effective.

"What I do is to mix 0.3 cc. of the commonly used influenza viral vaccine with 0.2 cc. of a long-used mixed respiratory bacterial vaccine, and inject the mixture intradermally to raise a wheal; then I give the remainder subcutaneously."

He told us that the vaccines would be given in a series, starting with three, then further vaccines as indicated. They would be given one week apart, then the interval would be lengthened to two weeks and longer until a maintenance program of once every three months could be established. The quarterly vaccines were merely to insure that no intervening infection might cause a recurrence of the arthritis once it was cured.

At this point in Dr. Bellew's description of the treatment, his nurse entered, bringing the vaccine for the first injection. The doctor injected into Randy's skin, then under the skin as he had described. "I expect," he said, "that your white count will be cut in half in three weeks. Now, you'll get a flare here, as I told you, and it will be tender to the touch."

We thanked him and went gratefully to our room. Randy was worn out and in terrible pain from the exertion of getting to the office.

Three days later Randy had his second treatment. He began to notice improvement very soon. The pain began to diminish and the swelling began to go down. He was able to encourage the new patients who arrived on crutches and in wheelchairs.

As Dr. Bellew had said, three weeks after his first vaccine Randy's white blood count had been cut in half—it was now 9,700. The sedimentation rate had dropped from 54 to 45. He was beginning to get strength back in his right hand as a therapist at the clinic, Helen Calmy, worked for hours on the muscles and tendons.

He had vaccines again on April 29 and May 13. Six weeks after he started treatment, Randy was well. How grateful we were that God had given us the answer to his need.

It was almost summer. The park had suffered without Randy's attention. He was way behind in his work. He had to force himself to work shorter days as he didn't want to overtax his body right away.

When the doctors at Loma Linda Hospital had painted such a grim picture of Randy's future, and while he was depressed, he sold our boat to Lorin Whitney. Now that he was well, he regretted it.

In July 1975, we went to Soap Lake and Randy got on water skis. It was the thrill of his life and mine. Tears came into my eyes when I saw him take off and watched his marvelous skiing form out there on lovely Soap Lake as he skied behind Bob Nacke's boat. When he turned in toward shore he smiled his broadest at me. He came up on the beach saying, "I wish you had the camera and could take a picture of me to send to the doctors at Loma Linda!"

Randy had his fifth vaccine on July 22. At that time his white blood count had gone down to 6,500 and his sedimentation rate to 18. From that time to the present, he has had the boosters every three months.

When we arrived home from Soap Lake, Randy couldn't wait to tell Mark about his water-skiing success. Mark was delighted, but he was bursting to tell about his summer also.

"You may have noticed that I haven't been happy for a long time," he said. "I just didn't know what direction to take—what to do with my life. You don't know how confused I was."

We had known. Randy and I had prayed much for Mark. What joy it was now to see his radiant face. His eyes glistened with joy as he said, "I was so lonely on the Fourth—so alienated and unhappy. I'd been holding onto a life style that I knew wasn't pleasing to God. I reached a fork in the road—it would be the path to destruction or the narrow path to Christ. I told the Lord, 'If you want me to give up the way I'm going, I will!' I gave my life to Christ and he turned my selfish desires into a desire to serve and love him."

Mark had gone forward at the Billy Graham Crusade in Anaheim years earlier. Now he explained, "I had made a commitment with my head. This time it was with my heart. God has made a new person of me!"

Randy and I rejoiced with him.

Mark has changed. Now he loves to study the Bible more than anything in the world, and enjoys long discussions with anyone who is willing.

Randy and I are usually willing, that is, at a reasonable hour of the day or night. But Mark gets most fired up over theology late at night. Even after Randy and I have retired for the night, Mark wants to sit on our bed and talk for hours. One night, he and I carried on a discussion on Bible prophecy regarding the end time. Randy had been lapsing into longer and longer silences. Suddenly Randy joined in. "Mark," he said, "do you know why Jesus didn't wear shoes?"

"No," Mark answered, completely off guard. "Why?"

"Because he wanted to save *soles*," Randy said.

Too kind to ask Mark to leave, Randy had completely broken the serious mood with a good laugh. Mark kissed us good-night and went to bed.

CHAPTER FORTY-FIVE

If mother was thrilled that I had sung for a president, I wondered how she would have felt when I was invited to sing for His Majesty King Olav V of Norway. What would my father's reaction have been? These were my thoughts as I accepted the invitation to sing at the royal banquet to be held in the Grand Ballroom of the Beverly Wilshire Hotel.

On the evening of October 23, 1975, we drove up to the front of the hotel. As we stepped out of the car we felt as if we were entering an enchanted forest. Thousands of tiny lights twinkled in the tall trees in the courtyard. We were surrounded by formally dressed couples—women in satins, silks, furs, and jewels; men in tuxedos. I wore a turquoise gown with a beaded bodice and a flowing chiffon skirt. I stole a proud glance at Randy—as handsome as any movie star in his black tux.

Holding hands, we entered the lobby and took our place at the end of a long waiting line. Some of the guests wore native costumes. Every face was alight with anticipation—eyes sparkling like the diamond necklaces we saw all about us.

Gradually we neared the reception table. Producing our formal invitation, we received a card showing our table assignment, and made our way toward the royal banquet hall.

Lined six abreast on each side of the archway were violinists, standing in perfect formation, playing a beautiful lilting waltz. The elegant setting transported us back over the centuries to days of medieval splendor. Each round linen-draped table held a tall candelabrum encircled with flowers. The crystal and silver glowed like jewels in the candlelight. Besides the many tables on the main floor, two tiers of tables rose at the sides of the immense hall. Satin valances of royal blue hung from a canopy above the throne, a splendid hand-carved work of art, where the king would sit. Flowers and candles lined the tables where dignitaries would take their places near the king. Animated voices rose above the music; laughter filled the room. I felt like a fairy princess, moving in a dream.

Our table was on the aisle near the entrance through which King Olav would come, and exactly opposite from his throne. Myron Floren, associate conductor of the Lawrence Welk Show, and his wife, Berdine, were already at our table.

As we waited for the king, the toastmaster, Mr. Twygwe Soyland, stood to instruct the guests in protocol. Everyone must have arrived before the king would enter...no one would be seated after his arrival...we must all stand facing the entrance. Everyone must have wine in his glass when the king entered...three toasts would be made and everyone *must* drink the wine! We waited eagerly for his coming.

"The king is coming!"

One after another, members of the royal party were announced. They slowly descended the stairs and passed by us to make their way down the center aisle to the head table.

Then His Majesty King Olav V stood at the top of the stairs. Tan and rugged, a little shorter than I had imagined him, but very broad shouldered, he wore a finely tailored black suit and stood straight and proud. Flashbulbs went off by the hundreds as he strode regally past us, his face expressionless. "For Kongen," was sung heartily by the guests as the king proceeded to his throne.

Next we sang "The Star Spangled Banner," then "Ja Vi Elsker."

Pastor Aagaard of the Norwegian Seamen's Church gave the invocation. A Mrs. Reinertsen greeted the king and all the guests. Toasts were made. "Olav! Olav! Olav!" the cheers rang out.

Then Myron Floren was introduced. As he stood with his accordion at the top of the stairs where King Olav had just entered, voices kept on a constant chatter. Myron announced his first selection and began to play a lively Norwegian folk song. We sat only twelve feet from him but even with the amplification we could hardly hear a note of his lilting artistry. For several minutes he continued to entertain a noisy boisterous crowd.

The toastmaster spoke to the audience begging them to give a little attention to Mr. Floren. There wasn't the slightest decrease in the clamor. Ending his part in the program, Myron introduced me.

I rose stiffly to climb the stairs and face the indifferent throng. As Myron played the intro to "Strange Music" from *The Song of Norway,* an experience of years ago flashed through my memory with all the force it carried so long before.

When I had first begun to solo, dad had arranged for me to sing before a Kiwanis group. Then, as now, it had been a great moment in my life. I had dreamed of standing before an appreciative audience. When the time came for my number, I had gone on stage and waited for the din to cease. I waited and waited. They never stopped talking. Finally, I had simply turned and walked off the stage!

Everything in me yearned to do that now. But I had to sing! Casting a glance at Randy, who looked stricken and pale, I began to sing the beautiful melody. Here and there a few people were looking at me but the babble of raucous voices continued through my entire program. Only the guests at our table, Randy, and King Olav gave me their undivided attention. The king smiled for the first time as I sang my last high note. He nodded in acknowledgment of my singing as I bowed.

I returned to the table to a smattering of applause. Randy gave me a weak, understanding smile. My heart thudded dully in my chest. I barely remember eating my meal, my disappointment was so intense.

The evening slipped away while a great mariachi group roamed through the aisles among the tables filling the air with vigorous Mexican tunes. That the king enjoyed this lively music was evident by his grin. The twelve strong-voiced men who sang with the band could have been heard above a locomotive.

King Olav's speech, delivered in almost perfect American-accented English, was very complimentary to our nation. Immediately following, he was ushered to a private meeting room.

Randy and I were invited to be introduced to him. He was extremely gracious and shook our hands warmly, saying, "Thank you for singing for me tonight, Mrs. Zimmer. You have a very beautiful voice." And he gave me a wonderful smile.

I've had to sort out my feelings about that momentous occasion. I have never been treated with such utter lack of courtesy as by that audience. Still, the king had been appreciative.

I hope I will always keep my eyes on the King of kings, and Lord of lords, Jesus Christ. I pray that whether in singing or speaking or whatever I am doing I will desire only to please him, that I may bask in *his* smile.

CHAPTER FORTY-SIX

I'm glad that Randy and I took that trip to Idaho soon after mother's death. If I had waited two years longer to view my birth-place, I would have found it entirely obliterated. Today, grandpa's farm is one of the largest silver mines in the state.

When I heard this, I had to call the only one left who had shared my early years in the log cabin.

"You don't mean it!" was Max's shocked reaction. "Dad was right all the time!"

We talked of how different it might have been for all of us if dad had discovered silver in the mid-'20s when he had "embarked on his hopeless venture." We imagined what dad might have been like if he had had no financial worries. Very likely he would have de-voted his life to teaching violin, as that was his first love, after the concert stage.

Remembering his absorption with "making something" of one's self, we agreed that dad would have gone to college and trained himself for a profession. I could easily imagine him as a professor in a conservatory of music. He would probably not have become so frustrated that liquor could gain control over him as it had for many years.

We wondered if the gypsy's frightening prophecies would have influenced him so much if he had not been intoxicated and brooding much of the time.

"So he was right all the time," Max repeated. "Isn't life strange?"

It is indeed. After talking to Max, I pondered what kind of a person I might have been if we had been wealthy...if dad hadn't drunk so much...if he had never been weakened by working in poisonous fumes. "Suppose," I mused, "mother had grown to love dad, which she might well have if he had been kind and gentle with her. She wouldn't have started to drink and smoke. With his encouragement she could have become an artist, a gourmet cook, an interior decorator."

I wondered if Kay might not have lived longer with good nutri-tion as a child; I remembered those arsenic-dusted vegetable leaves which may have damaged her liver.

What might have been...

But we must live instead with what has been and, even more im-portant, with what *is* and may yet be.

I am the person I am partly because my parents were the persons they were. I loved them both and am grateful to them. They both loved all of us children and did what they could for us, in their weakness. God used them to shape our lives and point us in the directions we went.

I can understand why they succumbed to the temptations they had—I wonder if I could have stood up to their problems and disadvantages without faith in God to sustain me. Our lives were characterized by quarreling and weeping, hunger and despair, yet through it all I sensed that my parents really cared for me. The cushion of love, though sometimes worn thin, was never jerked away.

How thankful I am that God used me to help them find more comfort and happiness in their later years, and to learn of Christ, the burden bearer. I hope to see them both again.

But what I have become is not only the result of my parents' influence. God came into my life in the person of his Son, Jesus Christ, and made me a "new creation" in him. All things became new, just as his Word promised.

Whatever the song I sing, it springs from a grateful heart in which there rings the new, new song of salvation.